Great Naval Battles of the Ancient Greek World

Contents

Acknowledgements

First and foremost, thanks goes to my editor, Philip Sidnell. He has dealt with my adapted time frames with support and good humour. His meticulous readings of various drafts have offered useful suggestions for refinement and more in-depth explanations. Indeed, if it was not for Phil, this book would never have come to light. Originally this book began as a section for my previous publication, Great Battles of the Classical Greek World, but from the moment Phil saw that heading in my prospective chapter list he shot me down. How could we waste an opportunity for a follow up book? I was apprehensive at first, but Phil's support encouraged me to jump in with both feet, the result of which is this book.

I am indebted to the community of academics, historians, and historical enthusiasts who I have used time and again to bounce ideas off, discuss narratives with, or ultimately lean on for motivation when the need arose. In particular, special thanks go to Dr Jason Crowley, who has put up with this book consuming much of my attention!

I am greatly appreciative of the enthusiastic support of David Bowen, who has vigilantly read over the drafts of this book and offered advice on edits. While military history is a passion of mine, my nautical experience is just a little more than zero. David's vast knowledge base has certainly refined this book accordingly. As always, any mistake and errors that are present here are mine and mine alone.

Finally, and most importantly, my thanks as always go to my wife Carly, and children Matilda and Henry. They have put up with me working from home to finish this book and have offered me nothing but love and support.

Introduction

The evocative and tranquil sight of the Mediterranean Sea is an intoxicating tableau of serenity to all who have witnessed it. But behind the calm, lapping waves and peaceful quiet, hides a story of bloody warfare and inhumane carnage. While the blood-soaked battlefields of the Greek mainland are so hard to ignore, the rouged-tint of the naval battle is quickly washed away by human memory almost as fast as it is by the waters.

To the ancient Greeks, naval battle was ubiquitous in war. The creak of the oars and the crack of a filling sail were as much noises of comfort and dread as the sound of thousands of armed men on the march. For some, the blistered hands of the rower was as much a mark of duty, and worthy of respect, as any battle-scar. Yet modern commentary on Greek warfare often leaves this vital part of the ancient Greek military ethos, and identity, on the side-lines, replaced by the more-glamorous land battles. I defy most enthusiasts to name as many sea battles from the Classical period as they can land battles. So the aim of this work is to bring the multitude of naval engagements, which pervade the ancient sources, into a broader modern awareness. By exploring the naval narrative it can reveal that Greek armies rarely, if ever, acted alone, and if we remove these naval narratives from our history we are removing a vital element of Greek military practice.

Triremes

By the time our ancient sources provide adequate accounts of specific naval battles (the earliest that is possible to reconstruct being Lade in 495 BC), there was one ship which ruled the waves: the *trieres* or, in its more common Latin form, the trireme. But the trireme was not an isolated invention, and must be understood as part of a logical evolution from its predecessor, the *penteconter*.

The *penteconter* was a ship originally powered by fifty rowers on a single rowing level, before it was adapted in the later eighth century BC to arrange the oars over two levels, thereby shortening the length of the ship without compromising its power. This ship is often referred to as a *bireme*, referring to these two levels, creating a neat parallel with the trireme, but it was not a terminology the Greeks used. In fact, this seemingly revolutionary design did not even warrant a name change so it was still referred to as a *penteconter*. The shortening of the length marked a change in emphasis for the *penteconter*; moving away from 'boarding' tactics which demanded more deck space to carry marines, this ship was better suited to concentrate its power on a single point – it was designed to ram.

The trireme was developed by adding a third 'layer' of rowers to the modified *penteconter*, and increasing the ship's length to about 35 metres to accommodate an increase in numbers on all levels. The trireme had two sails which were primarily used during general seafaring. When battle was imminent, the sails were removed and the rowers propelled the vessel by use of oars that measured just over 4 metres. By the fourth century we have evidence that the trireme was powered by a maximum of 170 oars: 62 rowers (called *thranites*) sat above the hull, sheltered by a removable cover or deck, with 31 rowers per side; inset from them sat 54 rowers (called *zygioi*) and below them all, towards the bottom of the ship, were the final 54 rowers (called *thalamoi*). These men gave the trireme thrice the oar power of the *penteconter*, and this powered the ram, a long wooden block protruding from the bow at the waterline. It was encased in bronze and edged with cutting blades out front, the impact of which could crush an enemy vessel or at the very least ensnare it.

The origins of the trireme are relatively obscure, with a general consensus pointing towards the Phoenicians as the creators, but this is not certain. The earliest images that can be reliably dated depict Phoenician triremes taking part in the evacuation of Tyre in 701 BC, whereas the clearest written reference we have for their appearance in Greece comes from Thucydides, who states that the Corinthians were the first to build them around 700 BC (dates given by scholars range from 721-654 BC). Interestingly, the two forms of trireme were not identical in design, with the Phoenician ship considered smaller and faster. The Alexandrian theologian Clement, writing in the second half of the second century AD, references a third century BC Greek writer called Philostephanus of Cyrene who attributed the ship's invention to the Phoenicians (*Stromateis*, 1.16.76) – specifically the Sidonians, who were described by Herodotus as having the fastest of all of the ships in the Persian fleet. But other sources, such as Plutarch and Diodorus, gave credit to the Corinthians. For this project, the obscure origins of the trireme simply show that there was a long tradition for their usage both in Greece and in the Near East.

Manning the Trireme

The make-up of Greek trireme crews is contentious, especially when it comes to the Athenian fleet. What I present here could be described as the orthodox consensus amongst scholars; however for those interested, I advise the titles listed under 'General' in the bibliography, many of which articulate the various scholarly interpretations of the evidence.

At full capacity, the trireme was said to have been manned by 200 men. We have already met the majority of this crew, the 170 rowers set over three layers within the ship. Of these, only the top layer, the *thranites*, could actually see out of the ship. While this was the most comfortable of the positions, it was also the most dangerous as they sat in a position exposed to missiles, merely protected by side screens hung down from the deck, but even these were not always used. The *thranites* seem to have been paid more than the other rowers, or at least so toward the end of the Ionian War (413-404 BC) when experienced crewmen were at a premium. The rowers consisted of citizens, slaves and mercenaries, and were highly prized by those *poleis* who held maritime power. This was especially true of Athens, who freed all of the slaves that rowed for them in the Battle of Arginusae (406 BC).

In addition to these rowers, the trireme was manned by marines. Conventionally the number is thought to have been fourteen per ship, ten hoplites and four archers, but as becomes evident in the early naval battles of the Peloponnesian War, different *poleis* manned their ships differently depending on the tactics intended. For instance, Athenian ships were smaller, lighter and faster than their counterparts, so the number of marines needed to be kept low to support these attributes, and maximize their tactical strengths of manoeuvring and ramming. The Corinthians, however, specialized in boarding their enemies' vessels and fighting on the decks, so they would have to have used more marines to facilitate this.

The trireme was commanded by a *trierarch*, the captain of the ship and often its owner. Being a *trierarch* was considered a civic obligation, for the richer elements of Athenian society in particular, and formed part of their liturgy. But, as naval warfare evolved and took on such importance in Athens, many a rich citizen paid for an experienced captain to take his place on the ship. The *trierarch* was joined by a helmsman (*kybernetes*), a rowing master (*keleustes*), a purser in charge of pay (*pentecontarchos*), a bow officer, a carpenter, and a flute player. In addition to these, there will have been extra men to handle the sails and so on.

The importance of the crew requires no explanation, but the reputation of a crewmember was not protected by this. The Greek philosopher Plato, in his work *Laws*, put in the words of his fictional Athenian a damning summary of a military sailor's character:

> [Sailors] are frequently jumping ashore, and then running back at full speed to their ships, and they consider no shame in not dying boldly at their posts when the enemy attack . . . what they describe as 'non-dishonourable flight.' These exploits are the usual result of employing naval soldiery, and are not worthy of frequent, infinite praise but precisely the opposite.[1]

Naval Tactics

In preparation for battle, a ship would remove much of its dead weight, including the main sails and mast, and leave them on the shore; where they became a viable target for the enemy. The ship would then row out with the fleet, which usually formed up line abreast, in other words side by side, with enough room for all of the ships to be able to turn around. Depending on the size of the fleet, and the surrounding geography, this would usually be a single line, but there are instances of a series of lines being used behind each other. As opposed to line ahead, which had the ships following one behind another, line abreast protected the flanks of each ship, which were vulnerable in the pre-gunpowder era (later ships, armed with a 'broadside' of cannon along each side, could protect their own flanks but were conversely vulnerable to attacks from the bow and stern).

As has been previously mentioned, and will become apparent throughout this book, different navies used different tactics. The Athenians built their tactics around their modified triremes. Unlike their Greek counterparts, the Athenians purposefully designed their triremes to be smaller, lighter and, therefore, faster. This pace and agility enabled the Athenians to use their mobility and exploit the space in the line abreast formation, and literally row circles around their enemy. Their preferred tactic was the *diekplous* (translation: sail through and out), in which a trireme would pass through the gaps in an enemy line and, when it came out the other side, the ship would turn around and ram the stern or the flank of an enemy target:

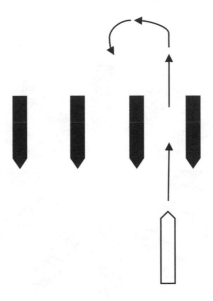

Fig. 1: The *diekplous*: One trireme breaks through the enemy lines and turns to attack the rear or flank of an enemy ship.

There is some debate between scholars about how many ships performed the *diekplous*: was it one ship on its own or did it lead a small squadron of ships in a line ahead formation? While our sources are never clear, in fact the *diekplous* is rarely mentioned other than to explain why it was *not* used, it seems unlikely that we are to envisage squadrons passing through the enemy lines. If for the simple reason that this would remove all military competence from the enemy ships. Surely those triremes being passed would not have stayed still, but instead engaged the triremes toward the rear of the offensive line, and attacked their vulnerable flanks. A long *diekplous* line removes the speed and surprise needed to exploit the gap available, so it should be thought of as a tactic for individual ships.

There were two methods for defending against the *diekplous*. The first is not regularly attested but can be seen in the Battle of Arginusae. Instead of deploying in a single line, the defending fleet formed some of its vessels into at least one reserve line, so that an attacking trireme which broke through would face yet more ships in front of him, nullifying its element of speed and surprise. Interestingly, this is a tactic that the Athenians adopted at the end of the Ionian War as a way of dealing with the now-superior Peloponnesian fleet. The second method was to adopt a circular formation:

Fig. 2: The *kyklos* (translation: circle): All of the ships form a circle, with their sterns pointed inwards and their rams outward.

The first time we hear of this formation is at the Battle of Artemisium (480 BC), when the Greeks were facing the Persian fleet. While it was an essentially defensive tactic, the Greek ships were still able, on a prearranged signal, to surge forward in attacks radiating outward from their position. This signal would have come in the form of flags, and crews may even have sung a paean as recognition that the signal had been received. This circle formation could work very well but it did have, however, one major flaw in its execution. If the enemy decided to circle around it, contracting their circle more and more, they would force the defensive position to tighten and the ships to start banging into each other. This effect can be seen in the battle of the Corinthian Gulf (429 BC), when the Athenian admiral Phormio sailed his fleet around a Peloponnesian circle in just this way. He also utilised his knowledge of the weather patterns so that defending ships were closest together when the wind began to blow, causing havoc for the formation and the defending fleet as a whole.

The second offensive manoeuvre that the Athenians mastered was the *periplous*. The term, given to us by Thucydides and described as a naval tactic, is frustratingly vague. It translates as 'sail around' which was used in as general a sense as one can imagine: one sailed around the Aegean Sea, and one sailed around a *kuklos* formation. It is a term that would also appropriately describe the end manoeuvre of a *diekplous*, in which the ship turns around to attack the enemy from behind. But there is one instance, seen again in the Battle of the Corinthian Gulf, which perhaps illustrates another technical sense for this term. An Athenian trireme was being chased by an enemy ship; when the enemy ship had been enticed far enough away from his own fleet, the fleeing trireme wheeled around a small merchant vessel and struck its pursuer in the flank:

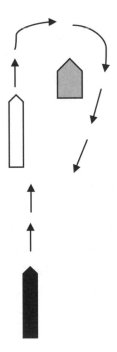

Fig.3: The *periplous*: The trireme purposefully wheels around, positioning itself to the flank of an enemy ship that was behind, and ramming it.

It seems unlikely that these offensive tactics were solely the remit of the Athenians, but it is the Athenian fleet who are most often described as performing them. The other, dominant form of tactic described in the sources was the purposeful binding of your ship to that of the enemy by grappling irons. This was easily achieved, because the impact of the original ramming often made it hard to separate the vessels anyway. Navies that did not want to fight in the old-fashioned way, according to Thucydides, needed to back water before the grappling irons were thrown. Once the ships were connected, the aggressors would board the enemy ship and fight it out hand-to-hand. This tactic neutralized the speed or agility of a superior vessel and enabled the battle to be fought out by marines and archers, rather than by helmsmen.

Great Battles

Naval conflict is rife throughout the works of the three main Greek historians – Herodotus, Thucydides and Xenophon – so in theory the choice of great battles should be made difficult by what should be omitted, but this is not the case. Naval warfare was omnipresent in Greek conflict, but for that reason it was rarely described in detail by contemporary writers, and very rarely given enough space for a modern writer to use the ancient testimony to try to reconstruct even a single battle. Fortunately, naval engagements were rarely solitary affairs. They were usually part of a larger campaign which saw the opposing fleets posturing and engaging again and again. Alternatively, a fleet was not just used to fight other fleets, but would also be used in conjunction with land forces. One example would be the Battle of Artemisium, which was fought at the exact same time as the famous land battle of Thermopylae by the two supporting naval forces. We also see the importance of a fleet during many sieges; either in a bid to control a major harbour, such as at Syracuse (415-413 BC), or as part of a joint force assault on the position by land and sea. As a result, in this work a greater emphasis has been placed on the context of the naval battle, and the strategic movements beforehand.

The battles that I have chosen follow a simple chronology through the classical period, beginning with the Persian Conflicts (499-489 BC), through the Archidamian War (the first part of the Peloponnesian War, 431-421 BC), and then the Ionian War (the second part of the Peloponnesian War, 413-404 BC). The Ionian War is also referred to as the Decelean War by many scholars, named after the fort at Decelea in Attica which the Spartans took control of and used as a base from which to raid the Athenian countryside. I have stayed with the term Ionian War because all of the naval conflict took place along the Ionian coast of Asia Minor, or the Hellespont further north, and very little actually happened on mainland Greece other than these Spartan raids.

A natural, and final, section to this book would have been the period of the Hegemonies and the naval battles therein. However, we do not have very much in the way of source material to reconstruct many naval battles from that period. Interestingly, our main source, Xenophon, either chose to not dwell on the naval engagements from that time, or else there ceased to be the naval campaigns that were so prevalent during the Peloponnesian War. This may be an oversight by the author, or may just reflect the growing powers of Sparta and Thebes, both of whom used land warfare to dominate their enemies. The final section here covers the Hegemony period, but you will find little continuity between the narratives. The Battle of Catane deals with the Syracusans and their conflict with the Carthaginians, and the Battle of Cnidus deals with a Persian fleet fighting against a Spartan one. Perhaps of the two, the most important is Catane, which shows the next evolution of naval warfare, and the design of a new ship which would shift the balance of control in the Mediterranean – the *penteres*, now known by its Latinized name, quinquereme.

Finally, as much as I may have wished to write this book without using the Latin name of trireme and quinquereme, I decided against making some pretentious stand and chose to use the term people are more familiar with. I have similarly transliterated Greek names into their Latinized forms. However, some tactical terms have been rendered as transliterations from the original Greek (see Glossary).

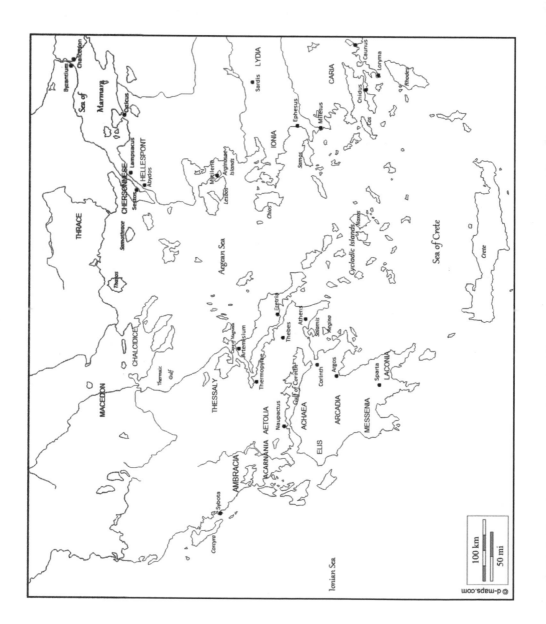

Chalcedon
Byzantium
Sea of
Marmara
Cyzicus
THRACE
CHERSONESE
Lampsacus
HELLESPONT
Sestus
Abydos
Samothrace
LYDIA
Sardis
Ephesus
IONIA
Miletus
CARIA
Cnidus
Caunus
Loryma
Rhodes
Cos
Samos
Mytilene
Arginusae
Islands
Lesbos
Chios
Aegean Sea
Cycladic Islands
Naxos
Sea of Crete
Crete
Thasos
CHALCIDICE
Thermaic
Gulf
MACEDON
Euboea
Artemisium
Chalcis
Eretria
Athens
Salamis
Aegina
Thermopylae
Thebes
THESSALY
ACARNANIA
AETOLIA
Naupactus
Gulf of Corinth
ACHAEA
Corinth
Argos
ELIS
ARCADIA
Sparta
LACONIA
MESSENIA
AMBRACIA
Sybota
Corcyra
Ionian Sea

100 km
50 mi

© d-maps.com

Glossary

aspides	–	a shield bearer.
diekplous	–	a naval tactic, sailing through the enemy lines.
ephors	–	a group of five Spartans who were elected on an annual basis to 'oversee' Sparta and her two kings.
Gerousia	–	the Spartan council of elders.
harmost	–	military governor.
hoplite	–	Greek infantryman, primarily armed with a large shield and spear.
karanon	–	commander-in-chief of the Persian armed forces in Asia Minor.
kyklos	–	naval tactic, to form a defensive circle with all of the rams pointing outwards.
Long Walls	–	giant parallel walls running from Athens to the Piraeus. The ability to indefinitely protect the road, for supplies to enter the city, turned Athens into a land based island.
medizer	–	to support the Persians, used to describe Greek *poleis*.
minae	–	currency, equal to 100 drachmae.
nauarch	–	naval commander.
paean	–	A type of chant that varied between Greek communities. It was used in naval warfare to communicate between ships, seemingly to confirm an order.
penteconters	–	a secondary warship that was superseded by the trireme, but was still in use throughout the classical period.

penteres	–	The Greek name for the quinquereme, see below.
periplous	–	naval tactic, circling around to attack the enemy ship from an unexpected angle.
Piraeus	–	the harbour of Athens, connected to the city by the Long Walls.
polis/eis	–	Greek city-state.
Pythia	–	the oracle at Delphi.
quadrireme	–	larger than a trireme, but smaller than a quinquereme, this warship is poorly understood by modern scholars. This is the Latinized name; the Greeks called it a *tetreres*.
quinquereme	–	the largest warship from this period, its exact design is disputed but it is thought to have had five men to every oar. This is the Latinized name. The Greeks knew it as a *penteres*.
satrap	–	a governor of a Persian satrapy.
satrapy	–	a province within the Persian Empire.
stades (singular *stadion*)	–	unit of distance equal to approximately 607ft or 184m.
strategos	–	a general. The title was used by the Athenians to also designate an admiral, unlike the Spartans who had the official position of *nauarch*.
talents	–	unit of weight and largest unit of currency, equal to 60 *minae* or 6,000 drachmae.
tetreres	–	The Greek name for a *quadrireme*.
triaconters	–	the smallest military ship described during this period. Little is known about it and it seems to have been used more for transportation than fighting.
trierarch	–	captain of a trireme. In Athens this title could also mean that you were the financier of the trireme.
trieres/trireme	–	the primary warship of the classical Greek world.

Part 1

THE PERSIAN CONFLICTS

At the turn of the sixth century BC, a vacuum of power had come into being, due to the catastrophic demise of the great Assyrian Empire. An alliance between the Babylonians and the Medes enabled the destruction of the ancient capital of Assyria, Nineveh, in 612 BC, leaving the Near East bereft of a single dominant power. By the 550s, the innocuous rise of one man would soon see an end to this vacuum.

Cyrus the Great was the architect for the Persian Empire, putting his Achaemenid Dynasty in a position of power to rule over this vast realm for over 200 years. In 550 BC, Cyrus won a great victory over the Medes, giving him control over the Iranian peoples; a tie that was so intrinsic to Persian power that Greek authors would regularly switch between the using the terms 'Persians' and 'Medes' when describing them. From here, Cyrus expanded west into the lands of Lydia, which at this time was almost all of Asia Minor.

The Lydian King, Croesus, was famous throughout the Greek-speaking world for his wealth, his opulence and, indeed, his arrogance. His failed resistance to Cyrus soon petered out and the expanding Persian Empire now contained the lands of Lydia. A failed uprising by another Lydian was quickly suppressed, but the rebel leader fled to the Greek cities in Ionia, taking with him the ire of Cyrus himself. The Persians were ruthless in their systematic punishment of the Ionian Greeks for the perceived support of the uprising, and Persia now held control over Greek cities. By the time Cyrus died, his empire stretched from the Aegean Sea in the west, to the northwestern border of India and included Babylon; already at this point, this was the largest empire ever seen in the Near East.

Cyrus' successors showed very little interest in the Greek mainland as a place for expansion. It held little value in the way of resources or even food supplies, compared to the lands of Thrace for example. But in 507 BC the growing *polis* of Athens sent word to the Persian King Darius I for help and support against the growing aggression of many stronger *poleis* in Greece. Darius agreed to support them, in exchange for a symbolic offer of subjugation in the form of earth and water. The Athenians complied and, perhaps unwittingly, placed themselves under the imperial authority of Persia. This submission amounted to nothing in real terms, Athens was a tiny prize worthy of little attention for Darius, who had greater interest in consolidating his advances in Thrace, and on many of the islands in the Aegean. However, the relevance of this symbolic subjugation came to the fore in 499 BC when the Ionian Greeks revolted against the Persians and looked to Athens for support. Athens sent a small military force to aid the uprising and in so doing broke a diplomatic agreement and solemn oath as a subject of the Great King – whether or not Athens saw it in such a way.

The failed Ionian Revolt ended and Darius began to show more of an interest in the Greek mainland. In 490 BC Darius sent a fleet to secure the south Aegean, with particular attention paid to the Cycladic Islands. Once this was secure, the commanders of the fleet had a secondary objective of punishing the Athenians for their betrayal. The Persians landed at Marathon, to the northeast of Athens, and were defeated in an epic land battle by the Athenians and their allies. For Persia this was barely a setback, they had achieved their main objectives and the added bonus of punishing Athens would just have to wait. Unfortunately for Darius, he never got his chance to try again. He died in 486 BC and the mantle was taken up by his son, Xerxes I.

Once Xerxes had subdued numerous rebellions in his empire, mainly in Egypt and Babylon, he was finally able to resurrect Darius' plans to attack Athens once again. Xerxes headed a gigantic army, the likes of which had never been seen in Greece. His brutal campaign lasted all of 480 BC, at the end of which he left to return to his capital, having fulfilled the expectation that he would lead the invasion for the first year. He left his forces in the capable hands of his general Mardonius, who continued the campaign into 490 BC when he was finally defeated and the Persian army was removed from Greece.

The Greek states, especially Athens, learned a great deal from their battles with the Persians. And the iconic naval victory at Salamis in 480 BC gave rise to Athens' reputation as a strong naval power. The Persian navy contained the greatest of naval forces in the Mediterranean, the Phoenicians. They also had access to Greek ships and sailors as well, through Ionia, so the fact that the Persians were defeated at Salamis tells us a great deal about the naval capabilities of the Greek resistance.

During the Persian Wars, there were three major naval battles covering a fourteen-year period. The first was the Battle of Lade (494 BC), during the Ionian revolt. This is the first recorded naval battle between the Persians and the Greeks. In fact it is the first Greek naval battle that can be reconstructed with any confidence. The battle highlights the poor state of Greek military discipline, and shows that even with good tactics and a strong fleet, a naval battle is often decided by the will of the crewmen. It also reveals a major weakness with inter-Greek alliances, their propensity to be undermined by the enemy.

The second battle was during the invasion of Xerxes, at the Battle of Artemisium (480 BC). The naval battle was fought at the same time as the famous land battle at Thermopylae. The battle was a huge undertaking, and forced the Greeks to face a numerically superior force head on. The Greeks planned a defensive strategy which worked well, forming a tight circle and also showing an ability to counterattack from this formation, which shocked the Persians no end. The battle ended in a stalemate, but the Greeks took a lot more from the day than the Persians did.

The third and final battle is, possibly, one of the most famous sea battles in world history. The Battle of Salamis (480 BC) was a last throw of the dice for the Athenians and their allies, but the Athenians especially. They had lost their city and, unless they could turn the tide of Persian success, they would be homeless. The battle is difficult to reconstruct due to the contradictory accounts. Salamis would be the battle that would epitomize Athenian resilience and resolve, as well as cement their place as the superior naval power in the Aegean. Thus our Athenian sources offer some very biased accounts of the day, but that is not to take away from the overall achievement. Vastly outnumbered and facing an elite Persian fleet with a strong Phoenician contingent, the Greeks, led by Athens, were able to force a battle in a narrow seascape and win a monumental victory. In terms of the wider campaign it did not push back the Persians, nor undermine their position in Greece. Yet the victory brought with it two important benefits: it prevented the Persian navy from having free reign around the Greek shoreline, and it uplifted Greek morale to ultimately face the Persians the following year and win the final land battle at Plataea.

Defeat of the Persians gave rise to a new sense of Greek identity; they had united against a common enemy and shown that together they stood strongest. The resistance formalized its existence into a Hellenic league, which was led by the great heroes of the Persian Wars, the Athenians. As time passed, Athens took a more aggressive line against the Persians and made greater and greater demands for men and ships from their allies. Soon it became possible for members to send money instead of men, enabling the Athenians to fund a ship-building project that would provide them with the largest of all the Greek fleets. The Hellenic League morphed into the Delian League, with Athens well and truly in charge. In essence, Athens had created its own mini-empire through the league, but it was not until cities tried to renege on their obligations that they discovered they were not donating funds to a panhellenic cause, but were paying tribute to the Athenians themselves. Athenian rule was harsh and demanding, but it gave them access to enough funds so that they could cement themselves as one of the two most powerful *poleis* in all of Greece, alongside Sparta.

Chapter 1

Battle of Lade (494 BC)

Background (Herodotus, V.30–55; 97–VI.6)

By the turn of the fifth century Persia ruled over an empire which stretched from the Indus River to the Danube, and from the Red Sea to the Ural Mountains. With an empire as large as this, the Great Kings of Persia chose to support local rulers in many of the more distant cities under their control, rather than impose their own ruling infrastructure. Inside the great cities of Greek Ionia, on the western coast of Asia Minor, this meant supporting local tyrants who were thus indebted to the Persians for their authority.[1]

For a time this arrangement suited both the Ionians and the Persians, with the Greek cities beginning to flourish under foreign auspices.[2] But, as affluence within certain Ionian cities began to outstretch their neighbours, one tyrant in particular became enamoured with the idea of extending his power outside of the city walls: Aristagoras of Miletus.[3]

Miletus sat on the southwesterly coast of Asia Minor and was by far the most prosperous city in Ionia. In the year 500 BC, Aristagoras, as tyrant, received a group of exiled aristocrats from the island of Naxos asking for military support to return to their homeland. Naxos was one of a group of south Aegean islands, called the Cycladic Islands, which had not yet been taken under the control of the Persians. Naxos was by far the most affluent island amongst them, so Aristagoras designed a plan to support the exiles, with the help of Persian man-power, and take control of the island for himself.

One small obstacle in Aristagoras' way was that Naxos would be a powerful enemy; it called upon a defending army of up to 8,000 hoplites and a great many long boats, which made it a formidable defensive position to attack.[4] However, there was a Greek social contract within the equation which forced Aristagoras to act.

Aristagoras was not the official tyrant of Miletus, he was an interim for his father-in-law, Histiaeus. Histiaeus had been a faithful servant of the Persians, but his loyalty had been called into question by the *satrap* Megabazus and so the Great King, Darius I, 'invited' the tyrant to stay with him in Susa indefinitely.[5] In fact, the only reason why the Naxian exiles had fled to Miletus was to meet with Histiaeus who was their former guest-friend.[6] This put Aristagoras in an interesting position. He was duty bound to uphold the exiles' guest-friend agreement with his superior and was obliged to help them in their endeavour. So he offered to go to the powerful *satrap* Artaphernes, who ruled over most of the west coast of Asia Minor, and gather support.

Aristagoras went to Artaphernes' capital in Sardis and presented the expedition to him as a way of making money; the exiles were offering to pay for the force's upkeep and Naxos was itself a very affluent island. The Ionian also speculated on the benefit of taking control of the Cyclades, which would enable the Persians to have a platform from which to push their influence into Greece. At Aristagoras' reckoning, the Persians needed to commit 100 ships. Artaphernes was convinced that the venture would be fruitful, but decided that 200 ships was a more realistic level of necessary forces.[7]

Word was sent to Darius for approval of the expedition, and with his approval Artaphernes supplied and equipped 200 triremes, while manning them with a vast mix of Persians and allies, and appointing Megabates to lead the fleet.[8] The fleet sailed to Miletus to pick up Aristagoras, the exiles, and a small Ionian army that would assist in the expedition, before heading north to Chios. Once they reached the southern side of the island the fleet pulled in to harbour, waiting so that they could use the north wind to head south to Naxos.

While in harbour tension began to rise between the Ionians and the Persian commander. Megabates was only acquainted with the Persian military system and was not prepared for the Greek approach to discipline, or lack thereof. As the Persian made his rounds, inspecting the boats, he found that one belonging to the Ionian city of Myndos did not have anyone guarding it. In a fury, Megabates ordered his bodyguard to hunt down the lax commander of the vessel, a man named Scylax, and tie him up so that his head would protrude out of an oar-hole while his body remained inside the boat. When Scylax was secured a close friend implored Aristagoras to intervene.

Aristagoras went to Megabates to defend the poor Greek commander, but it fell on deaf ears. So Aristagoras stormed on the ship and freed Scylax himself. When Megabates received word of how he had been undermined he flew into an almighty rage against Aristagoras, but was met with arrogant defiance – while Megabates was the commander of the fleet, Aristagoras was the leader of this expedition.[9] While he was still in a rage that night, Megabates sent a small dispatch to Naxos warning them of the impending attack.[10]

With the incoming intelligence, Naxos became a large hive of activity. Some Naxians brought all that they could within their defensive city walls, and prepared for a siege by stockpiling food, water, and wine, while others began to reinforce the walls. With preparations being made on the island, the Persian-led fleet crossed from Chios to Naxos and put the city under siege.[11]

For four gruelling months the Persians besieged the city without success. But their supplies were drastically dwindling, and Aristagoras' contribution was just as quickly consumed, leaving Megabates to acknowledge that the expedition was failing. The commander made the decision to pull his forces from the island, but not before building a fortification for the Naxian exiles that had travelled with him.

Aristagoras returned to Miletus full of anxiety. He had failed in his grand promises to Artaphernes, he had paid vast sums from his personal wealth, and he could have his authority in Miletus taken from him at any moment in retribution for the failed expedition. He had only one choice in his mind, he began to devise a revolt.

As his plans began to develop, Aristagoras received a slave sent to his home by Histiaeus with the simple instruction: shave my head. As the hair fell to the floor a message began to reveal itself tattooed on the exposed scalp; Histiaeus wanted Aristagoras to revolt as well.[12] With this seal of approval from the tyrant, Aristagoras took his proposal to his supporters who almost unanimously agreed. The one voice of consternation came from Hecataeus who warned of the size and power of the Persian Empire.[13] When this concern was ignored he relented and argued that they were better off trying to control the sea, and to do this they needed money – again he was ignored.

Instead of heeding the words of caution from Hecataeus, the followers of Aristagoras decided to revolt. First on their agenda was the acquisition of the Ionian contingent of the newly constructed Persian fleet which had attacked

Naxos. The ships were docked near Myous, a small town northeast of Miletus; it was here that the conspirators were able to arrest the ships' commanders and take control of the fleet. Parallel to this action, Aristagoras publically renounced his tyranny and declared a system of equal law for all. Once Mytilene gave him public backing he extended his 'revolution' to affect all of the Ionian cities. After appointing a general in each of the cities, Aristagoras knew his uprising would need support so he took a ship west to the Greek mainland.

Within a year Aristagoras returned from Greece with a mixed bag of results. Sparta had refused his request to send forces once they learned that the destination was three months' travel away, and not even the promise of riches was enough to stir their minds. Aristagoras had better fortune in Athens, where the assembly voted to send twenty ships to help the Ionians, whom they shared a common heritage with.[14]

With only the support of the Athenians secured, Aristagoras returned to Miletus with haste. As he waited for the Athenian fleet to arrive he sent a messenger inland, into Phrygia, to incite the recently uprooted Paeonians into revolt. The Paeonians had been dragged from their homes in the north Aegean, so when Aristagoras offered them both safety and an opportunity to return home, they welcomed his plans with open arms. The majority of the Paeonians hurried west toward the sea, managing to reach the island of Chios before the Persian cavalry sent after them were able to intervene. At Chios they were transported to Lesbos, then to Doriscos on the European mainland in Thrace, before they continued to march west back into their homelands. Aristagoras had scored no major victory against the Persians, but it was a morale-boosting venture for his allies, and proof that he would be true to his word: he would free the oppressed peoples of Ionia like he did the Paeonians.[15]

The Athenian fleet arrived, bringing with it five triremes from Eretria which had been offered as repayment for a military debt the small Euboean polis owed to Miletus.[16] Once all of Aristagoras' allies had come together he organized the first military expedition to Sardis, although he was conspicuous by his absence during the campaign. The tyrant had chosen his own brother and a second Milesian citizen to lead the forces of Miletus.

In 498 BC, the Greek army travelled north to Ephesus by sea, before disembarking and marching in full force northeast to Sardis where they swiftly took control of the city. With Artaphernes and his Persian force hemmed into the acropolis, the Greeks had the chance to loot the city without fear of retribution. Unfortunately, Sardis' buildings were not built from brick but were predominantly made from reeds, or at least had reed roofing; so, when one soldier set light to a house the flames spread throughout the city in minutes. The fire burned indiscriminately, as houses and temples alike became consumed by its ferocious heat.[17]

The flames drove the Lydian people from their homes and running in panic as many of them fled the flames right onto the point of a Greek weapon. With the outer edge of the city raging most, the Lydians and Persians herded themselves into the agora, which had the River Pactolus running through it, and made a stand with whatever arms they had managed to salvage. The Greeks saw the defensive position, as well as the vast numbers of citizens still flooding into the agora, and decided to retreat from Sardis.

The Greeks pulled back as far as Ephesus before they were finally confronted with a Persian relief force that had been directed in support of Sardis. The two forces lined up outside the city walls but the Greeks were no match for their Persian counterparts. The Greeks were broken into a rout and many of them slaughtered. After this defeat the Athenians withdrew all of their support for the Ionians, but this did not stop the momentum of Aristagoras' revolt.

By 497 BC the island of Cyprus had joined in an alliance with the Ionians and revolted against Persian rule. Uprisings in Ionia, Cyprus, Caria and the Hellespont showed that the rebellion was spreading like wildfire, so Darius sent Histiaeus to Ionia to try to subdue it, while simultaneously preparing a force to confront the rebellion on Cyprus first. They met a joint Cypriot-Ionian force on land and sea and, while the Ionians were victorious on the water, the Persians gained the upper hand on land and won the day. The Ionian fleet returned north, leaving the Persians to subdue the island and quell any possibility of a repeat performance.

The Persians continued to suppress their opposition in the Hellespont and Caria, bringing themselves closer and closer to addressing the source of the revolt, Miletus. Aristagoras realized his revolt was failing and fled to Thrace in 497/6 BC where he died besieging one of the Thracian cities.

Histiaeus' arrival at Miletus, in 496/5 BC, was not a welcoming one. Artaphernes immediately accused him of being the real force behind the revolt. Fleeing to Chios, he was similarly interrogated about his influence in the revolt by the Ionians. With little support to turn to, the tyrant sent messages to sympathetic Persians in Sardis, but they were discovered by Artaphernes and his Persian allies were executed for treason. With nowhere to turn, Histiaeus fled to Byzantium in 494 BC, leaving the Ionians to deal with the impending Persian forces that were gathering near Miletus without their leader.

The Ionian cities sent representatives to convene at the Panionian, a joint Ionian sanctuary north of Miletus. They knew the Persian land army was too large to confront in battle and that their best chance of survival was a siege. They decided to concentrate their collective forces on the impending naval battle that would ensue, so that they could keep their supply lines open and prolong the siege for as long as possible. They chose a rendezvous point for the various naval forces, a small island just off the coast of Miletus called Lade.

Forces

The Ionian fleet was the strongest Greek naval force assembled to date. On the eastern wing were 80 Milesian triremes. Next to them, stretching westward were 12 ships from Priene, 3 from Myous, 17 from Teos, 100 from Chios, 8 from Erythrae, 3 from Phocaea and 70 ships from Lesbos. Finally, on the far western wing were 60 ships from Samos. In all, the Ionians had amassed a force of 353 triremes, fully manned and equipped for battle.[18] They were led by the Phocaean commander, Dionysius, who was an experienced naval leader, but this was not an experienced force. Many of these men had not rowed triremes, nor experienced naval battle before; they were amateurs.

The Persian numbers are a little more complicated. They had accumulated 600 ships, which included a vastly experienced naval force from Phoenicia, as well as contingents from Egypt, Cyprus and Cilicia, but we do not know how many of these were actually triremes.[19] The Persian commanders were said to have been very concerned when they saw the Ionian fleet, which is unexpected for a force which held an advantage of almost 2:1. This may indicate that the Persians actually possessed a smaller number of triremes, which was at least closer in number to that of the Ionians. Whatever the case, the Persians definitely held a numerical advantage over the Greeks, we just do not know how large an advantage it really was.

Battle   (Herodotus, VI.7–VI.21)

When the Persian fleet arrived near Miletus and the commanders were able to assess the Greek force in full, they grew concerned by the number of triremes that the Ionians had been able to muster. In an attempt to undermine Greek morale, the Persians instructed those deposed tyrants of Ionia that were accompanying them on this venture to call on their former subjects to abandon the Milesian cause without fear of retribution. Every single Greek city refused.

The Greeks knew that this was a do-or-die situation, and their commander Dionysius likewise knew that they were not yet capable of winning the battle if it was imminent. He spoke in council and convinced the Ionians to let him train them for the fight ahead; to train them so they would be fully prepared for what would be expected of them. For seven days he drilled them in travelling out into the open sea in line-ahead, before realigning into the line-abreast formation which would be their battle line.[20] He also drilled them in the *diekplous*, which would have them drive forwards between the gaps of the Persian line and attack the vulnerable flanks and rear. While the rowers and trireme commanders (*trierarchs*) were learning their manoeuvres, Dionysius was also arming the marines who would be training on the moving decks.

Unfortunately for Dionysius, his regime was too gruelling for the amateur Greeks. When they were not practising in the ships he would put the men to labour for the rest of the day; never giving them any rest until nightfall. The Ionians were not used to this level of labour, nor discipline, and many became ill or injured as a result. By the eighth day at Lade, the men decided to refuse the orders of Dionysius and pitch tents on the island, thus refusing to board the ships.

When word of this reached the *trierarchs* of Samos they grew concerned about the discipline of their allies. They received another message from their former tyrant, Aiaces, imploring them to abandon the Ionian cause. This time the Samians were more receptive. If the Ionians could not be trusted to train how could they be trusted in battle? A vicious debate ensued between the [Samian] *trierarchs*, and not everyone agreed, but it was decided – the Samians would abandon the Ionian line at the first opportunity they had.

With at least one element of the Greek force resolved to abandon the battle line, the Persians felt confident enough to finally engage. As the Phoenicians began to appear at the head of the Persian fleet, pulling into an aggressive position, Dionysius gave the command. Just as they had practised, the Ionian ships pulled out to sea in line-ahead, with the Milesians leading the line. With drilled efficiency they each turned sharply and faced the Persian enemy with a line over 5km long.[21]

Both fleets began to advance on the other. The two lines edged closer and closer; gaps between allied ships spreading wider and wider. The Greeks watched with baited breath. Waiting for the chance to exploit the gaps, they would call upon a week of hard training and endless drills to defeat the greatest military force in the ancient world. Closer and closer they came, until a flash of white shot into the western sky. Then another. And another. The Samians had unfurled their sails. [22]

All but eleven triremes from Samos abandoned the left wing, those few who remained had refused the orders of their commanders and would fight to the bitter end.[23] The sight of the Samian flight had a harrowing effect on Greek morale, and the Lesbian contingent that floated next to them in the line quickly followed suit. In the blink of an eye Dionysius had just lost a third of his fleet, and yet more were abandoning their positions; but he had no time to dwell on such matters, contact was imminent – battle had begun.

The odds had quickly moved against the Greeks, and the Persians ruthlessly pursued their advantage. Only the Chians and the Phocaeans were able to cause any damage to the Persian line.[24] The 100 triremes from Chios followed the plan to the letter. They drove between the gaps of the Persian lines and started to cause havoc. Their triremes drove into the hulls of the outmanoeuvred Persian vessels. Once contact had been made the forty-strong teams of Chian marines engaged with their Persian enemy. As arrows flew through the air and sword clashed with shield, the men of Chios were able to take control of a handful of Persian ships. This victory came at considerable loss, for the Persians rendered the majority of the Chian fleet impotent. Those who had survived intact cut their losses and headed back to Chios; and those who were in the neutralized ships managed to flee north and disembark on the Mycale peninsula.

All Dionysius could do was engage with the Persians as best he could, but he soon realized this was a fight for survival. He needed to get his small Phocaean force out alive. His three triremes drove through the gaps ahead of them and turned back to ram the Persian ships they had passed. After a short mêlée, interrupted by the withdrawal of the Greek triremes and then a second round of ramming, three Persian ships fell into Dionysius' possession. But it was a hollow victory for the commander. He only needed the space to properly extract his force from the carnage that was ensuing. Having achieved his goal Dionysius steered the Phocaeans west and out of harm's way.

Aftermath

It is not known how many vessels were lost by either side, but the Ionian defeat brought about an even greater loss than any number of ships. With the sea at their disposal, the Persians pressed ahead and put Miletus under siege by land and sea. They dug mines under the walls, and used every available siege engine at their disposal. Miletus finally fell in that same year, and its people were enslaved.

As for the other Greeks, there were mixed fates. The Chians who managed to escape the disaster to Mycale began to march inland into the lands of Ephesus. Unluckily for them, they arrived during the night of the *Thesmophoria*, and the Ephesians believed this army had entered their lands to steal their women.[25]

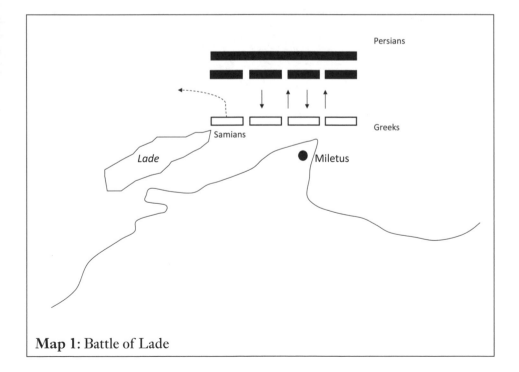

Map 1: Battle of Lade

The men of Ephesus marched out in full arms and slaughtered the Chians without ever knowing their story.

Dionysius was not foolish enough to take his men back to Phocaea. He already knew that the Persians would enslave all of Ionia, so he took his ships to Phoenicia, robbing and sinking some merchant ships. With a fortune acquired, he headed west to Sicily, where he established himself as a pirate.

As for Athens, the fate of Miletus caused great apprehension in the city. One playwright, Phrynichus, wrote a tragedy about the fall of Miletus for which he was fined on the charge of reminding the people of their own evils; it was ordered that the play should never be performed again. However, just because the Athenians were trying to forget does not mean that they were themselves forgotten. The Athenian role in the early Ionian revolt rested in the mind of Darius, and, as the dust began to settle in Ionia, Persian eyes began to look further west and to the Greek mainland. By 490 BC, Darius had arranged a small expedition to consolidate his control in the Cyclades before it headed north to Euboea and then landed a small force on the Greek mainland, to the north of Athens, by a small town called Marathon. Following the Persian defeat to the defending Athenian and Plataean army, the Persians returned home, having secured their foothold in Greek waters.

Chapter 2

The Battle of Artemisium (480 BC)

Background   (Herodotus, *Histories*, VII.3-147; VII.172-193;
Plutarch, *Life of Themistocles*, 4-7.)

I n 486 BC the Great King of Persia, Darius I, died and was succeeded by one
of his younger sons Xerxes I.[1] The empire that the young king inherited
may have been vast but it was on the verge of complete chaos. Even before
the death of Darius, the wealth-laden lands of Egypt were in revolt; so the first
action Xerxes took as king was to send an army into the Nile basin (485 BC) and
put down the rebellion with brutal efficiency.

Within a year Xerxes had established a stronger rule over Egypt, installing
his brother as the *satrap* of the region, before he returned home and began
preparations for an invasion of Greece. His plans were abruptly interrupted
by news of another revolt. This time the troubles were in the heart of the
Persian Empire: Babylonia had risen up against Xerxes' rule.[2] The revolt
was quickly dealt with, but Xerxes had a fondness for Babylon, a place
that had been his home for a few years of his life, so he was lenient in his
retribution on the city and the region as a whole. This leniency failed to
quell rebellious thoughts and within two years Xerxes was called upon to
send a second army into the region. Following this campaign, his army's
commander, Megabyzus, had the walls to the city destroyed and the statue
of Marduk removed from its home, symbolically removing the kingship of
Babylon from the city.[3]

These revolts constantly interrupted Xerxes' planning for his first military
expansion. Following the advice of Mardonius, and the petitioning of
aggrieved Greeks,[4] the King had begun preparations to punish Athens for their
involvement in the Ionian revolt, after he had exhibited control over Egypt
in 484.[5] The expedition took a full four years (484-1 BC) to arrange before he
could finally embark on his invasion of Greece.

Xerxes' plan was a bold one. He was to march at the head of his army north, through Asia Minor, and bridge the Hellespont. Once across and into Europe, the army would traverse the Aegean coast through Thrace, Macedonia, and then turn south into Greece. His march was to be shadowed for the entire journey by a strong naval fleet which would serve both as combatants against any joint-Greek navy, and as a supply chain to the men on land. For the Persian king, this expedition served as a statement of intent. He would launch one of the largest invasions that the world had ever seen. It would be an ostentatious display of his power as he completed the plans of his father and delivered retribution on the Athenian peoples that had wronged his family.[6] But Xerxes could not achieve this on his own, he needed the help of his *satraps* to amass the necessary numbers to achieve victory.

The king offered prizes to the contingent who was best supplied and equipped, which incentivised the *satraps* to do their best to impress the king, thus securing him a strong army. Yet the contingent did not need to be an army, per se: some of the *satraps* provided infantry and archers, others provided horsemen, some procured horse transports, while more still sent large ships to help bridge the Hellespont; some simply sent vast quantities of grain and small transport boats.

Xerxes' advanced planning extended even further than the procurement of men. Having identified an ideal crossing point on the Hellespont, in the lands outside the town of Abydos, he had the designs for the pontoon bridges he would construct ready. As early as 483 BC he ordered teams of Egyptians and Phoenicians to make ropes from papyrus and white flax that would be used to tie the ships together, and also to create a food reserve in anticipation for the march.[7] By 482 BC construction had begun on the pontoon which would span the narrow straits at the Chersonese (modern Gallipoli) in the mouth of the Hellespont, a distance of 7 *stades* (circa 1.3km). As the first two bridges were completed a violent storm broke out and destroyed them. When Xerxes learned of this he was furious and ordered that the waters of the Hellespont receive 300 lashes of the whip, and that a pair of shackles be dropped in for good measure. The unfortunate supervisors of the bridge construction were all beheaded for their troubles.

Xerxes swiftly assigned new supervisors to take up the task of rebuilding the two bridges. The first, which lay on the northern side of the chosen area for crossing, used 360 triremes and *penteconters* as support. They were aligned abreast, in the direction of the tidal streams and pointing north-to-south; with a gap between each vessel wide enough for smaller boats to pass through on their way into the Black Sea. Once in position they let down their very large anchors, some to the north and others to the south, to offset the tides and currents and various strong winds that blew there. Cables were made by twisting the four papyrus ropes and two of the heavier flax ropes; these were then stretched across the ships and attached to the European side of the straits. Planks of wood were cut to size, matching the width of the bridge of boats, and then tied into position between the taut cables. This walkway was covered in brushwood and trampled mud, before a fence was erected on both sides to stop the animals from panicking at the sight of water. The second, southern bridge was constructed in the same way but with 314 ships.

With the Hellespont removed as an obstacle, Xerxes had other concerns to deal with. Chief among them was a peninsula in Chalcidice, upon the promontory of which stood Mount Athos; for it was while rounding this point that the Persians had suffered a great loss of ships during their campaigns in Macedonia in 493/2 BC.[8] To counter this threat, Xerxes ordered an ambitious canal to be dug through the Mount Athos Peninsula.[9]

By 491 BC, the entire land army that Xerxes had enlisted assembled in the region of Cappadocia (north modern Turkey) before the long march west, along the great Royal Road.[10] They diverted south to Celaenae, most likely for supply purposes or else to gather more forces, and then headed back west to Sardis. At Sardis, Xerxes followed the behaviour of his father before him. He sent a team of heralds into Greece to ask for their supplication through the offering of earth and water. They also requested that the Greek *poleis* prepare feasts for the imminent arrival of the Great King. The messages were sent everywhere but for Athens and Sparta who had previously outraged Darius with the manner in which they dealt with his own heralds in 491 BC.[11]

In the winter of 481/80 BC news reached Sardis that the canal by Mount Athos had been completed, so at the arrival of spring the great army of Xerxes marched to Abydos. On arrival Xerxes sat on his recently commissioned marble throne atop a hill outside of the city, which allowed him to see all of his forces on land and sea: the sheer sight of them brought a tear to his eye. When the time had come, Xerxes crossed the northern bridge and watched as his soldiers followed suit, with the baggage train and beasts of burden crossing the southern bridge. From start to finish it took Xerxes' army seven days and seven nights to cross the waters and be ready to continue their march through Europe.

As Xerxes' army headed northeast to exit the Chersonese, his fleet sailed southwest and out of the straits into the north Aegean. They followed the coast around to Cape Sarpedon, where they were to rendezvous with the land army. On arrival they beached their ships to dry, so that Xerxes, after counting his land army, could finally review his fleet which had 1,207 triremes and a further 3,000 vessels of all shapes and sizes.[12]

As the army began its long and arduous march west through Thrace, the fleet shadowed it, following the coastline all the way to the Chalcidice peninsula. When they arrived at Acanthus the fleet broke away from the army and headed south to cut through the Athos canal. From here it headed round the last two peninsulas and into the Thermaic Gulf; recruiting benefactors, ships, and sailors all along the Greek lands of Sithonia and the Pallene Peninsula. Following the coast into the Gulf, the fleet stopped at designated cities: Therme, Sindos, and finally at Chalastra where they disembarked from their ships and set up a large camp to wait for the arrival of Xerxes and his army.

Reunited once more, the vast Persian force rounded south into northern Greece and the lands of Thessaly. It was about now that the envoys finally arrived back with the Greek responses to the demand for earth and water, and Xerxes was not disappointed as a large number sent their offerings.[13] The Greeks were scared; while much of Xerxes' rhetoric implied that only Athens was the target of his ire, it was believed that the Persian king would not be content with anything less than the complete subjugation of all of the Greek peoples. Concerns were raised by those who had not *medized* (joined the Persians) over the capabilities of the disparate Greek *poleis* to resist the Persians. Specifically, there was concern for the lack of suitable navies to be called upon to defend the seas.

The Athenians had already consulted the divine oracle of Delphi for help and guidance for the conflict ahead.[14] The Pythia at Delphi gave a harrowing prophecy telling the Athenians to flee their homes, for fire and blood would soon consume the houses and temples of not just Athens but many more cities besides. The Athenian delegates were in a panic; they would have to return home and deliver this portent of disaster. Before they could leave they were approached by Timon, a man of Delphi, who advised them to approach the oracle a second time but with an olive branch to identify themselves as suppliants. This brought a different response from the Pythia.

The oracle was unusually clear. Apollo told them that Zeus would grant Athens 'a wall made of wood' to defend its women and children. Unfortunately, when the delegates took the message back to the Athenian assembly, it was not easy to agree upon what a 'wall made of wood' actually meant. Some believed that the wall was a literal wall, that which encompassed the Acropolis in the heart of the city, while others believed it was meant figuratively and described the need for a strong fleet.

With little headway being made, an aristocrat by the name of Themistocles added to the argument for interpreting the oracle to be describing ships. He emphasized another part of the oracle which described a battle around the island of Salamis as proof that there would be a naval battle, and that ships were what was meant. Themistocles had already begun the construction of 200 triremes in 483 BC, for a planned attack on Aegina, so he argued that Apollo was telling them to build more ships and combine them with the vessels of any other Greek *polis* who would join them.[15] The assembly finally agreed with this point of view. After which, a meeting was held in the Isthmus of Corinth, where a Hellenic League was formed of all the *poleis* who would put their differences and squabbles aside and oppose the Persian invaders as a united body – at least this was the hope.[16]

During the meeting at the Isthmus, representatives from the *medized* peoples of Thessaly arrived declaring their allegiance to the Greek people. They said that Thessaly had submitted to Persia because of internal political pressure, but when they received word that Xerxes had crossed into Europe they had sent these envoys post haste. They called upon the League to defend the pass of Tempe at Mount Olympus and stop the Persian army, or else the Thessalians would be forced to surrender to the Persians in their entirety.

The League's response was resolute and an army 10,000 strong was sent by boat to land just south of Thessaly and continue on foot to the pass of Tempe. The army waited for a few days, but word soon reached them from Alexander of Macedon which relayed the full scale of Xerxes' invading force, which was at present crossing the Hellespont, and warned the Greeks that they would be simply overrun. This unwelcome news was followed by a second realization: not only was the Greek army too small but it was guarding one of two main routes south from Macedon into Thessaly. This meant that Xerxes could simply avoid their position entirely by using the other route or, worse still, surround and attack the pass from both sides.[17] The Greek army returned to the Corinthian Isthmus to plan a new strategy, and the Thessalians finally conceded to the Persian demands and *medized* without further hesitation.

The Greeks re-evaluated their position and decided to make a defensive stand slightly further south than Tempe. They chose the ill-fated pass at Thermopylae, and the land army would be shadowed by a fleet which would moor on the northern tip of Euboea, Artemisium.[18]

Xerxes' army continued its route south from Therme, but the king had already sent ten of his best ships to race ahead to Sciathus, an island just northwest of Artemisium, to clear the route. Once word was received that the Persian fleet could proceed they set sail, twelve days behind the land army, and waited at Sepias on the Magnesian coast.

The beach that had been chosen was very short, so only a small number of ships could be moored near to land while the rest lay at anchor offshore in rows eight ships deep, facing out to sea. But, as day broke from their first night, a ferocious storm came from the east and destroyed much of the fleet. The storm lasted for three long days, costing the Persians 400 ships. Once the sea had calmed, Xerxes' fleet took to the water once more and anchored at Aphetai, on the southern coast of Magnesia, opposite Artemisium.

The Persian arrival at Magnesia had driven the Greek fleet away in fear, but as the events proceeded in their favour, the Greek fleet returned to Artemisium in the expectation that they would face a much smaller Persian force – they were wrong.

Forces

The naval force of the Persians is frustratingly ill-described. Assuming, for a moment, that Herodotus' original figures were correct, then Xerxes' original fleet of 1,327 triremes (this figure includes 120 new triremes that joined him from Thrace) and 3,000 'others' ships lost 400 vessels in the last big storm.[19] We do not know what forms of boat were lost, or if this had a greater impact on the fighting strength or on the logistical strength, so any assessment of a fighting strength is difficult. Suffice to say it was still very large. What we are told is that the composition of the navy was based around three strong naval traditions: the Ionian Greeks, the Egyptians, and the Phoenicians.

Each trireme was manned by a crew of 200 men, inclusive of the Athenian standard complement of 10 marines and four archers. The Persians added an extra marine force of 30 Medes and Sacae, who were renowned archers, to ensure that Xerxes had a presence on every trireme, making them less likely to flee. The smaller ships had crews of roughly 80 men with 50 rowers and the remainder being petty officers, deckhands and marines.[20]

For the Greeks we know a great deal more. The entire fleet consisted of 271 triremes, and an unspecified number of *penteconters*. Athens supplied the bulk of the ships, 127 in total, some of which were manned by the Plataean allies; Corinth sent 40 triremes; the Megarians 20; Chalcis manned a further 20 which were provided by the Athenians; the Aeginetans provided 18; the Sicyonians 12; the Spartans sent 10; with smaller contributions sent by Epidaurus, Eretria, the Troizenians, the Styrians, the Keans and the Locrians. It was a vast fleet in Greek military terms but most definitely outnumbered by the Persians.

Again, each trireme would have been manned by a crew and marine force numbering 200 each. Interestingly, the overall command of the fleet was given to the relatively under-represented Spartans and their *nauarch*, Eurybiades, due to their dominant military reputation.[21]

While the triremes from each fleet were, by and large, of the same design, we are told that the Athenians had the fastest ships among the Greeks, possibly due to a specification in the designs made by Themistocles.[22] Similarly we are told that the fastest of all the triremes, Greek and non-Greek, were those of the Phoenicians.

Battle   (Herodotus, *Histories*, 7.194–195; 8.1–8.22; Plutarch, *Life of Themistocles*, 7–9; Diodorus, XI.12–13.)

As the Greeks were moored at Artemisium, staring at the vast flotilla that opposed them at Aphetae, their fears and apprehensions for the inevitable battle that was to ensue were quickly abashed by a peculiar sight. Heading toward them from the Cape of Magnesia were fifteen seemingly barbarian ships. They had obviously departed later than the rest of the Persian fleet and were heading directly toward the Greeks, mistaking them for the Persian fleet. The Greek commanders watched with some bemusement. A number of Greek ships put out to sea and quickly captured all fifteen of the vessels. The captive marines were interrogated and, after the Greeks had learned all they needed regarding the size of Xerxes' fleet, the prisoners were sent in chains to the Corinthian Isthmus.

The realization of exactly how superior was the Persian fleet caused great trepidation within the Hellenic crews. The storms had not removed the Persian advantage as much as had been expected and there was talk of the allied fleet turning back from their position for reassessment. The Euboeans were particularly concerned about this as their island would be the first contact point for the Persians. Originally they went to the *nauarch* Eurybiades, imploring him to give them time so they could evacuate their families from the island, but they were refused. Following this rebuff, they went to Themistocles and bribed him with thirty *talents* to convince the fleet to stay. [23] The Athenian in turn bribed the Spartan *nauarch* and the commander of the Corinthians with five and three *talents* respectively – keeping the rest for a nice personal profit. [24]

To the Persians, the presence of the large Greek fleet offered an opportunity to eradicate any significant Greek presence on the sea, freeing them up to offer more support to the army which was now fighting in the pass at Thermopylae. To that end, the Persian commander needed to cut off any escape route before he engaged in a head-on battle. A detachment of 200 ships was sent out to sea, around the isle of Sciathus so they could not be seen, and down the Euboean coast, with the aim of travelling up the narrow straight of Euripos and cutting off the inner channel. Until a signal came to tell the main fleet that the Greeks' escape was blocked, the Persian commander simply waited and counted his ships.

During this wait, the Greeks received a Greek informant from the Persian camp called Scyllias. Having swum the 9 miles from Aphetai to Artemisium he relayed news of the Persian losses during the storm, and he warned them of the plan to surround the Greek position that was already in motion. The Greek commanders took stock of their situation and, with nightfall imminent, they chose to wait until daybreak and then attack the 200 ships that were coming from the south.

With dawn came a re-evaluation of their situation, and Eurybiades decided that they would not turn their back on the main Persian fleet but attack it head on. The plan was to assess the Persian resolve and fighting capabilities; it was an intended skirmish and the *nauarch* knew his limitations. A part of the

Greek fleet set out late in the day, preventing the possibility of a long, drawn-out confrontation which would only favour the Persian numbers. The Persians could not believe what they were seeing, the Greek force was tiny in comparison and so the Persians sent out a detachment to deal with them swiftly.

The Persian ships maintained their column and set in motion a *periplous*, encircling the Greeks. A signal finally came from one of the Greek triremes and all of the ships moved simultaneously, bringing their sterns together at a central point with their bows pointing out, forming a naval hedgehog of lethal points. Once everyone was in position they waited for the second signal. When it came, each ship shot forwards at full power. The perfectly timed *diekplous* had a devastating impact on the Persians, breaking their lines and ensuring that carnage reigned supreme. Thirty Persian ships were captured, along with many important commanders. Night fell before the Persians could regroup and turn the tide of Greek momentum, with both forces returning to their main fleets.

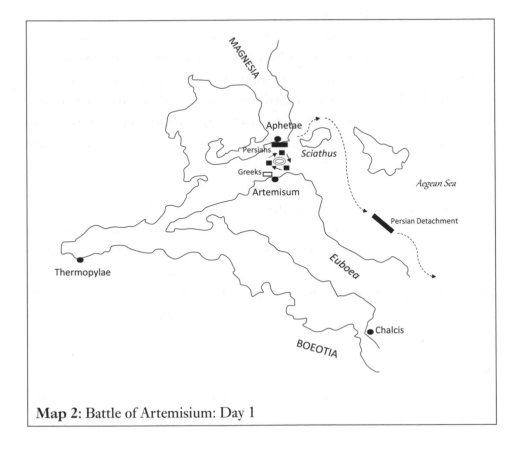

Map 2: Battle of Artemisium: Day 1

It was not the skirmish the Greeks had in mind, but the sight of thirty Persian ships in tow brought renewed optimism.

During the night heavy rains began to fall and booming thunder filled the ears. The corpses and splintered wreckage of the battle began to float ashore at Aphetae. The Persian sailors began to panic as the corpses collected around the prows of their ships, and became entangled in the blades of their oars. Much worse was to befall the 200 ships travelling around Euboea as they were caught by the storm before they had reached the safety of the inner channel. Carried off by the wind they were smashed into the dark rocks along the Euboean coast and destroyed.

At daybreak the Greeks received word that the 200 Persian ships sailing off Euboea had been destroyed. This was greeted with further good news as the morning brought with it a further fifty-three ships from Attica to join them – the two fleets were now a lot closer in fighting strength. [25] A small Greek skirmish party was sent out late in the day and destroyed some Persian ships before retreating as night fell.

As day three began, Greek morale was very high. But for the Persians it was their day of reckoning. Xerxes was beginning to make ground at Thermopylae and would not tolerate any failure from his fleet. They had to act, and decisively. The Persian fleet drew up line-abreast and advanced on the Greeks, who remained motionless. It was not until the Persian line began to move into a crescent shape – attempting to encircle and trap the Greeks – that the order was finally given for the Greek triremes to attack.

The fighting was ferocious and chaotic as rams crashed into wood, arrows flew from deck to deck, and marines fought in an unrelenting mêlée. Panic and confusion, allied with the narrow space involved, meant allies crashed into allies as the manoeuvring of ships became more and more hazardous.[26] Neither side could gain the upper hand, with the Egyptians and the Athenians bearing the brunt of much of the combat. Neither side would relent until the daylight started to fade and they both broke off from each other and returned to land and the safety of anchorage.

Aftermath

At the end of the battle there was no victor. The Persians had lost more ships, but they had substantial strength to allow them to fight again. The Greeks,

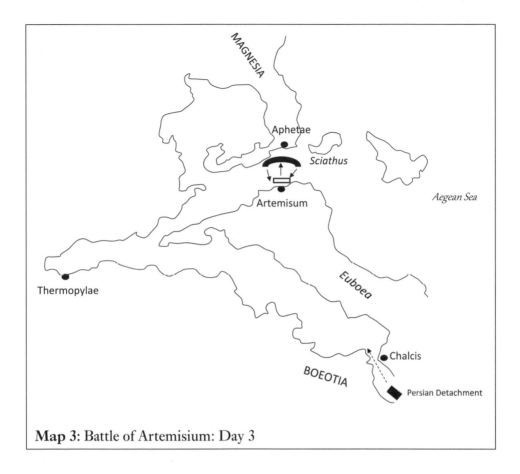

MAGNESIA

Aphetae

Sciathus

Aegean Sea

Artemisum

Euboea

Thermopylae

Chalcis

BOEOTIA

Persian Detachment

Map 3: Battle of Artemisium: Day 3

for their part, held sway over the corpses and wreckages in the water, a Greek sign of victory not necessarily shared by the Persians, but Athens alone had lost the use of half of their ships. With the inner channel free of a Persian blockade there was a victory of sorts and the Greeks decided to retreat from their position.

As the Greeks prepared to leave Artemisium, a lookout from Trachis arrived with harrowing news. Leonidas was dead and Thermopylae had fallen. Xerxes had a clear route into Greece. The Greeks could not delay any longer, they had to regroup around Athens and the Peloponnese to plan the next phase of their resistance to Xerxes.

Chapter 3

The Battle of Salamis (480 BC)

Background   (Herodotus, VIII.19-80; Diodorus, XI.13-17;
                   Plutarch, *Life of Themistocles*, 10-13.)

In the height of summer in 480 BC, bad news flooded the resistant Greek *poleis*.[1] The Spartan king Leonidas had fallen and the position of Thermopylae had been lost. The vast Greek fleet at Artemisium had fought heroically but was soon forced to abandon their position and sail south and around toward the Corinthian Isthmus. This allowed Xerxes to regroup his forces before continuing his advance south into central Greece.

The Persian fleet remained waiting cautiously at Aphetae. Reports that the Greek fleet had fled their position at Artemisium were not believed in an instant. To validate the rumour the Persian commander sent a few of his fastest ships to find out, and it was not until their return that the Persians finally relaxed. They lingered until noon of the day when the swift ships had returned and then sailed to Histaea, to the southwest of Artemisium, taking the city and overrunning all of the coastal villages in their path. While in Histaea they received a message from Xerxes inviting any of the men who so wished to take a small period of leave from the ships and join him on the battlefield of Thermopylae to see the evidence of his victory against the Greeks who resisted him.

Before the marines arrived on the battlefield, Xerxes had already begun proceedings to orchestrate the sight which his sailors would eventually see. The Great King ordered large ditches to be dug, and for the majority of the Persian bodies, maybe as high as 19,000 in total, to be buried – leaving just 1,000 dead above ground.[2] The move was designed to maintain the morale of his men; his army had no reason to be despondent, they had been marching at a steady pace, plundering as they went through Thrace and down into Greece. They had only met one pocket of resistance which had been overcome in a mere three days, and their fleet was similarly undefeated even though it had suffered at the hands of numerous storms. However, Xerxes seemed aware that the visual shock of the costs of attrition that had won the day at Thermopylae may have created doubts in the hearts of his men. The Great King's ploy did not convince everyone. The sailors came in their droves and walked across the battlefield to view the corpses. 4,000 Greeks lay slaughtered, but Xerxes could not keep the secret of his deception, for the sheer absurdity of it is said to have caused the truth to be known. But the lie did not have any great effect on the sailors, with many of them returning to their ships in Histaea, while the rest stayed with the army to continue the march on land.

Xerxes' march south was uncontested, as the Greeks were celebrating the Olympic festival which ostensibly forced a pan-Hellenic truce for the games. So, with the guidance of their Thessalian allies, the Persians headed west into the pro-Persian lands of the Dorians, before steering south into the resistant lands of Phocis, looting and razing towns as they went. Towns and sanctuaries were put to the flame, not even the oracle of Apollo at Abae was safe from the carnage. Any men that were found were killed, and women were raped to death by the sheer volume of assailants. When Xerxes' army had reached the Boeotian border with Phocis, he split his army in two. The larger force stayed with him to march through the pro-Persian lands of Boeotia, to be shadowed by the reinforced fleet at Histaea. The smaller force headed west to plunder the rich temples of Delphi, but was defeated at the sanctuary and fled, beset by rockslides and supposedly divine apparitions.[3]

Meanwhile, the Greek fleet that had departed from Artemisium was heading around Attica and most likely bound for Troezen on the Peloponnesian coast to meet up with the rest of the ships which had been brought together by the Greeks. But they soon received a message from Athens to assist in the evacuation of the city. The Athenians had not waited to discover the fate of the Greek forces at Thermopylae and Artemisium, since the Delphic oracle had clearly warned them that Athens would be taken and an evacuation of this magnitude needed as much time as possible to orchestrate.[4] It was also known that the Peloponnesians were building a wall across the Corinthian Isthmus, in essence cutting Attica and Athens adrift, so the city was no longer a safe haven for its people. This point was emphasized by the priestesses from the Acropolis when they announced – possibly under the influence of Themistocles – that the protector of the city, the goddess Athena, had abandoned her temples and left the city.[5] Whole families were packed onto ships and sent to Troezen and the islands of Aegina and Salamis, and only a small garrison and the treasurers of the temples were left to defend the Acropolis.[6] Once the fleet from Artemisium had aided the Athenians in their move, they sailed to Salamis to await the rest of the Greek ships moored at Troezen. On convening at Salamis, the Greeks held council to decide on their next move, with a strong set of voices arguing for the Greeks to sail to the Isthmus of Corinth and fight the Persians at sea there. As the debates continued, news came of the Persian advance through Thespiae, south past Plataea and into Attica. Athens was their next destination.

Since crossing the Hellespont, Xerxes' army had marched for over four long months. While it was not the sole aim of the invasion to punish the Athenians, the target of Athens must have been a focal point of Persian planning, and it was finally there for the taking. On arrival, the Great King discovered the city deserted and simply marched his men inside the defensive walls. It was not until his men reached the Acropolis that they found a hastily constructed rampart fortifying the sacred precinct, made from doors and random planks of wood. The Persians set themselves upon the rocky hill of the Areopagus and laid siege to the Acropolis that lay opposite.

The siege protracted for many days, if not weeks, with the Athenian garrison defending with all their might. Persian arrows were wrapped in hemp and set alight, burning the palisade to the ground, but still the Athenians resisted. Around this time, Xerxes sent a family of Athenian exiles, the Peisistratids, to negotiate a surrender, but they were quickly rebuffed. The Athenian garrison reacted by creating new forms of defence, such as rolling boulders down at the Persians to prevent access to their position. The siege continued until the Persians were finally able to reach the top of the Acropolis, probably through the impact of attrition on the defenders, and the vast numerical superiority the Persians possessed.[7] Some Persian soldiers had ascended a steep cliff face to the eastern face of the Acropolis and struck panic in the hearts of the Athenians, with many throwing themselves from the heights to their deaths, while others took refuge in a holy sanctuary. The Persians threw open the gates for the rest of their forces to join them, while those already at the summit entered the sanctuary and slaughtered the suppliants. Once the Athenians had been duly killed, the Persians then set fire to the entire Acropolis precinct.

News of the disaster reached the Greeks on Salamis and caused a major division between them. Some of the commanders made their own decisions; not waiting for the discussions to conclude they embarked onto their ships and fled. The majority who did remain further pushed their cause for a tactical withdrawal to the Isthmus shoreline. Only the Athenians, embodied by the charismatic Themistocles, argued for Salamis to be their arena for a naval battle but with little effect. Themistocles emphasized the tactical advantages of the narrow straits of Salamis rather than the open waters around the Isthmus, but to no avail. He was forced to threaten that the Athenians would simply depart for Italy rather than the Isthmus if the decision was made to abandon Salamis. This threat was enough to postpone a mass withdrawal, as the official leader of the naval forces, the Spartan Eurybiades, was frightened by the prospect of losing 200 fully manned triremes.

While the Greeks waited at Salamis, the Persians were discussing their plans in Attica. Xerxes knew that the first confrontation would be at sea and had joined his fleet at the Athenian harbour at Phaleron to talk with his naval commanders. Almost all of the commanders offered the same advice, take to the sea and fight the Greeks at Salamis; all except one. The female commander Artemisia, tyrant of Halicarnassus, disagreed with the need for a naval confrontation, predicting that the Greeks would not hold their cohesion for long and would soon end up dispersing back to their own cities.[8] Xerxes was impressed by her honesty and sage advice, but decided to follow the majority of his commanders and gave the command for the fleet to put out to sea and sail to Salamis. On arrival they deployed into battle lines but it was too late in the day to expect the Greeks to come and face them so they returned to land and prepared to do battle the next day.

The sudden appearance of the Persian fleet caused panic within the Greek camp, especially for the Peloponnesian contingent who never wanted to be caught at Salamis. The panic caused whispers, whispers which grew to grumbling dissent, but those grumbles were soon vehemently aired at a meeting of the Greek commanders. The same old arguments were put forward but Themistocles was losing his influence. The Athenian surreptitiously withdrew from the council and called for a trusted aide, a house-slave named Sicinnus, to make his way to the Persian camp and pass on a message. Pretending that Themistocles wanted Xerxes to be victorious, Sicinnus informed the Persian commanders that the Greeks were frightened and looking to depart, giving the Persians a great opportunity to win a massive victory against a disillusioned enemy. His message was believed and the Persians reacted quickly.

Forces

Confusion surrounds the fighting strength of both fleets at Salamis, but the Persian numbers are particularly problematic. The main reason for this is that Herodotus, our main source for the battle, does not give them. All we are told by the historian is that the naval strength of the Persians was depleted in the lead up to, and subsequent battle of, Artemisium, but that they received reinforcements from various pro-Persian *poleis* which returned their strength to roughly the number which they had before the storms, that is 1,327.[9] A similar number can also be deciphered from an earlier source than Herodotus, in Aeschylus' play *Persians*. Aeschylus, who himself fought in the battle, described the Persian fleet as having 1,000 ships, while those excelling in speed numbered 207.[10] Yet it is not clear whether those 207 are in addition to, or included within, the 1,000. As always with Persian numbers, these should be taken with a large pinch of salt; however, the Persian fleet would have been very large indeed.

The Persians had a force of 400 men on the island of Psyttaleia, but no other land forces are mentioned.[11] The fleet had four admirals who commanded distinct contingents based upon territorial identity: Ariabignes commanded the Ionian and Carian ships, Xerxes' brother Achaimenes commanded the Egyptian ships, while Megabazus and Prexaspes commanded the rest. Finally the entire battle was watched by Xerxes himself on the Attic coastline.

The Greek numbers are similarly confusing. Our two main sources, Herodotus and Aeschylus, both give numbers for the Greek fleet but they just do not agree. Herodotus claims that 380 ships fought on the Greek side, but if you add up the breakdown he gives of the contribution for each of the *poleis* the Greeks only provide 366 ships, and 180 of those were Athenian. Aeschylus describes the Greek fleet in a similarly ambiguous style to his description of the Persian fleet: 300 ships, or possibly 310.[12] Ctesias gives the remarkable figure of 700 Greek ships, which is not generally given credence, but he preceded this by remarking that the strength of the Athenian contingent was only 110 triremes.[13] It has been suggested that some numerically nuanced work can combine these three sources to present the Greek strength as approximately 300–310 strong and the Athenian numbers to make up 110 of these, taking into account that roughly half of the Athenian triremes which fought at Artemisium were put out of action as a result of the battle (i.e. roughly 70 ships) – something Herodotus maybe forgot to factor into his figures. But it is speculative and, while not implausible, cannot be proven.[14]

The Greek fleet was made up of ships from all over mainland Greece, many of the Greek islands, and one trireme was supplied by a rich aristocrat called Phayllus from as far afield as Croton in southern Italy. This mixed force was officially led by the Spartan *nauarch*, Eurybiades, but tactical credit is most frequently given to the Athenian Themistocles and, on at least one occasion by Ctesias, jointly with another Athenian called Aristides.[15]

Battle   (Herodotus, VIII.76-96; Aeschylus, *Persians*, 353-471; Diodorus, XI.18-19; Plutarch, *Life of Themistocles*, 13-15.)

The Persian commanders wanted to capitalize on their information quickly, and immediately placed a force of infantrymen on the small island of Psyttaleia at the southern entrance to the channel between the mainland and Salamis. Then, waiting for night to fall and midnight to pass, they sent the Egyptian contingent on the western wing of their fleet to circle clockwise around Salamis to cut off the Greek retreat; while the main bulk of the fleet blocked off the escape route south and out of the channel.[16] If what Sicinnus had said was true, Xerxes was ready to catch any Greek ships trying to flee in the night; if not, then his ships were poised for the signal to attack the Greek station on Salamis in the morning.

As for the Greek commanders, they were still arguing amongst themselves, unaware of the proverbial net that was being cast around them. It was not until the warnings of a recently returned exile of Athens, and political enemy of Themistocles, by the name of Aristides came, that the situation was revealed. Aristides approached the council's door and called Themistocles to him. In private conversation, away from non-Athenian ears, the two politicians put aside their personal differences and discussed the matter at hand. Aristides told him that Persians had cut off all possible exits from Salamis, unaware that it had all been Themistocles' own doing. When Themistocles revealed his secret he asked Aristides to relay his news to the rest of the commanders, through fear that his own standing among the group may lead to accusations of deception and lies on his part. But Aristides suffered a similar fate in his attempts until the arrival of a solitary trireme of deserters from the island of Tenos, who had abandoned their position in Xerxes' fleet and relayed the truth about the situation that the Greeks faced. With the words of the Tenians ringing in their ears, the Greek commanders realized that their fates were set and that battle was imminent. With this shift in mindset, they made their preparations.

At the break of day Xerxes stood on the Attic coast overlooking the channel of Salamis. He was ready to move and follow the battle, allowing himself the best vantage point as the contest evolved; with him stood his secretaries ready to record the battle as it transpired.[17] In the Persian fleet the day started slowly as they stood by for orders to advance. On Salamis, the scene was somewhat different.

As dawn was breaking, the Greek commanders convened another meeting and invited the marines to join them. Themistocles spoke to the men, encouraging them ahead of the battle to choose the best facets of human nature, rather than succumb to the worst. They then moved out to the shore, where, it is claimed by one source, Themistocles and a seer named Euphrantides made a sacrifice alongside the triremes. Their rite was interrupted by the arrival of three Persian prisoners taken from a skirmish on Psyttaleia. When the seer saw them he immediately identified positive omens and called upon the Greeks to sacrifice the prisoners to the god Dionysus Eater-of-raw-flesh. Themistocles was both terrified and mortified by the notion, but the fear of the battle ahead drove the masses to ignore the Athenian and do as the seer suggested, dragging them to an altar and shedding their blood for the god.[18]

The Greek triremes were manned and prepared and, with the omens on their side, the Greeks sang their paean. The words carried across the choppy waters to the Persian ships, unsettling the men, most of whom were unable to see the Greeks. Once the *paean* went quiet, the silence was broken by the blasts of a trumpet, giving the Greeks their order to move offshore and form their battle lines. The Athenians and the Spartans took the left wing pointing toward Eleusis, facing the best of the Persian navy in the Phoenicians and the Ionians. The triremes from Aegina and Melos took the right wing while the remainder of the ships formed the centre, except for the Corinthians who had been sent north to stop the Egyptians from joining battle at the rear. The Persian lines were formed and organized, but when the order came to advance through the narrow channel their lines proved too wide and some of their ships had to drop back, causing some confusion and disorder.

The Athenians moved first against the Phoenicians opposite them, where the trireme of the Athenian Ameinias made first contact against the great ship of Ariamenes, a son of Xerxes himself. Ariamenes was a formidable enemy, and his marines littered the Greek decks with arrows and javelins, until the two ships struck each other head on, their rams penetrating deep and binding the hulls together. The close proximity allowed Ariamenes to attempt a boarding of the Greek trireme but he was faced by Ameinias and, after a short mêlée, was stabbed by the Greek's spear and fell into the sea. The first blood was taken by the Greeks, but amazingly most of their ships were not there to see it.

As the Athenians and Aeginetans had advanced on the wings, many of their comrades had decided against rowing out and were instead backing water. The exception to this was the Corinthians to the north of the channel who had been engaged in their own fighting with the Egyptians, holding the rear against superior numbers with a mammoth effort. For the Egyptians it was not a catastrophe, their job was to cut off the northern exit in the case of a Greek rout and, in all likelihood, the fighting was little more than a skirmish in their eyes. But for the Corinthians it was a great struggle against a strong enemy, and one they succeeded in fending off.[19]

Once word spread of the Athenian successes the centre of the fleet finally joined them. The Greeks rowed out to the Persians who had slowed their advance, as they had become more and more wary of the narrowing channel. With momentum behind them, and a distinct weight advantage, the Greek triremes ploughed into their now-disorderly Persian adversaries. Persian rams were torn off by the clashes, and oars were shattered by the collisions.

The Persians fought valiantly and held the upper hand when the ships were locked together and boarding tactics were implemented; but, without the space to manoeuvre, their ships soon began to obstruct one another.[20] The Greek ships were able to hem them into the narrows and battered them from all angles. From his stool on the mainland promontory Xerxes watched the carnage unfold. Hulls of Persian vessels began to roll, throwing the men into the sea to be skewered by Greek spears like fish. The Greeks struck any enemy they saw in the water, using weapons and broken oars they smashed the bones of the Persian sailors who were unable to swim. Many of their bodies washed up against the reef and shorelines, lapped over by the crimson surf.

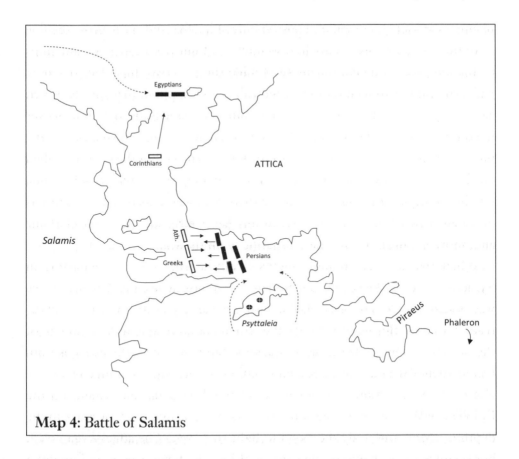

Map 4: Battle of Salamis

The Persian ships turned and fled as best they could, and in the confusion the ship of the female commander Artemisia was trying to escape from an Athenian ship that was chasing her down. Due to the confusion she was unable to navigate free from the mass of ships around her and so took drastic action by ramming one of her ally's ships. By doing so the Athenian *trierarch* believed Artemisia's to be a Greek ship and abandoned his pursuit. This action secured Artemisia her safety and also caught the attention of Xerxes who was impressed by the actions of his only female commander. Any of those Persian ships that were able to break free and retreat south out of the channel were greeted by the awaiting Aeginetans who had successfully routed their opposing wing and lay in ambush toward the channel's exit. For the Persians it was a fighting retreat until they could reach the safety of Phaleron.

As the confusion of battle began to subside, Aristides turned his attention to the Persian force on Psyttaleia. He collected Athenian hoplites who had been waiting and watching the fighting from the coast of Salamis and dropped them onto the island. The men jumped from their ships and encircled the island, giving the Persians nowhere to turn. The stranded Persians loosed their arrows and, when they had run out, threw stones at the hoplites and killed some of the Greeks from a distance; if they were going to die they were not going out without a fight. But when the Greeks had closed in far enough they charged the Persians from every direction, piercing them with their spears before letting go, drawing their swords and hacking away at the remaining combatants. Not a single Persian left the island with his life.[21]

As night descended over the faces of the dead and dying, the Persians finally cleared the channel of their ships, aided by a strong westerly wind. The Greeks hauled their vessels onto the shores of Salamis and, with them, as many of the Persian wrecks as they could manage. Finally, they could relax after a long, gruelling, and hard-fought twelve hours. They had lost at least 40 triremes in the fight, but in the process they had destroyed 200 of the Persians'. Yet the war was far from over. Both sides had lost roughly a fifth of their naval force, but Persia still held a vast numerical advantage on the sea as well as their hitherto undefeated army on the mainland.

Aftermath

Following his defeat at Salamis, Xerxes consulted with a few of his commanders and decided to leave Greece. The reason for his withdrawal is not known, but the campaigning season was swiftly coming to an end since Salamis was fought at the end of September. Thus it could simply have been his intention to spend the winter back in his palace. He left his trusted general Mardonius with a strong army to continue the conquest of Greece in his absence and left, never to set foot in Greece again.

Mardonius went on to fight the Greeks at the decisive encounter of Plataea where he was finally defeated and the Persians were pushed out of Greece. This did not bring an end to the Greco–Persian conflicts which continued to be fought, on and off, for a further 150 years up until the definitive success of the Macedonian king, Alexander the Great.

To the Greeks, Salamis was the victory which typified their heroic stand against the Persians. Every *polis* involved wanted credit for their achievements; unlike Marathon which was a victory for Athens, or Thermopylae which was a heroic stand for the Spartans, Salamis could be claimed by all who took part.

Part 2

ARCHIDAMIAN WAR

The Archidamian War was a conflict which lasted ten years, between 431 and 421 BC, and forms the first part of the much larger Peloponnesian War (431-404 BC). In reality, the Peloponnesian War as a single entity is a fiction, and consists of two distinct wars separated by a finely balanced peace treaty that lasted from 421-413 BC. Yet, because the main protagonists are consistent throughout both wars, namely the Athenians and the Peloponnesians, it is often referred to as a continuous conflict in the ancient sources.

The Archidamian War did not begin because of tensions between the two powerhouses of ancient Greece, Athens and Sparta. It began in the 430s BC because Athens was encroaching on the authority of another strong *polis*, Corinth. Corinth was itself an important Peloponnesian ally of Sparta, due mainly to its powerful navy. Corinth's fleet was considered one of the strongest aside from Athens' own, but the Athenians were putting that all under threat by forming an alliance with the Corinthian colony of Corcyra. The navy of Corcyra was the second largest, larger even than Corinth's, and if it united with Athens, they would form the largest navy imaginable in the Greek world. Corinth needed to intervene, which resulted in the Battle of Sybota (433 BC). The battle was a gigantic affair, with both the Corcyraeans and the Corinthians amassing well over 100 ships each. But the Corinthians were not expecting a naval battle, and had prepared for an invasion rather than combat. As a result, the battle turned into the perfect example of a style of combat that focussed on boarding and fighting on the ship decks.

Corinth was able to win the day, but their problems were not over. Although this was not yet the official outbreak of the Archidamian War, our main source for the period, Thucydides, pinpoints this conflict in the northwestern theatre as one of the main causes for it. The second flash point also concerned Athens and Corinth, and it focussed on the small town of Potidaea, in Chalcidice. Potidaea had been founded by Corinthian settlers, but it had also been absorbed, over time, into the Athenian empire as a tribute-paying member – so each *polis* felt a legitimate claim to it.

Potidaea was a point of concern for Athens. There was growing discontent in northern Greece against Athenian influence. Potidaea was in a perfect position to become a focal point of resistance, a well-defended base from which a large rebellion could easily grow. To the west and north of Chalcidice were the lands of Macedon, which was in a state of unrest due to its own internal conflicts. The Macedonian king, Perdiccas II, was trying to defend his crown against both his younger brother and another pretender to the throne, both of whom had just received support from the Athenians. Perdiccas needed to redirect Athenian attentions, so he hoped to start an inter-Greek state war. Originally he petitioned Sparta to begin a war against Athens, but the Spartans were reluctant to do so without good cause. Not being put off by this rejection, Perdiccas decided instead to focus on the northern Greek towns of Chalcidice and the Thracian tribes in the area. He encouraged them to revolt and thus forced the hand of the Athenians.

A strong Athenian presence was sent north and, after their heavy handed threats were not heeded, they fought a battle outside of the walls of Potidaea. The Athenians won a simple victory and put the city under siege. However, what Athens had not reckoned on was that this siege would last a further two years, it would cost them a third of their entire war chest, and it would not succeed in subduing feelings of resentment in the region, nor the desire for revolt. All that Athens had achieved was to give Sparta a reason to enter a war, a war that would be named after the Spartan king himself, Archidamus.

The war on land was quite a passive affair for long periods of time. The Spartans used a system of raiding campaigns to attack Athenian lands, but could never induce the Athenians to engage with them in battle. The Athenians, instead, utilized their greatest strength, their navy, to cause havoc all along the Greek coastline. They focussed their attentions in the Corinthian Gulf, to try and nullify their main rival for control of the sea, Corinth. In 429 BC this culminated in a two-part battle, with the Athenian fleet led by the great admiral of the period, Phormio. In this battle for the Corinthian Gulf, Phormio was able to exploit the experience of his crews and the speed of his ships to turn what should have been a shattering defeat into a glorious victory against a far larger enemy fleet. During the battle we see the tactical capabilities of a well-managed trireme, and we witness the utter devastation that can result from a *kyklos* being contracted by a circling enemy.

In 427 BC, Athenian interests had moved to the northwest and around Corcyra once again, which needed support following an internal revolt before the Peloponnesians could exploit their weakened state. However, the Peloponnesians were more dynamic and assaulted an ill-prepared Corcyraean fleet, which had with it only a small Athenian contingent. The Athenians were still able to influence the battle of Corcyra, but the Peloponnesians had learned from their defeat in the Corinthian Gulf. When they formed a *kyklos*, and the Athenians began to circle around them, the Peloponnesians were not destined for destruction this time. They waited patiently for a separate squadron to come and help them, using this formation to buy themselves some time. When support did arrive, they immediately opened up the *kyklos*, into line abreast, and pushed the Athenians back.

These three battles show the range of fighting systems available to Greek fleets. While our sources denigrated what they describe as the 'old fashioned tactics' of boarding and fighting amongst marines, that does not mean that we should as well. Our sources were mainly written by Athenians, or else produced in Athens, and it was not a style of warfare that the Athenians were very good at employing. However the naval purist will get to appreciate the tactical ingenuity show by the Athenians, who preferred to ram and move within the enemy lines, exploiting the weaknesses of the enemy, while maximizing their own strengths. What is also obvious from these battles is the interconnected nature of naval campaigns. The entire naval theatre was finely balanced, so that if the Athenians moved a fleet from one point to another, it would often have a knock-on effect. The clearest instance is the Battle of Corcyra, when the Peloponnesian fleet that was defeated in Lesbos continued their journey home, before venturing round to Corcyra to exploit a revolt in the city, which the Athenians could not tackle in time, because of their own commitments in the east.

Chapter 4

The Battle of Sybota (433 BC)

Background   (Thucydides, I.24–47; Diodorus, XII.30–33;
Plutarch, *Life of Pericles*, 29)

By the year 435 BC the coming of war was considered, by the Athenians at least, to be inevitable. Athens had successfully created an empire for itself in the guise of a Hellenic defence league, it held power over the Aegean and the trade routes therein, and its power had the capability of growing almost continuously unless an external military intervention occurred. However, the only *polis* strong enough to take Athens head on was that of Sparta, which held greater concerns for its own internal affairs and stability than it did for Athenian expansion.[1] Thus, the blue paper would not be lit by direct opposition against Athens, but instead by an innocuous event on the periphery of the Greek world.

In the northwest of Greece, on the periphery of the Hellenic world, stood the city of Epidamnus, just at the entrance of the Ionian Gulf which separates the Greek mainland and the 'heel' of Italy. The city had a mixed lineage as a colony of the island of Corcyra (modern Corfu), which had in turn been called upon to found the colony by its own mother-city, Corinth. Corinth also sent some settlers to join the venture and supplied the overall leader who would be considered the city's founder. The early life of Epidamnus was one of growth and prosperity, but its situation was always precarious, isolated as it was within the lands of the Illyrians, a non-Hellenic, tribal based culture. As the city expanded, and the prospect of power grew, internal factions arose during a period of extended conflict with a number of Illyrian tribes. The dual factors came together and weakened the city, forcing the citizens to react. Just before the year of 435 BC the people of Epidamnus rose up and overthrew the oligarchic leadership that had been in place, installing a democracy in its place.

The exiled party made contact with the Illyrians and joined forces with those tribes who were engaged in the war with Epidamnus. With the help of the exiles, the Illyrians began a raiding campaign both by sea and by land. As their confidence grew, and their numbers swelled, the exiles put their former city under siege;[2] forcing the Epidamnians to look for outside help. The logical choice was their nearest ally, and mother-city, at Corcyra, so ambassadors were sent to the temple of Hera on the island as suppliants. Unbeknownst to them, the exiles had already made a similar plea to the Corcyraeans and had garnered favour for their reinstatement into Epidamnus, which was their ultimate aim.[3] The ambassadors begged the Corcyraeans to intervene, to stop Epidamnus from being destroyed, to arbitrate between the democrats and the violent exiles, and most of all to help bring an end to the war with the Illyrian tribes. But the Corcyraeans had already made their decisions, and without further word refused the supplication, dismissing the ambassadors back to their fate.

When news returned to Epidamnus of the refusal, the ruling party did not know where else to turn; their only realistic option was to send a plea to their other, partial, mother-city of Corinth, but they likewise knew that Corinth would want greater control of the city as a result. With no solutions freely offering themselves, the people sent for divine intervention. An enquiry was sent to the oracle at Delphi asking Apollo whether they should offer their city to the Corinthians in exchange for their assistance. The god was uncharacteristically clear in his answer: they should deliver the city and place themselves under the protection of Corinth.

With divine instruction, ambassadors were swiftly sent to Corinth and pleaded their case, offering to deliver their city as well. For the Corinthians, the decision was an easy one. Pragmatists would have argued that the city sat on an important sea route to Italy and Sicily and would enhance Corinthian naval prospects and trade. Those Corinthians whose motives were more duty bound would have found more than enough cause to vote in support: the request for help came not only from fellow Greeks, but from a city founded by a Corinthian; Corinthians were among the original colonists to the city; Corinth had a special relationship with their colonies anyway; and lastly the oracle at Delphi had approved the action.[4] Add to this a growing animosity between Corinth and its colony of Corcyra – due in part to Corcyra's growing power and influence which consequently allowed it to act as an equal to its mother city – and Corinth became eager to help Epidamnus.

After advertising for settlers to join the expedition, a modest Corinthian force departed, acquiring allies from Ambracia and Leucas. From Ambracia the allied force took the route over land to another Corinthian colony called Apollonia, just south of Epidamnus. When the Corcyraeans discovered the presence of the Corinthians they put on a show of force, sending a strong fleet to the city and demanding that the Epidamnians received the exiles back, while dismissing the newly arrived Corinthian settlers and garrison. Their demands fell on deaf ears so the Corcyraeans sent out a naval force of forty ships, taking with them the Epidamnian exiles in the hope of re-establishing them in the *polis*, and also securing the support of numerous Illyrian tribes. The Corcyraean army stood at the gates of Epidamnus and offered safe passage to any citizen, or foreigner, who wished to depart, or else be prepared to be treated like enemies. Once this offer was refused, the city of Epidamnus was put under siege.

When intelligence was received in Corinth of the happenings in the northwest they called for volunteers to go to the defence of Epidamnus, offering political equality to all who took up the offer. For those who did not want to go, a further offer was announced allowing men to pay fifty drachmae in exchange for a share in the colony. Huge numbers of people took advantage of the generous offers, giving the Corinthians the necessary manpower and a healthy fraction of the running costs to launch their forces. However, the situation was politically volatile, and if the venture was mishandled Corinth could be accused of breaking the treaty that held a precarious peace over Greece. So Corinth called on more allies to offer a convoy in the hope of avoiding conflict with Corcyra before they arrived at Epidamnus.[5]

During these preparations at Corinth, Corcyra was not inactive. It launched a full-on political offensive, sending envoys to Corinth via the Corinthian-allied *poleis* of Sicyon and Sparta. Corcyra called for the withdrawal of Corinthian forces in Epidamnus, and if this demand was not met then Corcyra was willing to invite arbitration from an agreed select committee of representatives from various Peloponnesian cities, agreeing to honour their decision as to who had authority over Epidamnus. In addition to this, Corcyra offered to refer the matter to Delphi and accept any judgement from Apollo. They threatened, in turn, to break ties with Corinth and look elsewhere for support in the forthcoming conflict.

To the Corinthians the offers from Corcyra may well have raised as many alarm bells as their threats. For Corcyra to bring Spartan envoys with them implied that Sparta had already decided on whom to support; and the arbitration on offer would obviously fall at the feet of the Spartans as the most powerful *polis* in the Peloponnese, creating a forgone conclusion.[6] Similarly, why did Delphi need to be consulted again, having already answered the question? Could the oracle be corrupted into supporting Corcyra? Corinth could not afford to find out and so retaliated in a political manner: they would approach the negotiations on offer, after Corcyra withdrew its fleet and Illyrian allies from around Epidamnus, but not while the city was still under siege. Corcyra's reaction was predictable: they would withdraw their troops only after Corinth had withdrawn her garrison from the city, or else allow both forces to remain under an armistice while negotiations took place.

The Corinthians ignored these compromises and, with their forces ready for departure, sent a herald to declare war on Corcyra. The Corinthian fleet swelled from the 30 ships they had sent, to 75 ships when their allies joined them on route to the Ambracian coast, plus 2,000 Corinthian hoplites. When the fleet stopped at Actium, at the mouth of the Gulf of Ambracia, they received a Corcyraean herald sent in a light boat to warn them against sailing north. Corcyra had prepared itself early, its ships were ready to be manned and older vessels had been upgraded to increase the number of available ships. When their herald returned without success the Corcyraean fleet, eighty ships strong, sailed out to meet the Corinthians.[7] After forming their lines the two fleets engaged, resulting in a resounding defeat for the Corinthians, who lost fifteen ships in the process. The Corcyraeans erected a victory trophy on Cape Leucimme, and took the Corinthians as prisoners, while massacring all the other captives. That same day Epidamnus surrendered to their besiegers under condition that the foreigners would be sold into slavery and the Corinthians kept as prisoners of war.

With the Corinthian fleet defeated, and the remaining ships returning home, Corcyra moved on the offensive. They terrorized the Corinthian colony of Leucas, and burned the harbour of Cyllene which belonged to the Corinthian allies at Ellis in the northwest Peloponnese. For months, any ally of Corinth was being harassed by Corcyra who acted with the impunity that came with their victory. But they had underestimated Corinthian naval strength, and by the end of the summer in 435 BC, Corinth established a naval base at Actium and another at Chimerium which was further north and closer to the island of Corcyra. Corcyra reacted by establishing a naval base at Leucimme, with neither fleet making any major offensives.

For the next two years Corinth invested in its naval force by building more ships and drawing rowers from throughout the Peloponnese. Having established a standoff against Corcyra, one of the strongest navies in Greece, with its original fleet, Corinth's investment drove its navy to a level second only to Athens'.[8] Meanwhile the rulers of Corcyra were growing concerned; they could not match the level and speed of investment of Corinth and, to make matters worse, the island was cut off and isolated by its own policy of not participating in either the Peloponnesian or Delian leagues. In an attempt to not pick a side, Corcyra had left itself without any allies for any forthcoming conflict, so a quick decision needed to be made.[9] Sparta may have supported their cause in arbitration but there was little chance of their military support against one of the Peloponnesian League's strongest members. Corcyra's only chance was to convince the Athenians to come to their aid.

So, in 433 BC, the Athenians accepted envoys from both Corcyra and Corinth to put forward their cases before the assembly would make a decision. The choice was by no means an easy one. By now wide-scale war in Greece was considered imminent and it was important for the Athenians to not be considered the protagonists of the conflict.[10] Likewise, both sides had valid cause for support; for Corcyra their independence was under threat, but Corinth was entitled to defend their colonists at Epidamnus. Furthermore, the immanency of war made this situation all the more precarious for the Athenians. Corcyra and Corinth were the two strongest naval powers of Greece, behind Athens itself. Individually they were not a serious threat to the Athenian maritime monopoly but if Corinth took the island and combined the two navies then Athens had a serious rival for its control of the sea. Yet, could Corcyra be trusted after this conflict was neutralised? They had never formed an alliance like this, maintaining a policy of self-imposed isolation thanks in part to its strong geographical position.

Having heard the cases, the Athenians called two assemblies. In the first the general feeling was to support the claim of Corinth, but when the second assembly was held the public opinion had moved to sympathise with Corcyra. The problem remained as to what action Athens would take, but a solution did finally present itself. It was in Athens' best interest that Corinth did not establish itself at Corcyra, but it was also prudent to damage the lasting power of Corcyra as well. The Athenians voted to enter into a defensive alliance with Corcyra, which committed them to only helping if Corcyra was attacked. As proof of their alliance, Athens sent a measly ten triremes to Corcyra's immediate assistance.[11] Furthermore, the commanders of the 'fleet' were under strict orders to not engage with the Corinthians except under very strict circumstances: the Corinthians needed to attempt, or threaten to attempt a landing on Corcyra itself or any of its possessions.

Forces

The Corcyraean fleet consisted of 110 triremes split into three squadrons, each commanded by a single admiral, and powered predominantly by slaves.[12] In addition to the 10 Athenian triremes, Corcyra had received a force of 1,000 hoplites from their allies at Zacynthus to help repel any Corinthian landing party. These hoplites were united with a Corcyraean land force which was stationed at Leucimme.

The Corinthians had succeeded in amassing an allied fleet of 150 ships: Elis and Leucas provided 10 each, Megara 12, Ambracia supplied 27, Anactorium gave 1, while Corinth supplied the majority with 90 from its new triremes. This was, however, not a battle fleet but an invasion force, so many of these ships were carrying more men than would be expected from purely combat-ready triremes.[13] Each individual contingent was led by its own commanders, with the Corinthian command held by Xenocleides and four colleagues. On land, the Corinthian fleet was supported by an unnumbered barbarian force, who were longstanding allies of Corinth in the region.

Battle   (Thucydides, I.48-55)

The Corinthians sailed to the island of Leucas, off the west coast of Ambracia, where they met with their allies' contributions. Sailing from Leucas, the fleet followed the coastline north until it reached their furthest northern base at Chimerium by the second day at sea.[14] Anchoring in the harbour, the Corinthians disembarked and formed an encampment that could make good use of the lush hinterland for food, and ample water supplies from a nearby river. But their arrival did not go unnoticed, so Corcyra quickly mobilized their own fleet and stationed them on one of the Sybota islands which lay off the Thesprotis coast, directly opposite the southern tip of Corcyra. From this position the Corcyraeans held the access into the channel between the island of Corcyra and the mainland, allowing them to force a battle on their own terms in the mouth of the channel if the Corinthians decided to continue their advance north.

At Chimerium, the Corinthians had completed their preparations and ensured that each man took three days' rations with them to prepare for the invasion of Corcyra.[15] The plan was to sail before the dawn, hoping to catch the Corcyraean fleet off guard and force a landing on the island before a major resistance could be launched. For all of the Corinthian expertise on show, particularly that of navigating the seas at night, they had not appreciated how well prepared the Corcyraeans were. The islanders' lookouts spotted the Corinthian movements in the dark and raised the alarm early, so that as the fleet arrived at the mouth of the channel they were greeted by the dawn-lit image of 120 enemy triremes blocking their access.

The Corinthians had already planned for this eventuality and their fleet quickly formed into a pre-arranged line abreast formation. Opposing them were the three squadrons from Corcyra, with its right wing (nearest Corcyra) reinforced by the Athenian contingent either on the end or perhaps supporting behind. The Corinthians had already chosen to take the left wing of their formation, with the aim of breaking through the Corcyraean lines and cutting off the enemy's escape route home. Next to them, in the centre of the line, were the contributions from Elis, Leucas and Anactorium. The right wing, nearest the mainland, held by the Ambraciots and Megarians.

Signals were raised by the opposing command ships, greeted by the loud *paeans* from the ships confirming their orders. The creak of the oars broke through the vocal cacophony, and the loud splashes from the lapping sea signalled the building momentum of the two forces as they headed towards each other. However, the Corinthians were not set for a conventional sea battle – their ships were laden down by the weight of an invading army – and the

Corcyraeans seem to have anticipated a land battle on the sea by imitating the presence of large land forces on their ships. This could not be a battle of speed and ramming, there was no ability to perform *diekplous*-style breakthroughs, so this would have to be an old-fashioned slugging match determined by the strength and determination of the marines.[16]

As trireme crashed against trireme, the fleets became compacted and ensnared due to the sheer volume of ships involved. For the marines on board this was ideal, giving them a stable platform from which to release their arrows and throw their javelins. With missiles flying overhead, opposing hoplites dropped the gangplanks and attempted to board the enemy vessels, with vicious fighting the result of obstinate resistance. The battle became one large scene of confusion, mayhem and death.

The Corinthians on the left wing were making good progress against the Corcyraeans opposite them, but would pull back every time the Athenian contingent arrived to offer their support. The Athenians in turn refused to actually engage in the fighting, they were instead happy to use their presence as a deterrent from extended Corinthian aggression in any given area. The Ambraciots and Megarians on the Corinthians' right wing were not faring as well. Corcyraean aggression was beginning to overwhelm the Corinthian allies who, being unable to sustain any more losses, pulled back and fled to the main land, pursued by a breakaway group of twenty Corcyraean ships. When the pursuing ships made it to the Corinthian camp they burned the empty tents and plundered the equipment that had been left there as excess weight in battle. This included not only cooking equipment and clothing, but also the sails and masts of the ships in battle.

Unfortunately for the main Corcyraean fleet, the Corinthian left wing was winning a decided victory. The scattered and outnumbered triremes from Corcyra could ill-afford to lose the twenty ships that were absent by way of their pursuit. The Corinthians were on the verge of accomplishing their breakthrough on the wing when the Athenians finally relented and joined in the battle with full vigour. Their addition was enough to stem the breakthrough, but not enough to turn the tide of the battle. After a period of prolonged mêlée, the battle lines finally broke apart, resulting in a race to the island of Corcyra. However, the Athenian intervention had manufactured enough time for the Corcyraeans to land first, allowing them to regroup and recover from their defeat. The Athenian action prevented a devastating pursuit by the Corinthians, but it did not in any way win the battle.

The Corinthians used this time of rest to deal with the survivors, rather than the usual ritual of hauling back the hulls of defeated triremes. As they sailed back out of the mouth of the channel they butchered any living man that they saw. Unluckily for some, the Corinthians did not know the true extent of their right wing's defeat, and many of the survivors killed where in fact their allies. As they returned to their original position they turned to their own wrecks and the dead, most of which were recovered from the sea, and moved to Sybota, the harbour of Thesprotis, where they rendezvoused with their allied land forces.

Once the dead had been successfully reclaimed and placed under the protection of their allies, the Corinthians called their men to muster once more. The battle had been won, the Corcyraeans had been shown inferior to the might of the Corinthian fleet, Athens had failed to support their ally in any worthwhile manner, and Corcyra would be theirs after one more concerted effort, one more bloody battle to decide the fate of the island. The fleet from Corinth headed across the channel, on a direct course for the depleted Corcyraean fleet, and the ten Athenian triremes, that had set off to confront them once more. There was no longer a pretence of Athenian abstinence, Corcyra was under serious threat of an invasion force landing on its soil and this was the best chance of stopping the island falling into Corinthian hands.

As the two forces moved closer and closer, the sounds of the sea suddenly changed. The rhythmic sounds of oars cutting through the water was broken by the booming sounds of an invigorated *paean*. The sounds broke the concentration of the Corinthian commanders, for it did not come from the approaching enemy but from the south. As their eyes turned to the source they were faced with a sight they did not anticipate; heading towards their lines were twenty new Athenian triremes. The commanders had to make a decision, could they afford to confront thirty Athenian triremes? Were they the front of a much larger fleet following behind which would be too strong for the Corinthian fleet to handle? The one thing the commanders did know was that this signalled Athenian resolve to protect Corcyra. Even if Corcyra could be taken, Athens had shown its true intentions and success on the day would likely result in all-out war.[17] Furthermore, and more pragmatically, night was soon to fall, so any

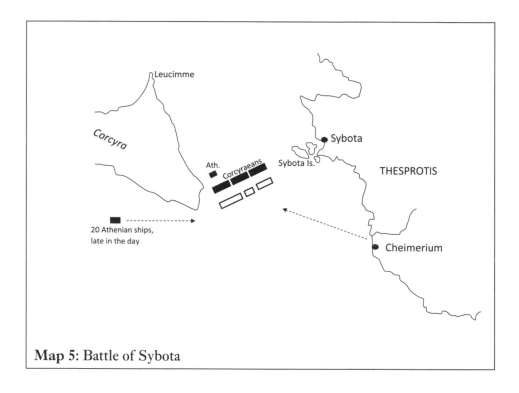

Map 5: Battle of Sybota

action would have to be resolved quickly. Was this worth it? The Corinthian commanders decided that it was not, and began to retire back to Sybota.

To the Corcyraeans, the scene playing out in front of them was both confusing and joyous, for they could not see the Athenian force arriving from the south. So, to their minds, at the point when their fate had seemed sealed, their superior enemy were backing water for no discernible reason. Daylight was fading and some of the Corcyraeans could just make out the silhouettes of the new Athenian triremes, but could not identify who they were there to support. Rather than take any chances, the Corcyraean commanders ordered their men back to their camp at Leucimme, followed swiftly by the twenty Athenian vessels.

The following day, the Athenians sailed out, along with all the Corcyraean ships that were still seaworthy, and went straight to Sybota harbour to try and force another sea battle. The Corinthians obliged, putting out from land and forming their battle lines, but this day was different. To the Corinthians, this was tantamount to an open battle with the Athenians, which was never their intention. To the Athenians, their enemy had absolutely overwhelmed the second strongest navy in Greece and a defeat here, even for a small Athenian force, would send shockwaves through their empire and beyond.[18] This reticence manifested in a standoff, with neither side wanting to act the aggressor.

The Corinthians grew weary of waiting, and became anxious to depart for home. They sent heralds to the Athenian ships challenging their actions and accusing them of trying to start a war. The Athenians denied any wrongdoing and said that they would not obstruct the Corinthians if they wished to leave. Receiving this answer, the Corinthian commanders prepared for departure; they set up a trophy in the mainland harbour, Sybota, and abandoned their position. When the Corinthian fleet began its journey home, the Corcyraeans, likewise, erected a trophy on the island of Sybota to commemorate their victory. For, although the Corinthians had won the main battle – destroying nearly seventy enemy ships and taking over a thousand prisoners, while only losing thirty ships themselves and being able to collect their dead[19] – the Corcyraeans were able to collect their dead the following day, plus they had seen the Corinthians flee before them on the second day, so victory was as much theirs as the Corinthians'.[20]

Aftermath

Our main source for this period, Thucydides, was very clear in his words: the conflict over Corcyra was the first cause of the war that Corinth would later have with Athens.[21] The Athenians were very aware that the Corinthians had not been defeated, contrary to the erection of the Corcyraean trophy. The Athenians were also aware that Corinth had a strong relationship with its many colonies, some of whom were a part of the Athenian Empire. The Corinthian colony of Potidaea, in Chalcidice, was one such city, paying tribute as a member of the Athenian empire, so it soon became the indirect battleground between these two heavyweight poleis.

The Athenians ordered Potidaea to raze its walls, to give hostages to Athens, and to turn away any magistrates from Corinth who were sent annually while dismissing the ones already serving their year. The Athenians were afraid of a rebellion in the north, but their heavy-handed tactics forced the likes of Potidaea to look for help against this new level of imperial interference. By the year 432 BC, Potidaea joined a coalition of *poleis* in Chalcidice, led in part by the king of Macedon, Perdiccas, and revolted against Athenian rule. Athens sent a force to deal with the uprising and, after a swift victory outside the walls of Potidaea, put the Corinthian colony under siege. So began the first action of a war that would consume the attention of the Greeks for twenty-seven long years.

Chapter 5

The Battle of the Corinthian Gulf (429 BC)

Background   (Thucydides, II.69–II.82)

The first two years of the Peloponnesian War were filled with frustrations and setbacks for the Athenians. Their leader, Pericles, had adopted a pragmatic strategic approach to the war but it was not a popular decision. Pericles realized that Athenian strength lay in its navy and in its tribute-paying empire, whereas the Peloponnesians, led by Sparta, held superiority over land. So, his plan was simple, he drew all of the Athenian populace within the city walls and refused to meet the enemy on land. Athenian action focussed on unsettling the enemy, by way of sea-based raids, and ensuring the solidity of its own empire by sending a strong fleet to Corcyra and, more importantly, subduing the potential revolt in Chalcidice by besieging Potidaea in 431 BC. But this action in the north proved to be the first of two major frustrations and setbacks for the Athenians.

The siege of Potidaea was still raging at the end of 430 BC and had cost the treasury of Athens nearly 2,000 *talents*, approximately a third of their entire funds in just under two years.[1] Back in Attica the Athenian citizenry were forced to live in squalor behind the walls while they could see the Peloponnesian forces enter their lands and ravage their farms, homes, businesses and livelihoods. To further exacerbate the problems being endured, the large concentration of people in such a cramped environment created the perfect environment for a plague to afflict the people for four years, killing nearly a third of the Athenian population. Meanwhile, the only impact that Periclean strategy had on the Peloponnesians was through a series of small-scale raids; while these were wholly successful and resulted in accumulating plunder and striking fear in the hearts of the enemy, they did little to raise the morale of the Athenian people.[2] These were not victories, they did not relieve the situation in Attica, nor did they turn the tide of Peloponnesian pressure.

On the northwestern frontier, early Athenian progress was unravelling. The events of 431 BC had seen the Athenians successfully nullify the Corinthian sphere of influence in the region by forming a wider alliance with the people of Zacynthus, Corcyra, Acarnania and Cephallenia, and subduing three *poleis* with strong links to Corinth. The Corinthians did not take this affront lightly, and sent a fleet of 40 ships and 1,500 hoplites in the winter of 431/30 BC to help a tyrant in Acarnania who had been expelled by the Athenians. The venture started well, with the tyrant fully restored by the Corinthians, but further assaults in Acarnania and Cephallenia were repelled with relative ease. While this was by no means a disaster for Athens, since they still held the strongest level of influence in the area, they could not afford to let the Corinthians attack Athenian allies at will, and no other *polis* was capable of resisting the Corinthian navy.

In the winter of 430/29 BC the Athenians acted to cut off Corinthian actions at their source by posting their best admiral, Phormio, with a small fleet of twenty triremes inside the Corinthian Gulf (what Thucydides calls the Crisaean Gulf). Phormio stationed his fleet at the Athenian-friendly city of Naupactus, near the entrance to the gulf. The position made strategic sense, it enabled Phormio to interfere with Corinthian traffic in and out of the gulf, as well as giving him a strong position from which to observe Corinthian naval developments. Equally, Phormio's decision to station his force at Naupactus was well considered, politically: the city had been a long-time supporter of Athens, and during the 460s the Athenians had resettled there a large group of Messenian *helots* who had revolted against their Spartan masters, meaning that it was the most secure place for the Athenian fleet to be.[3]

The summer of 429 BC brought with it a Peloponnesian initiative in the northwest. The Ambracians, and their allies the Chaonians, had designs to reduce the lands of their enemies, the Acarnanians, but they lacked the manpower to be able to overthrow the Athenian-supported forces in the area. Envoys were sent to Sparta by the allies, who succeeded in persuading the Spartans that a combined assault on Acarnania by land and sea would make any resistance nigh-on impossible. Once Acarnania was subdued, it was argued, the islands of Zacynthus and Cephallenia would quickly follow suit, which would result in the Athenian fleet being unable to circumnavigate the Peloponnese with the ease it had thus far enjoyed. As an added incentive, the Ambracian envoys postulated that from this position of dominance in the west, it would even be possible to capture Naupactus.[4]

For the Spartans, the benefits were great: they could move to stop the Athenian raids on their homeland, they could take control of the northwestern route to Italy, and they could even avenge their elders by punishing the Messenians who had escaped their justice and now lived in Naupactus. The *gerousia* agreed to send a small force of 1,000 hoplites under the command of that year's *nauarch*, Cnemus, while simultaneously sending orders to their allies to prepare the joint fleet and meet at the island of Leucas, just off the Acarnanian coast.

Cnemus arrived in the Ambracian gulf, having avoided the watchful eyes of Phormio, and disembarked his forces, which had swelled due the arrival of land forces sent from Ambracia, Leucas Anactorium, and various non-Hellenic northern tribes including the Chaonians.[5] Rather than wait for the allied fleet, as planned, Cnemus grew restless and chose instead to march his army south, through the lands of Amphilochian Argos, before sacking the village of Limnaea and then heading straight for the Acarnanian capital at Stratus.

The Acarnanians were taken aback by the speed and the power of the invasion. A decision was quickly made, they could not face the Peloponnesians by themselves so they would defend their own homes and send a message to Phormio asking for naval assistance. Unfortunately for them, Phormio had been watching the Corinthian preparations for their contribution to the allied fleet and was afraid for the safety of Naupactus if he left his position to help in the north – his answer was no.

Cnemus' forces moved south in three divisions; the centre was held by the Chaonians and their non-Hellenic allies, the right was held by the Leucadians and Anactorians, while on the left were the Peloponnesians and Ambracians led by Cnemus. The three groups marched independently of each other, separated by great distances at times, meaning that they were poorly coordinated and reliant on individual discipline from the three relevant commanders. When they all neared Stratus, the Greeks set up a strong camp from which to plan their assault on the city, but the Chaonian commander had different plans. The Chaonians were a confident and brave tribe from the northwest and saw Stratus as a perfect opportunity to gain a glorious victory for themselves. They decided to rush the city walls and launch an immediate attack against the unsuspecting

Stratians. But the people of Stratus had not been caught unawares, they were very well prepared.

When news had arrived in Stratus of Cnemus' progress south they quickly realized that their city would be the main target of their aggression and prepared themselves for battle. They did not intend to resist in a prolonged siege if they could help it, so sites for ambuscades were identified if not constructed: they were going to take the fight to the enemy. So when they heard that the Chaonians had bypassed the Greek camp and were heading to the city, the defenders jumped into action. The chance of defeating one third of the enemy's forces was enticing, it would shatter the morale of the Greeks sat in their camp and maybe even stop this invasion in its tracks.

When the Chaonians arrived they did not even reach the city before they were attacked by the city's defenders who fought from outside the walls. The Chaonians were in disarray, they had not expected a pitched battle like this, and when men came screaming out of their ambuscades the fragile morale of the Chaonians and their allies simply broke. The Stratians were merciless in their pursuit, they needed to send a message to Cnemus – this is what happens to anyone who tries to take our freedom. What was meant to be a glorious battle for the walls of Stratus turned quickly into a chase and massacre.

The Greeks in the camp knew nothing of these events, the camp did not overlook Stratus, and they assumed the Chaonians and their allies were still on the way to the camp. The sight of their allies charging towards them in disarray caused confusion but the Greeks took them into their ranks and prepared for the expected attack from the pursuing Stratians. But the Stratians were not foolish enough, they knew they were not strong enough to take on a Peloponnesian army without their Acarnanian allies. They did not offer battle but instead utilized a weapon for which they held a reputation for excellence, the sling. Hurling their bullets from a safe distance they made it impossible for the enemy to rest, they could not relax their formation, nor could they take off their armour. They were stuck in situ until night when the Stratians relented in their attack, giving Cnemus time to swiftly withdraw his forces to safety, nine miles away from Stratus.

The following day Cnemus sent the request to collect the war-dead and, with the arrival of his allies from Oeniadae, the Spartan commander ordered his army to pull south, toward the coast of the Corinthian gulf, where he disbanded his army and sent his allies home. But his were only the land forces of what was meant to be, but for his own impetuousness, a joint-force enterprise. Yet, the great fleet produced by Corinth, which was to make up the bulk of the allied naval force, had problems of its own. Before they could even hope to join Cnemus, they first needed to pass by Phormio who still lay in wait at Naupactus.

Forces

The battle for the Corinthian Gulf actually consisted of two separate battles, often separated as the battles of Patrae/Rhium and Naupactus.[6] In both battles the Athenians, led by the experienced commander Phormio, had a small fleet of twenty battle-ready triremes. Phormio's triremes were fast and agile in the water, manned by hardened rowers, so his tactics would be based upon this speed and manoeuvrability, for which he needed space and to avoid the narrows of the entrance into the gulf.

The Peloponnesian fleet was different for each battle: in the first battle (Patrae) they had forty-seven ships which were transporters for carrying soldiers and were predominantly commanded by three Corinthians; in the second battle (Naupactus) they had seventy-seven ships, only some of which were Corinthian, under the overall command of Cnemus and three advisors he was sent from Sparta. Of this second force, we are also told that twenty from its number were 'fast' triremes which implies that they were the best and most experienced crews in the fleet. This small squadron would be used as a mobile strike force outside of the main fleet, allowing the Peloponnesians to match the Athenians at their own game.

Battle   (Thucydides, II. 83-92; Diodorus, XII.48)

While Cnemus was campaigning through Acarnania, the Corinthian contingent of the allied fleet was prepared for assisting Cnemus by means of troop transportation and logistical support. When the fleet was ready, the Corinthians assigned three experienced commanders, Machaon, Isocrates and Agatharchidas, to lead them west out of the gulf.[7] The fleet followed the Peloponnesian coast west, all the while being watched intently by Phormio. As the Peloponnesians continued on their journey, the Corinthian commanders became aware of a line of ships directly north of their positon, shadowing their journey. The commanders were confused, surely Phormio would not attack a force of ships so much larger than his own small fleet?

Phormio's plan was well constructed. He knew that his position at Naupactus was inside the neck of the gulf and that any advantage he held would be best utilized in the open water, so he bided his time, knowing that the enemy would, at some point, attempt to cross the gulf. The Athenian fleet shadowed the Peloponnesians before moving ahead and anchoring on the River Evenus at Chalcis. The Peloponnesians lost sight of Phormio's ships and continued with their set course. They arrived at Patrae from where they intended to cross over to southern Acarnania.

Knowing that Phormio may have still been in the area, and that the Peloponnesian fleet was really one built for logistical support, not battle, the Corinthian commanders decided on a night departure. So the Peloponnesian ships slipped their moorings in the night, but their movements had been spotted and, by the time the sun had risen, the Peloponnesians were only half way through their crossing and were suddenly faced with Phormio's twenty triremes bearing towards them. The Peloponnesians reacted quickly, manoeuvring their ships into a circle, with their prows pointing out and their sterns in. They left a space inside the circle in which they put their five fastest ships, who could move out at a moment's notice to strengthen any point that was being threatened by the Athenians. Phormio, for his part, ordered his triremes into line ahead and sailed around the Peloponnesian's floating hedgehog formation.

The Athenians kept sailing, round and round the formation, each time contracting the size of their circle, each time edging closer and closer to the Peloponnesians. With each contracted circle, the ships in formation grew more and more concerned about an Athenian attack against them, so they tightened their circular formation, drawing their sterns closer and closer together. The Corinthian commander must have known what was happening, Phormio was intent on causing panic and mayhem before launching his attack; the Peloponnesians were going to cause their own destruction through their fear. All Phormio needed was a catalyst, one final event that would cause the disorder he so desired, and the early-morning weather duly obliged.[8]

In the early morning a strong wind rose and caused havoc upon the narrow formation of the Peloponnesians. The smaller craft were dashing against the

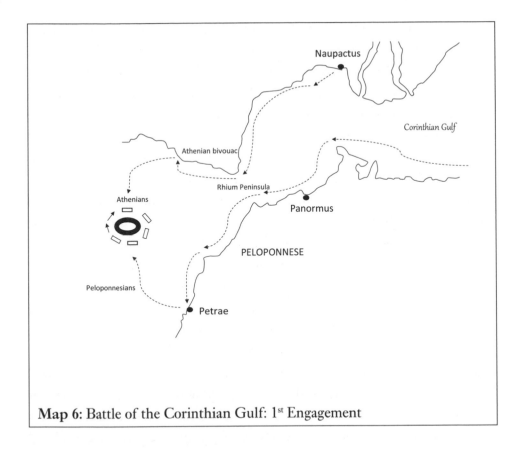

Map 6: Battle of the Corinthian Gulf: 1ˢᵗ Engagement

larger, and the panicked crews began to scream, shout and swear as they tried to push boats apart with poles. The din of the sailors overwhelmed the calls from the boatswains and commanders, meaning that orders were going unnoticed. This chaos was the moment Phormio had been hoping for. He gave his signal and the Athenians attacked. The first ship to sink was the flagship of one of the Corinthian commanders. Then the Athenian attack became more efficient, with more and more vessels being disabled by them. The attack was so fast and so effective that the remaining Peloponnesians lost any will to attempt a defence and instead broke formation, fleeing to Patrae and Dyme at the entrance of the gulf. The Athenians did not relent, giving chase and capturing twelve more ships before they finally disengaged and sailed to Molycrium. Here they set up their victory trophy at the promontory at Rhium. They dedicated one of the captured ships to Poseidon, god of the sea, and then returned to Naupactus with all of their ships intact.

The Peloponnesian fleet left the gulf and followed the coast of Achaea west, arriving at the Eleian seaport at Cyllene.[9] Here they were met by Cnemus, fresh from his defeat at Stratus, and the ships from Leucas that had been due to join the Corinthian-led fleet. The Athenian victory in the gulf redirected Peloponnesian intentions. Knowing that any land-based operations in the north would need a strong fleet to support it, allied with the knowledge that Corinth was the strongest naval ally in the Peloponnesian league, meant that Phormio's blockade needed to be dealt with, and quickly.

Sparta, for their part, sent Cnemus three advisors, Timocrates, Brasidas and Lycophron, to whom orders were given to prepare the fleet for battle against Phormio.[10] The navally inexperienced Spartans had been shocked by news of the defeat in the gulf; not realizing the wider factors involved, they merely focussed on the numerical disadvantage held by the Athenians in the region and believed that the defeat must have been due to a weakness in the hearts of the Peloponnesian crew. On their arrival, the advisors worked with Cnemus to order more ships from their allies and to fix up the vessels they already had so that they would be battle ready. These preparations did not go beyond Phormio's notice so he sent word to Athens, telling them of his victory and of the amassing enemy fleet at Cyllene. He requested that the Athenians send him as many ships as they could, as quickly as they could, because he considered battle to be an imminent possibility. The Athenian assembly agreed to send him twenty triremes, but the commander of these reinforcements was given instructions to take a detour via Crete to aid an Athenian ally in Gortys. While this small fleet had success in Crete, it was to the detriment of Phormio who had to prepare for battle with just the twenty ships he already controlled.[11]

Phormio's fears of imminent battle were justified. Once Cnemus was joined by more allies, he took his fleet of seventy-seven ships along the north Peloponnesian coast to Panormus, directly opposite Naupactus, where they were met by a supporting land army. Phormio stationed his fleet at Molycrian Rhium, resulting in a stalemate across the narrow mouth of the gulf for six or seven days. But neither side were idle. That week was spent training and practising their drills and coordination, preparing for battle and planning their tactics. Phormio wanted to catch the Peloponnesians in the open, like he had last time, knowing that he still held the advantage of speed and agility with his ships. Whereas Cnemus did not want a repeat performance, and realized that his strength in numbers, and the size of his ships, offered a better advantage within the narrower straits, where they could neutralize the enemy's speed and agility.

Cnemus also knew that his best chance for success was to engage with Phormio before he received any reinforcements from Athens. This battle would be decided by whoever controlled the opening movements.

As twilight crept into a slow sunrise, both fleets were preparing themselves for battle, as they had at the beginning of every day that week. Cnemus chose to act first and seize the initiative from Phormio. He noticed that the Athenians were slow to move and did not want to sail into the gulf through the narrows, so the Spartan acted quickly. With the sun still rising, he ordered his fleet to sail four abreast towards the direction of Corinth, led by their right wing which contained their twenty fastest ships.[12] Phormio was in a panic, the Peloponnesians were seemingly heading straight for Naupactus, the garrison of which was supporting Phormio, meaning that the city was completely undefended.[13] Phormio acted predictably and hurriedly embarked his men onto their ships and set sail for Naupactus as quickly as they could, with their Messenian land force following them along the shore. The Athenians had taken Cnemus' bait and begrudgingly entered the narrow strait.

On seeing the Athenian ships in file heading along the northern shore, the Peloponnesian commanders gave their orders so that, on one signal, all the ships turned suddenly and, by bearing down on them, hoped to cut off Phormio's route to Naupactus and safety. Thanks only to the speed advantage held by the Athenian triremes, eleven of the leading ships were able to escape beyond Cnemus' right wing and reach more open waters towards the city. However, the remaining nine ships were overtaken and overwhelmed as they tried in vain to flee. The Athenians were left helpless against the enemy, and their ships were driven ashore and disabled, while any of the crews who had not been able to jump ship and swim for land were duly killed. The Peloponnesians lashed the enemy ships to theirs, claiming their trophies; even when faced with Messenians from the land who had jumped into the surf in full armour and climbed onto some of the decks in the hope of salvaging something from this tactical disaster.[14] They failed.

While the main bulk of the Peloponnesian fleet revelled in their victory, the twenty triremes that held the right wing had turned off and were still in

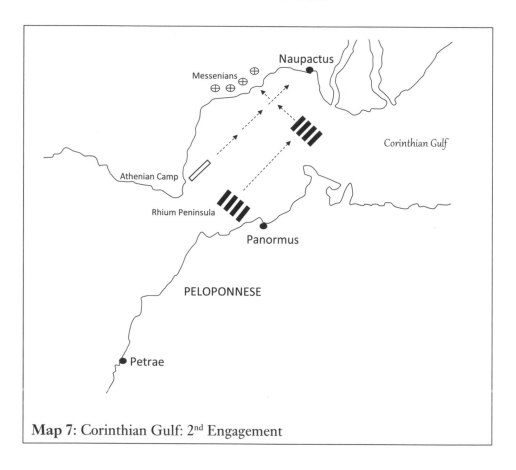

Map 7: Corinthian Gulf: 2nd Engagement

pursuit of the eleven Athenian ships that were fleeing towards Naupactus. Ten of the Athenian ships were able to speed ahead and reach the port, whereupon they turned around, facing their prows out toward the Peloponnesian fleet, ready to fight should the enemy attempt to sail against their position. The final surviving trireme must have been in bad shape, perhaps it had been obliged to fight its way out of the Peloponnesian attack as opposed to outrunning it completely like those ahead of it. This ship was coursing slowly through the sea, losing distance between itself and its pursuers with every stroke of the oars. The Peloponnesians were filled with the euphoria that comes from a successful hunt and, prematurely, struck up a victory paean as they closed the gap further. But, in the path of the Athenian trireme lay a small merchant boat which had anchored in the roadstead, sheltering it from the tides and the ocean swell. The Athenian *trierarch* thought fast and decided on a drastic solution to his problem.

As the Athenian trireme rowed past the small merchant vessel it continued to pass around the vessel and then reversed course back into the path of the Leucadian ship which led the pursuit. Catching the Leucadian trireme off-guard, the Athenian trireme ploughed straight into it amidships and put it immediately out of action. The commander of the Leucadian ship was none other than the Spartan advisor, Timocrates, and the dishonour of losing his ship was too much for him to bear so he promptly killed himself. The brazen counterattack stopped the remainder of the pursuers in their tracks, they had already lost their order due to the euphoria from thinking they had already secured victory, and now they lay isolated from the main fleet and staring down the prows of eleven highly motivated Athenian triremes, in relatively open waters. The decision was a simple one, the Peloponnesians turned and fled.

Buoyed by the turn of events following their embarrassing defeat a mere couple of hours earlier, the Athenians gave a loud cheer and set off after their fleeing foes. Their mere presence caused confusion and panic amongst those ships commanded by men unaccustomed to the region, with a small handful running aground in the shallows. The Athenians were able to capture six enemy vessels and reclaim a few of their own. Any survivors from the Peloponnesian crews were either killed or taken prisoner.

The Athenians set up a trophy around the harbour of Naupactus, at the point where they had set out and seemingly turned the tide of the battle, and then went about collecting the wrecks and the bodies of the dead on their shore, which they returned to the Peloponnesians under a truce. The Peloponnesians did not consider this a defeat, having successfully defeated the Athenians first and disabled almost half of Phormio's fleet. So they also set up a trophy and put a captured ship alongside as a dedication to a god. The Peloponnesian fleet, excluding the Leucadians, sailed further in to the Corinthian gulf and anchored at Corinth. In the meantime, Phormio tried to recover from the shock of almost complete destruction; the twenty Athenian triremes that had been sent via Crete, finally arrived, but far too late. So, as winter arrived, the power balance within the gulf was still as precarious as it had been at the start of the year.

Aftermath

Before Cnemus was allowed to disband his fleet, he and his Spartan advisors were convinced by the allies from Megara to attempt an audacious attack on

Athens' own port, the Piraeus. To avoid detection from Phormio, and to utilize the element of surprise, the Peloponnesians chose to cross the Corinthian isthmus by land, carrying their rowing equipment, and use forty ships that were already harboured at Nisaea. When they arrived at Nisaea the Spartan commanders swiftly set sail for the Piraeus, which was not guarded by any fleet. However, either due to a change in winds, or because of a grave error of judgement, the Peloponnesian fleet stopped at the northwestern point of the island of Salamis.

There they found a small Athenian garrison and fleet, which were easily dealt with, and the marines decided to lay waste to the surrounding countryside. The north of the island became a scene of panic and mayhem, and the warning beacons were soon lit to warn the people in Athens of the danger. Athens became a hive of commotion and, when the Piraeus was suitably garrisoned, a strong fleet was launched to relieve Salamis, but by the time they had arrived the Peloponnesian force had departed back to Megara. The Athenians had been taken completely off guard and it was not a mistake they intended to make again, so the Piraeus was reinforced and a more diligent guard was allocated.

By the end of the winter in 429/8 BC Phormio had taken a force of 800 hoplites, half Athenian and half Messenian, under his command and headed north to Acarnania to reaffirm Athenian influence and secure continued support from the region. On his return from this venture, Phormio was able to wait in Naupactus for the coming of spring, when he returned home to Athens, carrying in tow the captured ships he had taken, and the captive freemen he held. All of which were later exchanged for Athenian prisoners.

Chapter 6

The Battle of Corcyra (427 BC)

Background   (Thucydides, III.1-19, III.25-76; Diodorus, XII.55)

Periclean strategy had thus far proved successful, if frustrating, for the Athenians. Yet the balance of power had not yet swung in their favour. The Peloponnesians were still unopposed on land, and the battle for control of the western sea was undecided. Furthermore, Athens' empire was growing more and more precarious. Having only just succeeded in putting down the revolt in Potidaea, a new outbreak of unrest had appeared in 428 BC on the island of Lesbos, which lay just off the coast of Asia Minor.

The Lesbians had begun plans for a revolt prior to the outbreak of the war in 431 BC, but the Spartans refused to support them through fear of causing a war with Athens.[1] Yet, with the war entering its fourth year and the Peloponnesians beginning their annual invasion of Attica, the people of Lesbos were ready to revolt, knowing that Sparta would now, surely, support them in their uprising. The main protagonists on the island were found in the southeastern city of Mytilene, who had begun preparing for an Athenian countermeasure to the revolt-in-waiting. Ships were being built, walls reinforced and moles built in the harbours; they were also waiting on the arrival of mercenary archers and grain from Pontus (the Black Sea).[2] These preparations did not, however, go unnoticed, nor indeed did the growth of Mytilenian influence over the island. The authorities on the small island of Tenedus, just north of Lesbos, went to the Athenians with word of the developments on the big island. Their information was rightly corroborated by the Methymnians, from a *polis* on the north side of Lesbos, and by some Mytilenian citizens who served as representatives of Athens in Mytilene.[3]

The Athenians could not believe what they were being told. The size of fleet that Lesbos, as a unified island, could hold, and the untapped resources at their disposal – not to mention their strong geographic position which could compromise the Athenian grain route from the Bosporus – made them a very unwelcome new addition to the Athenians' growing list of enemies. It was not until an Athenian envoy returned from Mytilene, having demanded that they break the union on the island and give up their military preparations and been refused, that the Athenian assembly decided on pre-emptive action. Forty triremes were reassigned from a squadron of fifty that were soon to embark on a raiding sortie around the Peloponnese. The remaining ten ships happened to be from Mytilene (as per their agreement as an ally of Athens) so they were detained in Attica and their crews kept in Athenian custody. The plan was for this fleet to rush across to Lesbos in time for the Mytilenian festival of Malean Apollo, which took place outside of the city, so they would be unprepared for the Athenians' sudden arrival. However, the Athenians were cautious and ordered their commander, Cleippides, that, if the plan did not work and the Mytilenians did not immediately desist in their revolt, then he was to demand the deliverance of their ships and the dismantling of their walls. Only on the refusal of this could the commander officially declare war.

Unbeknown to the Athenians, their plans had leaked out of the city. An unnamed man sneaked out of Athens and crossed over to Euboea, travelling across the island and gaining passage on a merchant ship that was about to sail. In this way he was able to reach Mytilene, a mere three days after leaving Athens, and warn them. The Mytilenians reacted pragmatically. They had been caught short in their preparations, but this warning stopped them from being immediately overrun, so they cancelled the festival to Apollo and barricaded the unfinished sections of their harbour and defensive walls, while also setting up permanent garrisons at these weakest points. By the time the Athenian fleet arrived they found an orderly defence ready to oppose them. The commander of the fleet followed his orders and made his demands upon the Mytilenians; these were swiftly refused, and hostilities commenced.[4]

The Mytilenians sent out their fleet in a show of strength, without any real intent to make battle. A small naval skirmish took place outside the city's harbour, but it was merely posturing from both forces. Neither wanted the fighting to begin until their respective allies had arrived to support them, thus a parley was quickly agreed. Mytilene used this time to send out envoys to their allies, both on Lesbos and to Sparta on the mainland. Simultaneously they despatched other envoys to Athens in the hope of persuading the Athenians to call back their fleet. The envoys to Athens were the first to return, having accomplished nothing, and fighting resumed.

The Mytilenians organized a sortie from the city, and attacked the Athenian camp, inflicting some casualties. While they were victorious, it was only a small victory, and the commanders did not feel confident enough to stay outside of the city walls, so the army soon retreated back inside. After this excursion, the islanders decided against further action until more allies arrived to support them. Recent arrivals, a Laconian and a Theban in particular, raised the morale of the Lesbians and urged them to send another ship of envoys to Sparta, which they swiftly did. All the while, the Athenians had become buoyed by the lack of bite to the Lesbian resistance. They moved their ships to the south of Mytilene, using Malea as a station for their ships 9 miles south of the city, and blockaded the city's two harbours.[5]

On the mainland, the Mytilenian envoys sent to Sparta had been invited to Olympia where their message would be heard by the rest of the Spartan allies as well. The envoys delivered an impassioned speech, declaring their revolt against Athenian oppression to be just and legal, and imploring the Peloponnesian league to send help. Their words were heard and the Peloponnesian League agreed to enter an alliance with Mytilene and also embark on an invasion of Attica, as the envoys had also suggested. Thus, each ally was ordered to bring two thirds of their fighting force to the Corinthian Isthmus. The Spartans arrived first, and began preparations to move their fleet from the Corinthian Gulf into the Athenian waters by dragging the vessels over land, and organized a joint assault by land and sea. However, the rest of the Peloponnesian allies failed to show the same level of enthusiasm, having already grown tired of these expeditions as well as having a harvest to bring in,[6] so they were much slower in their mobilization.

The Athenians, in turn, were aware of the preparations being made against them and used the opportunity to make a show of force. The Peloponnesians, on the information of the Mytilenian envoys, did not believe that the Athenians had the manpower to blockade Mytilene and raid the Peloponnesian coast, as well as deal with a naval assault on Athens itself.[7] They were grossly mistaken. The Athenians ordered a further 100 triremes to be fully manned by citizens, excluding the two richest property-classes, which then sailed toward the Isthmus and raided the Peloponnese whenever it wished. During this raiding campaign the Athenians held the largest active fleet in the entire war: these 100 new triremes were added to the original fleet of 100 ships that were already raiding the Peloponnesian coastline or guarding Attica, and 50 more engaged elsewhere throughout their empire.[8] The Athenian response at sea, allied with news of further Athenian raids on the Spartans' own coastline, forced the Spartans to withdraw back to Laconia. On their return to Sparta, a new *nauarch*, Alcidas, was appointed and placed in command of an allied fleet of forty-two ships that were to sail to Lesbos and aid the Mytilenians.[9]

On Lesbos, Mytilene had been trying to assert its authority over the entire island with limited success. After an unsuccessful assault on Methymna they withdrew to some of their allies and helped secure the defences before heading back to Mytilene. When the Athenians received word of Mytilene's growing hegemony on the island they sent a force of 1,000 hoplites to besiege the city, building a circumvallation and thus blocking the city off by sea and land. However, this blockade did not stop the arrival of a Spartan commander, Salaethus, sent to deliver a message to the Mytilenians to not give up hope as a fleet was on its way.

The spring of 427 BC brought with it a new invasion of Attica by the Peloponnesian League that was coordinated with the sailing of Alcidas' fleet to Lesbos, in the hope of unsettling the Athenians with two operations occurring simultaneously. Unfortunately Alcidas' journey took longer than expected, for some unknown reason, and the Mytilenians became concerned. Provisions in the city were quickly running low, the Athenian siege had caught them by surprise and cut off the trade routes to their Lesbian allies. Even the Spartan commander was growing concerned, so he decided to take matters into his own hands.[10] Salaethus designed a sortie with which he could break through the Athenian siege, and so he armed the rest of the male citizens with hoplite armour, something they were not accustomed to.[11] Regrettably for him, when he armed the people they simply turned on him and refused to fight, preferring instead to demand that the authorities in the city release all of the grain held in the reserves to dole out evenly among the people, or else they themselves would make terms with the Athenians. The Mytilenian authorities had no choice: they invited the Athenians into the city and sent an envoy to Athens to plead their case.

A full week had passed since the fall of Mytilene before Alcidas arrived off the Ionian coast. He received the news of its demise and decided to land at Embatum, on the mainland of Asia Minor directly south of Lesbos. It was only then that he discovered the true extent of what happened, and that the Athenians held a strong position inside the newly fitted defences of the city. The *nauarch*'s allies attempted to persuade him to still proceed to Mytilene and attack the city, but he refused. He wanted to return to the Peloponnese as soon as possible, having failed in his mission.

Putting out from Embatum, Alcidas' fleet followed the Ionian coast south before following the islands back toward Attica via Samos. Along the way he captured vessels that had approached the fleet, assuming them to be Athenian ships, but Alcidas took to executing the prisoners before he was reprimanded by the Samians and, instead, released them back to their homeland. The Peloponnesian fleet did not have an easy journey home, as an Athenian fleet appeared off the Ionian coast and, on hearing of Alcidas in the vicinity, set off in pursuit but were never able to overtake him. Following the Peloponnesian fleet's departure, the Athenians were able to re-establish control over Lesbos, leaving them with a dilemma as to what punishment to exact upon Mytilene. The original verdict was to condemn the city to death, but this was later adjusted to only include the main protagonists in the uprising, which still numbered over 1,000 men. The walls of the city were destroyed and harsh financial restraints were placed on the Lesbians as a whole. This Athenian success was quickly offset by a development closer to Athens: their allies at Plataea, in Boeotia, had just surrendered after a brutal two year siege (429-427 BC).

Athens received yet further troubling news, there were rumblings of dissent at Corcyra. A single envoy was sent to the island, but it coincided with the arrival of a Corinthian envoy, so the Corcyraeans quickly became unsure of what to do. The debate became heated between populists, who felt that they should continue in their alliance with Athens, and the oligarchs who believed the old stance of neutrality was a better course of action. Disagreement turned into political murder and, ultimately, civil war, before the oligarchs were able to loosely take control of the city after a day of fighting.[12] The battle had broken out in the streets of Corcyra and the populists were forced atop the Acropolis, with brief skirmishes breaking out with great frequency. The following day, both sides sent messages to the slaves outside the city, offering freedom in exchange for their support. The slaves chose to help the populists, but the oligarchs soon received 800 mercenaries into the city as reinforcements. After a day of rest, battle recommenced but the numerically superior populists finally gained the advantage, with the help of the slaves and even the women, sending the oligarchs into a rout. The fighting ceased at nightfall and both the Corinthian envoy, and the mercenaries, were able to remove themselves from the city without detection.

The following day saw the arrival of the Athenian commander, Nicostratus, from Naupactus, with 12 triremes and 500 Messenian hoplites. He was able to broker a peace between the two factions and restore the status quo, but on the point of departure he was requested to leave five Athenian triremes and crew with the Corcyraeans, to dissuade the oligarchs from trying to restart the troubles. Nicostratus agreed, in exchange for five fully manned Coryraean ships. Unfortunately, the Corcyraeans decided to fill their ships with oligarchs or else their supporters, which created an atmosphere of fear and distrust among the population. The oligarchs were afraid they were being sent to Athens as prisoners, and no amount of promises from Nicostratus would change their mind. Nicostratus was able to stop civil war from breaking out again, but the oligarchs had to be moved onto an island that lay just north of the city for their own safety.

Four or five days passed before a new sight appeared on the horizon. A large fleet of fifty-three triremes were heading toward Sybota from the south. In command of the fleet was Alcidas once again. He had survived his journey back to Sparta, via Crete to avoid the Athenian ships, and had arrived at Cyllene where he was met with thirteen allied triremes and the Spartan commander Brasidas, who had been assigned to him as a counsellor. The Spartans had decided to act fast following the failure at Lesbos. On hearing that civil war had broken out in Corcyra, the Spartans aimed to exploit the situation before the Athenians could send reinforcements to Nicostratus. The fleet, having duly arrived, dropped anchor at Sybota for the night, ready to face battle the following morning.

Forces

The Corcyraean fleet consisted of sixty triremes, but the sudden and unexpected arrival of the Peloponnesians meant that they were ill-prepared.

Nicostratus had not yet left the island, so his twelve experienced triremes were there in support of the islanders. Also within his fleet were the two official state triremes, the *Salamina* and the *Paralus*. No overall commander was ever decided upon, and when Nicostratus attempted to assert some tactical authority he was ignored by the Corcyraeans.

The Peloponnesian fleet had forty experienced triremes made up from the various allies of the Peloponnesian League that had served in Ionia. To this were added the thirteen ships from the island of Leucas and the westerly Greek region of Ambracia. Overall authority lay with Alcidas, who was himself advised by Brasidas. It is possible that the triremes were carrying a larger number of marines than the Athenians and Corcyraeans, which would mean they would be heavier and therefore slower in the water.[13]

Battle   (Thucydides, III.77-79)

The arrival of Alcidas' fleet sent shockwaves through Corcyra. They had been caught completely unprepared. The preparations for a defensive action were hastily cobbled together. Their crewmen were called to muster, and sixty triremes were swiftly fitted out for battle. Nicostratus understood the potential danger here. If the Corcyraeans maintained this flustered behaviour at sea they would be utterly destroyed by the numerically superior Peloponnesians. He made the wise suggestion that the Athenian contingent should lead out the fleet, which would allow all of the Corcyraean ships to prepare and follow them together. He was ignored.

The Corcyraeans set out to sea the moment each ship was ready. This was not an organized fighting force but a multitude of scared squadrons without any discernible leadership. As the enemy ships came into sight, two of the Corcyraean ships immediately deserted. Others still did not even notice the enemy coming into view, as they were too busy fighting amongst themselves. In contrast, Alcidas had his fleet organized and, on seeing the great confusion amongst the Corcyraeans, arranged for twenty ships to be placed on that flank, while the remainder would be ranged against the Athenians who had, characteristically, held their order.

The Corcyraeans attacked the Peloponnesians that faced them, but in complete disarray. The attacks occurred in small detachments, without any form of coordination or impetus. It was a panicked display from what was a strong naval power, and the small Peloponnesian squadron was able to resist the assaults with ease. The fighting was only drawn out due to the sheer quantity of Corcyraean ships, but the Peloponnesians were able to beat them back, immobilizing many triremes in the process.

Nicostratus, with his Athenian ships, soon realized that this battle would have to be about damage control rather than victory. He decided against launching his ships into the main bulk of the Peloponnesian fleet, nor even into the centre of the detachment that directly faced him. Nicostratus reasoned that the Peloponnesians would struggle to maintain their composure in the face of Athenian successes, so he aimed his squadron against the furthest wing of the enemy, swiftly sinking one of the Peloponnesian triremes.

Alcidas was prepared for such a move. His advisor, Brasidas, had seen the impact that Athenian manoeuvres could have on even a strong Peloponnesian fleet in the Corinthian Gulf; so, at the sight of Athenian progress on their wing, Alcidas gave the order for the forty-two triremes with his to form a large circle, their prows pointing outwards. The Athenians began to circle around the formation, attempting to create disorder and to exploit the gaps it would produce. The Peloponnesians did not falter, but their tactic could not last forever.

The twenty Peloponnesian triremes who still faced the disorganized Corcyraeans were called to join the bulk of the fleet and break up the Athenian offensive.[14] The arrival of these reinforcements saw the Athenians withdraw from their circling and they quickly reassessed their next move. The moment the Athenians withdrew in front of them, Alcidas ordered the circle formation to open out into line abreast, and joined by the extra squadron, the entire Peloponnesian fleet bore down on the Athenians.

Nicostratus had to think quickly. If he tried to hold his position he would be defeated. If he fled now, his ships would survive because of their speed, but the Corcyraeans would be left at the mercy of the enemy. The commander ordered a controlled retreat, backing water at a leisurely pace but never allowing the Peloponnesians to lose interest in pursuing them. At the sight of the Athenians backing water, the Corcyraeans withdrew with as much composure as they had embarked on this disastrous battle. The retreat lasted until sunset, when the Peloponnesians stopped in their pursuit.

The Corcyraeans were in a panic. They were convinced that the Peloponnesians would follow up in their victory and attack the city, or that

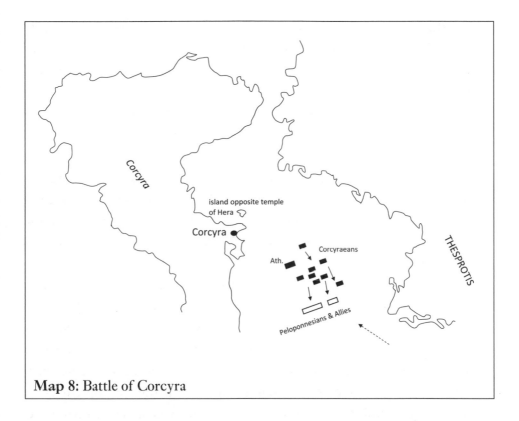

Map 8: Battle of Corcyra

they would release the oligarchs who were still captive on the island off the coast. Their concern was so great they sent men over to retrieve the oligarchs from the island and imprison them in the temple of Hera in Corcyra. However, Alcidas had no such intention to attack the city, choosing instead to collect the thirteen Corcyraean triremes that had been captured and recover the only one of the Peloponnesians that had been bested by the Athenians. With these ships in tow, he returned to Sybota. The following day Alcidas ignored the reports coming from the city about unrest and panic, and decided to land a force at Leucimme, to the south of the island, where they laid waste to the country. Not even the urging of Brasidas could convince Alcidas to change his mind; he would not attack the city of Corcyra.

Aftermath

The people of Corcyra were so afraid of Alcidas' fleet they came to terms with the oligarchs, and even convinced some to join the crews of the thirty remaining triremes in defence of the city.[15] But there was no need, for the Peloponnesian raid on the island only lasted until midday before they withdrew to Sybota. By dusk Alcidas was informed by beacon signals about the impending arrival of an Athenian fleet, sixty triremes strong, which had been sent from Leucas to support Nicostratus.

Alcidas withdrew from his position, following the coast south to avoid the Athenian advance. The fleet went as far as dragging their ships over the isthmus of Leucas, all with the intention of avoiding observation by the strong Athenian fleet. When the news of an Athenian fleet reached the Corcyraeans the atmosphere in the city drastically changed; not to euphoria or relief, but to vengeance and murder. The oligarchs who had been convinced to join the trireme crews were murdered in cold blood, while those still in the temple of Hera took it upon themselves to kill each other or else hang themselves, rather than face the summary courts and pseudo-legal executions that awaited them. For seven days the city was beset by death and atrocities. Sons killed their fathers, debtors killed their creditors, screaming men were torn from the altars at which they had sought sanctuary, or simply killed at them, while some were even walled up in the temple of Dionysus to die a slow and agonizing death.[16]

For the Athenians and the Peloponnesians, the battle for supremacy in western Greece still raged. This victory for Alcidas accomplished little, except for the injection of morale that came from sending an Athenian fleet into retreat, albeit an orderly and calm retreat. This defeat did little to dent Athenian ambition, and the continued political alliance with Corcyra allowed for a simpler journey to Sicily where they had plans to support allies on the island and attempt to incorporate this large wheat-growing island into their empire.

Part 3

THE IONIAN WAR

The Archidamian War ended in a stalemate. The Peace of Nicias, named after its architect, was put in place because neither the Spartans nor the Athenians could maintain the pressure that the war was exerting on their respective cities. However, the peace was a sham almost from the start. Conflict and battle persisted, and by 418 BC the Athenians joined an alliance of *poleis* who took to the field against Sparta at the Battle of Mantinea, which the Spartans won. But this did not bring with it open war between Sparta and Athens; not yet.

Athens was still in recovery from the war, and the plague which had devastated its population in the 420s BC. During this time, the Athenians decided to take firm control of their empire, resulting in the harsh treatment of some rebellious factions. The worst example being the small island of Melos, which was put under siege by its Athenian overlords. When the Athenians finally broke through, and following a long and famous political discussion about what punishment to exact on the rebels, the men of Melos were all brutally slaughtered and the women and children were put into the slave markets.

By 415 BC Athens had gained a new generation of men to fill its army's ranks. They did not want to exert their growing power on mainland Greece, but an opportunity came to help an ally in faraway Sicily. A large expeditionary force was sent to the great Sicilian city of Syracuse, and it was duly put under siege. But the expedition started to encounter some major setbacks, and when word came to Athens that the Spartans were sending one of their own commanders to help the Syracusans, they knew that the situation was only going to get worse. In 413 BC, Sparta broke all pretence of peace. They set up a permanent military presence in the small fort of Decelea, which was situated in Athenian territory and only a few miles away from the city itself. This gave the Spartans and their allies a foothold from which they could now launch their raids into Attica all year round, rather than the seasonal raids that defined the Archidamian War. Our Athenian sources refer to this as the beginning of the Decelean War (413–404 BC); but, because most of the fighting would revolve around the Ionian coastline, it was also, more accurately, called the Ionian War.

413 BC went from bad to worse for the Athenians. They had placed a small fleet in the Corinthian Gulf to try and dissuade the Peloponnesians from sending reinforcements to Syracuse. The Corinthians, however, decided to take the opportunity to test out a new design for their triremes. In what is often considered a very innocuous event, the Battle of Erineus in fact witnessed a vital shift in the balance of naval power. The new Corinthian designs, allied with the tactical nous of the commanders, revealed the great weakness of the Athenian navy: they could not handle a direct assault. The battle was not really a victory for either side, but the Corinthians were definitely the ones who took the most from the day.

Later that same year the Athenians witnessed their most crushing defeat to date. In Syracuse, the siege had been going on for two years. Due to the geography of the area, one of the most important positions to control, as the attackers or the defenders, was the Great Harbour. It was the site of many skirmishes but in 413 BC the harbour bore witness to one of the great naval battles of the period. The Syracusans had copied the designs of the Corinthian prototypes which had been so successful at Erineus. The Syracusans were able to use the element of surprise to force the Athenian fleet into a confined area, and suffer heavily at the direct method of battle that faced them. The battle sees the use of smaller boats to move in between the larger triremes, so that projectiles were being thrown at Athenian sailors from all angles. It also shows us the ingenuity of the Athenians, who set up a safe area for their ships to return to and defended it using an innovative weapon called a 'dolphin'. This was a heavy weight which could be dropped from one ship, through the hull of an enemy ship. Finally the Syracusans show how important joint-force operations could be to the outcome of a battle, by coordinating to perfection their land assaults with their naval movements.

The expedition in Sicily ended in a catastrophic defeat for Athens, but it could not lick its wounds and recover because the war in Greece was only just beginning. The Spartans maintained their momentum, focussing their intentions on destroying the Athenian empire, and thus the source of Athenian finances. Therefore attentions went east, to the Ionian coast and the islands around it. Political manipulations soon moved into armed conflict once again, and the years of 412 and 411 BC were consumed by naval battles in the area. This culminated in the Battle of Cynossema, which saw the Athenians win an important, but hard-earned victory. The battles of the Ionian Coast show just how much the balance of power had shifted at sea. The Athenians were no longer guaranteed easy victories, even when they were able to use their great advantages of speed and mobility. They also show how naval battles were rarely decisive affairs, but part of larger more complex strategies to garner control of an area.

Athens began to hold the advantage in the Aegean once again, but Sparta soon gained the confidence of the Persians and, with their vast supplies of money, were able to recover from their defeats quickly. By 406 BC the Spartans were trying to gain control of the Hellespont, to cut off the grain supply that was feeding the perpetually besieged Athenians. A large battle took place off the island of Lesbos, the Battle of Arginusae, and resulted in a great Athenian victory. However, that victory was to be marred by the manner in which the commanding officers were then treated on their return to Athens. In the battle we see the Athenians go to extraordinary lengths to neutralize the direct assaults of the Peloponnesians. No longer content in their own superiority, the Athenians had been forced to adapt and set themselves out in a deep formation. The depth of their lines absorbed the power of the Peloponnesian assaults, giving the Athenians time to recover and fight back, to great effect.

Even after such a victory, the Athenians put their commanders on trial for a failure of duty, and killed them. The impact of such an act must have been hugely influential, and it is perhaps not surprising that in the following year the Athenians were finally defeated in the Battle of Aegospotami (405 BC). This battle was an enormous affair, consisting of over 300 triremes. The Peloponnesians were heavily outnumbered, but the Athenians were poorly commanded. The Spartan commander, Lysander, orchestrated a great joint-force operation which caught the Athenian ships off guard, with many of them never making it out to sea. Uniquely, this battle sees the use of spy ships, and shows us the importance of intelligence gathering before battle. This battle basically brought an end to Athenian resistance, and by 404 BC Athens was finally defeated.

Chapter 7

Battle of Erineus (413 BC)

Background   (Thucydides, VI. 30-32, 96, VII.10-20, 26-31)

The summer of 415 BC saw the Athenian harbour town, the Piraeus, abuzz with excitement and activity. The Athenian assembly had finally reached an agreement to help their allies in Sicily, who were struggling under the growing influence of the great city of Syracuse. They had decided to send a great armada to the island. Men answered their call to muster, and streamed into the Hippodamian *agora* in search of food supplies, weaponry and equipment, followed by their family and friends.

It seemed like all of Attica had come to see the new fleet depart, for this was the first, large-scale, military venture that Athens had committed to since the Peace of Nicias had brought the Archidamian War to an end in 421 BC. The crowds watched as 100 Athenian ships were boarded by their crews, and an additional 1,500 hoplites and 700 marines. Once the ships were fully equipped a large trumpet sounded, bringing silence to the vast crowd that huddled close to the waterfront. A herald offered prayers to the gods for the expedition, while bowls of wine were mixed on each of the vessels. The men were able to offer their own libations in the ornate gold and silver goblets, joined in voice by the citizen crowd. When the choral hymns came to an end, and the libations spilled, the fleet finally put out to sea, carrying with it the hopes and expectations of the Athenian people.[1]

For a year, Athens heard little word from Sicily, except for a request in the winter of 415 from their generals for more funds, and more cavalry. All was going well, it seemed.[2] However, in Greece proper, the summer of 414 BC witnessed more disturbing news beginning to arrive from the Peloponnese. Sparta had mobilized an army and marched on Argos. Fortunately for the Argives, the Spartan force never arrived; turning back, as it did, due to an earthquake. This show of strength by the Spartans was not welcome news in

Athens, but as long as things did not escalate further, there was little need for alarm. Unfortunately, Argos did not take to the Spartan threat very kindly, and mobilized an army of its own.

Marching on the Spartan held territory of Thyrea, due south of Argos on the eastern coast, the Argives caused havoc in the surrounding lands and took twenty-five *talents* worth of booty for their troubles.[3] With a watchful eye over events around Argos, as well as incoming reports from Sicily, Athens was distracted once more by the arrival of some populist rebels from Thespiae. They had attempted to overthrow their government and implement a democracy in line with the Athenian system, but had failed. The Thespiaean authorities received support from Thebes and chased down the rebels, those that escaped fled to Athens. But still, the official peace was able to hold out over the summer. Sparta had no reason to resume any hostility with Athens, and all reports from Syracuse brought promising developments: the Sicilians had been defeated in every single battle and skirmish outside of the great city walls, the harbour was under Athenian control, and the city was being circumvallated. It was not until the winter of 414/13 BC, that the situation began to turn.

Unbeknownst to the Athenians, Sparta had received advice from one of Athens' own exiles, Alcibiades, and the year of 414 BC had seen Sparta send a Spartiate commander to support the Syracusans in their defence against the Athenians.[4] By the time that this news had reached Athens it was too late. The leading commander in Sicily, Nicias, sent a letter to update the assembly, warning that Gylippus was beginning to turn the tide of Athenian success on the island. As the Athenian expedition was coming to the end of its second year, its original strength was beginning to diminish; while Gylippus was able to recruit more and more men to his side. Furthermore, a graver threat was beginning to appear; the Syracusans were evidently planning to take back the Great Harbour by investing in a more powerful naval force, effectively cutting off the Athenian land forces. Nicias' letter ended with two requests, the first was for reinforcements to be sent, or else for orders to be given to withdraw from Sicily. The second was perhaps more telling, he requested the right to resign his post and return to Athens.[5]

The Athenian assembly voted to persevere with their original plans. It was agreed to send reinforcements in the coming spring of 413 BC, but they immediately sent one commander with ten ships, and a necessary injection of funds around the winter solstice, to inform Nicias of the decisions made. The commander also informed Nicias that his resignation had been refused. Athenian concerns did not simply rest with reinforcing the expedition, they also voted to try and stem the movement of Spartan allies from the Peloponnese who could add to Gylippus' manpower. Twenty ships were sent around the Peloponnese to monitor the sea routes from Greece to Sicily. Their concerns were well founded, for Corinth and Sparta had begun to mobilize hoplites and board them on merchant vessels, in the hope of evading Athenian attention. Corinth also manned a fleet of twenty-five triremes and arrayed them in the Corinthian Gulf, with the intention of contesting the Athenian naval stronghold at Naupactus, in the mouth of the Gulf.[6] The Corinthian show of strength had a secondary aim of distracting the Athenian fleet's attention away from the merchant ships carrying their hoplites to Syracuse.

More concerning for Athens, was that this naval aggression from the Corinthians was not the greatest threat to their position in Greece, and the official peace that still technically persisted. For the Athenian traitor Alcibiades had also advised the Spartans to renew their raids on Attica, and he was joined in voice by the Corinthians and the Syracusans. The reasoning was infallible, Athens would not be able to fight two wars, one in Sicily and the other in its own lands. It would not take long for Athens to be brought to its knees, and for Sparta to hold the greatest influence throughout Greece. However, the Spartans had a problem with this scheme. They did not wish to be seen to break the sacred oath by which the Peace of Nicias had been sworn. The Spartans had reasoned that their own poor fortunes in the Archidamian War were, perhaps, down to such a violation of religious propriety, and it was not a mistake they intended to repeat.[7] Fortunately for the Spartans, excuses for conflict were easy to come by. The Athenians had continued raiding the Peloponnese from their position at Pylos, on the west coast of Messenia. Thus, theoretically the Athenians had broken the peace almost as soon as it was agreed, and continued to violate it on a regular basis. To add wood to the fire, the Athenians sent thirty ships out from Argos and ravaged parts of the eastern coast of the Peloponnese.[8]

Once the Spartans had voted to send a force into Attica in the following spring, they spent the winter requesting supplies from their allies in preparation. But they did not require thousands of men, or hundreds of cavalry; instead they requested as much iron as their allies could acquire. The Spartan intention was not to simply raid Attica, like they had in the previous war. On the urging of Alcibiades, the Spartans resurrected an old plan and decided to fortify the position at Decelea, which lay just over 13 miles northeast of Athens itself.[9] This fortified position would be situated to perfection. Located on one of the main roads from Thebes to Athens, the fort would be able to be reinforced by the Thebans, who would help build and man it also. Furthermore, the position would cut off the route from Athens to Euboea, a region from which Athens relied upon for much of its food supplies. Finally, the fort would allow for a constant relay of raids, without the need to withdraw back to the Peloponnese or Boeotia for the winter.

The first days in the spring of 413 BC saw a joint Peloponnesian and Boeotian army invade the undefended lands of Attica, under the command of King Agis II of Sparta. After a brief period ravaging the countryside, the joint forces set to work fortifying Decelea. With Athens suitably distracted with issues so close to home, Sparta and its allies sent off their assigned troops to Syracuse, aided by the Corinthian fleet that succeeded in distracting the Athenian ships that had been assigned the role of blocking the reinforcements heading west.

The impact on the Athenians of the fortification of Decelea was almost immediate. The Attic countryside was awash with enemy forces of varying sizes destroying Athenian property. Whether it was the ever changing garrison of the fort, which rotated between the allies on a regular basis, or marauding armies under the command of Agis, the Athenians could not take back control of their lands. With food supplies over land being cut off, Athens became more like a fortress than a city, its only source of supply came through its heavily fortified harbour at the Piraeus. The costs of the constant raiding forced the Athenians to review their imperial income, replacing their old tribute system with a tax of a twentieth imposed on all imports and exports as a way of raising enough funds. Meanwhile, Decelea itself swiftly became a beacon for slaves in Attica, with over 20,000 slaves reported to have deserted their Athenian masters.[10] Yet, amazingly, Athens was able to resist and also continue its military actions in Sicily.

Athens still intended to send another force out to Sicily to help Nicias, under the command of Demosthenes, but it was given a further tactical goal before embarking on its long voyage. Demosthenes was charged with raiding the Peloponnesian coast as he circumnavigated it. Furthermore, he decided to fortify a small isthmus on the tip of the southern coast of Laconia, opposite the island of Cythera. This formed a permanent base in the Spartan heartlands, from which the Athenians and their allies could launch their own raids. From there, Demosthenes headed north around the Peloponnesian coast to the island of Cephallenia where he met with more troops to join him in on his expedition to Syracuse. It was here that he also met with Conon, the Athenian naval commander at Naupactus. Conon was growing more and more concerned about the twenty five Corinthian ships in the Gulf, believing that they intended to attack him at any moment. Conon requested that Demosthenes send him some of the ships under his command, otherwise Conon did not feel he could resist with only the eighteen triremes under his command. Demosthenes could not refuse, so he sent Conon back with ten of the fastest that he had under his command, before leading the rest of his forces to Sicily.

Forces

The Athenian fleet was thirty-three triremes strong, moored at Naupactus. This means that a further five ships had been acquired by the Athenian commander, in addition to his original eighteen and the ten sent by Demosthenes. Although it was Conon who officially held command, he was not present at the battle, which was instead led by an Athenian named Diphilus. Conon's absence is not commented on by Thucydides; perhaps he had been sent to garner more reinforcements from elsewhere, or else the Athenians had replaced him with a new commander in the middle of the summer season, which would be strange timing on their part but not impossible.[11] The Athenian ships were sleek and fast, with experienced crews.[12] They also knew the Gulf very well, having been stationed there since the outbreak of the Archidamian War. They knew its geography, they knew its weather and its tidal patterns. If they were to be surprised by anything, it would have to originate from the Corinthians themselves.

The Corinthians had planned for this battle long in advance. The twenty-five triremes they had originally assembled, under the command of the Corinthian Polyanthes, were supplemented by a few more as a way of narrowing the Athenian numerical advantage. But, interestingly, the Corinthians still chose to fight while outnumbered, against the strongest navy in the Greek world. They were not foolish in this decision, but were experimenting with a new ship design. Each of these triremes had been reinforced in its bow-timbers, giving the Corinthians a great advantage when ramming the lighter-built Athenian vessels. This small battle would be decided by tactical decision-making: either the Athenians would utilize their greatest asset of speed and mobility, or the Corinthians would force the Athenians to fight head-on and beat them with their reinforced ships.

Battle   (Thucydides, VII.34)

The Athenian command at Naupactus had received concerning reports, rumours really, of Corinthian activity since the end of 414 BC. Gossip floated on the winds of an innovative weapon, a new form of trireme that the Corinthians intended to test out on the small Athenian fleet. Rumours about such an unknown quantity led to unrest and concern among the Athenians, crews and officers alike. When the Corinthians put their twenty-five triremes to sea, Conon was forced to wait and watch as merchant ship after merchant ship passed him by, carrying Peloponnesian troops to Sicily. Uncharacteristically, the Athenians were no longer sure of their superiority, so the assessment was quickly made that the Athenians were not prepared to face such an unknown, with only eighteen ships in their number. Having been sent to gain a greater number of ships, Conon had almost doubled the fleet's strength, but still there was an element of unease.

The Corinthians had already shown themselves capable of fighting the Athenians at sea, and giving them a bloody nose in the process, but Athenian superiority in crew and ship design had always seen them safe from defeat. If Corinth had taken the lead in the naval arms race, then Conon's fleet was under real threat. Conon understood this risk and realized the vulnerability of his fleet and had moved to nullify it as best he could. Conon planned to wait until the timing was opportune. But Conon was not in charge of the fleet when battle commenced. For command had passed to a rather impetuous man called Diphilus, who lacked the composure and patience of his predecessor.

Diphilus decided to force a battle as early as possible, confident in his numerical and technical superiorities over the enemy. Polyanthes, perhaps in reaction to news of Diphilus' intent, decided to take the initiative and choose a location that suited him best. He took his Corinthian fleet west, along the northern coast of the Peloponnese, until he reached the bay of Erineus, in the

Rhypic country of Achaea. The bay was a perfect location for the defensive strategy that Polyanthes had devised. He needed to secure three vital elements by his choice of geography, and this bay achieved those aims: he needed his fleet to be near to land and a strong land-army presence in case there was a disaster and his ships needed to beach quickly; he needed to place his ships in a landscape that neutralized the superior mobility of the Athenians; and he needed a seascape that forced the Athenians to meet his rams head-on. The bay at Erineus was ideal for all three of these requirements due to its crescent shape. Polyanthes situated his land forces on both projecting headlands at either end of the bay. Stretching between these two points, he formed his triremes in line abreast, appearing a continuous line and effectively closing off the bay.

At the sight of the Corinthian ships lining up for battle so close to Naupactus, Diphilus decided to act. He led his fleet in line ahead across the gulf to face Polyanthes. What Diphilus saw on arrival did not surprise him, since he would

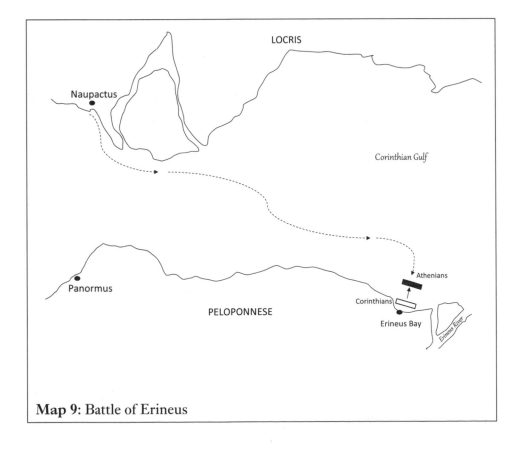

Map 9: Battle of Erineus

have expected the Corinthians to hold a defensive position, but it did cause a delay to his plans. For as long as the Corinthians were moored just inside the mouth of the bay, the Athenians could not attack in their usual fashion. There was no space to attempt an encircling *periplous*; Diphilus would have to attempt to lure them out into the open water, but his was no simple matter. Not only would the Corinthians resist entering the open water anyway, they would certainly have no intention of doing so while they were outnumbered.

We are not told by Thucydides what actions were taken by Diphilus in his attempts to entice Polyanthes into advancing. But we are told that the Corinthians did not move for a very long time. More importantly, when the signal flag was finally raised by Polyanthes, we are told it was due to a visible opportunity. For the Corinthian commander's plan to work, the opportune moment must have presented itself. The Athenian ships would have needed to be grouped together and to have ventured too near to the Corinthian fleet, possibly as a way to entice the enemy to attempt to chase them into the open water. Polyanthes saw the opportunity, in whatever guise, and raised the signal.

With the strain of the oars, the stationary naval wall was transformed into a juggernaut of both intent and power. The Corinthian rowers pulled with all their might, Polyanthes knew his window of opportunity was small and closing fast. The Athenians knew they had been caught off guard and decided to resist the first wave of attack, but their ships were no match for the new trireme design. Polyanthes' ships drove their bows directly into the bows of the Athenian ships, rather than the usual tactic of manoeuvring to strike the sides of the enemy ships.

On contact, a pair of opposing ships ran along the other's ram and their projecting bow timbers finally made contact; in usual circumstances this could mean disaster for both vessels, but the new design gave the Corinthians the greatest advantage possible. The Athenian bow timbers, which covered much of the foreparts of the ships, were smashed on any of their ships unfortunate enough to suffer direct contact. With these timbers broken, the outrigger become dislocated and with it the third deck of oars which powered the ship.[13] This had an added benefit in that it did not destroy the ship, leaving it in need of some great restoration, but merely disabled it until some relatively simple repairs could be made by the victors.

The Athenians quickly realized their mistake in trying to face the Corinthians. After a period of obstinate fighting between the ships, the Athenians were finally able to break away from their adversaries and flee into the open water. Only then did their superior speed come to their aid, saving them from certain disaster. In the brutal fight, Diphilus' fleet was able to neutralize three Corinthian ships, but they in turn saw seven of their own disabled in a short space of time. With the help of fortuitous winds, the Athenians were able to escape the Corinthians, who in any event decided to return to their position just inside the crescent bay.

Victory for the battle was claimed by both sides. The Athenians saw themselves as victors because they had control of the disabled vessels from both sides, which all floated outside of the bay. However, the lack of pursuit or the capture of any prisoners, by either side, made the result ambiguous in Greek minds. The Corinthians considered themselves victors because they had disabled the most ships and the Athenians had been forced back from their position. Both sides set up trophies of victory, and neither considered themselves defeated. However, victory surely rested with Polyanthes who had masterminded the first defeat of a numerically superior Athenian fleet in recent history. Ultimately, this battle was a Corinthian experiment. Their new trireme design had been tried and tested, and won victory. They had finally found a way to neutralize Athenian naval superiority, and they could now use this battle as a blue print for a much larger venture the Peloponnesians, as a whole, had in mind.

Aftermath

Seemingly, the battle had little or no outcome in the Corinthian Gulf. The Athenian fleet returned to Naupactus and policed its entrance as before. However, there was a great lift in confidence for the Corinthians, knowing that they no longer needed to fear the Athenians, even if they could not remove them from the gulf. In reality, this battle was a precursor to events in Sicily, and it is to the island that our historian, Thucydides, immediately directs our attention. The question was, which of the two forces had learned most from this small encounter?

Chapter 8

The Battle for the Great Harbour of Syracuse (413 BC)

Background (Thucydides VI.1–VI.98; Diodorus, XII.82.3–XIII.6; Plutarch, *Life of Nicias*, 12–16)

Since the year 421 BC there had been an official, if uneasy, peace in Greece.[1] This peace had been strongly tested in 418 BC, when the Spartans took to the field and defeated an allied army of Argives, Athenians, Mantineans and Arcadians at the Battle of Matinea.[2] The subsequent Spartan victory left an uneasy feeling in Greece, and in Athens especially. Sparta had asserted a sense of authority over the Peloponnese and Athens needed to respond, or else face the potential loss of many allies. The problem was complex, however. Athens could not simply restart a war; the same war that had seen the Athenian lands of Attica ravaged, that had brought an unrelenting plague into her city walls, and that had ultimately ended in a stalemate. Furthermore, if they were seen to bring war to Greece, then the Athenian reputation would truly be in tatters as it would confirm to the minds of many that Athens was on a quest for imperial control over her fellow Greeks.

In the winter of 416/5 BC Athens played host to envoys from the Sicilian town of Egesta, situated on the northwest of the island. The Egestaeans had engaged in a conflict with the neighbouring town of Selinus, and the Selinuntians had recently secured the support of Syracuse, the largest Greek *polis* on Sicily. In an attempt to counteract this, the Egestaeans decided to call upon an old alliance they held with the Athenians, and it did not take long to convince them to give their support. There were two main thrusts to their speech. The first warned of the threat of a Syracusan monopoly on Sicily which, the Egestaeans pointed out, would allow them to send a large army to support the Spartans in any approaching conflicts. The second thrust was a promise to finance the Athenian fleet, removing the financial strain of a distant war from the Athenian war chest. The Athenian assembly voted to send a fleet, but first they agreed to send scrutineers to Egesta with the job of assessing whether the town was honest in its ability to fund the war.

When these scrutineers returned, in the spring of 415 BC, they brought with them news of Egestaean temples filled with valuable objects, and treasuries full of money. They had travelled with some Egestaeans, who had also brought sixty *talents* of un-minted silver to provide the first month's pay for sixty ships.[3] The Athenian assembly voted again to send a fleet, ignoring the negative overtures from the old statesman Nicias, who did not think it prudent to begin a new war, particularly one so far away. Amazingly, accounting for his negative views on the expedition, they nominated Nicias to lead the force, seconded by Lamachus and the young Alcibiades. Five days following this vote a second assembly was required to vote on more pragmatic matters, such as the fastest way to equip the ships. It was here that Nicias tried one last time to convince his fellow Athenians that this venture was ill-conceived.

Nicias was a well-liked and well respected veteran of Athenian politics, and indeed of their military. While he was considered quite cautious by nature, his opinions were always sought and listened to, even if his view opposed the common consensus. His opposition to the expedition was well thought through, and actually caused some discontent in the assembly. He pointed out that the peace in Greece, the peace he had played such a large hand in creating, was very frail at that point. If Athens sent a strong fleet far to the west, would she not be left vulnerable if the Spartans and their allies decided to attack? Moreover, he lambasted the assembly for trying to expand their empire, at a time when Athens did not have firm control over the areas it already held. The previous year, 416 BC, had just seen an arranged massacre of the island of Melos, an island who had dared to try and resist Athenian authority;[4] and 415 BC continued to see the northern region of Chalcidice in rebellion against Athens. Finally Nicias appealed to the older members of the assembly, the men who had lived through the Archidamian War, men who remembered the horrors of the plague, and he appealed to them to cool the hot-headed actions of the younger men. He finished by requesting a second vote on the expedition, to give the assembly the opportunity to rectify this error of judgement.

To counteract this rhetoric of Nicias, his would-be joint commander, Alcibiades, stood to address the assembly. Alcibiades spoke in favour of the expedition, emphasizing the prestige that such a successful mission would bring to Athens. He highlighted his own youthful exuberance, which he believed would work well alongside Nicias' good fortune, and argued that the Spartan fleet was too weak to offer any threat to Athens while the Sicilian expedition was under way. His speech was convincing, and the assembly became more resolute in their desire to send the fleet.

Nicias attempted one last throw of the dice. Knowing that his old line of arguing would not work, the experienced orator attempted to overwhelm his audience with the sheer scale of the task at hand. Nicias painted a picture of a possibly united Sicily, populated with independent Greek *poleis* that would join forces against the Athenians if they were to invade. He argued that the Athenian force would need to be much larger than the sixty ships originally voted on. It would need to include all arms of the military, including mercenaries and allies. It would need to be very well provisioned, and include a team of bakers, in case the expeditionary force became cut off by bad weather and was unable to import supplies. Unfortunately for Nicias, his plan backfired. On hearing the size of the venture ahead of them, the Athenian assembly were enthralled by the prospect and asked Nicias to declare what forces he would need. With reluctance, Nicias conceded that he would have to discuss the matter with his fellow commanders, but to begin with he would need 100 triremes, 5,000 hoplites (both Athenian and from their allies), as well as cavalry, archers and slingers.

The day of the fleet's departure was one to behold. Crowds of people swept into the harbour at the Piraeus as they watched the grand splendour unfold before them. So unique was this event, that religious protocol was adapted to incorporate the crowds. The ships were united in communal rituals of prayers and libation, which was usually contained within each individual ship.[5] Moreover, the crowd joined in with the marines and commanders as they made their prayers and sang their *paean* hymns. The ships sailed out of the harbour, racing as they went, and the hopes and fears of the Athenian population went with them.

As the Athenian fleet moved west to Corcyra, meeting with the remainder of its allies, news of its impending arrival reached Syracuse. But the city was beset by much political turmoil and the Athenian threat was not taken seriously. One Syracusan who understood the threat was Hermocrates, but his warnings were shouted down as being driven by some political machination. It was believed that the Athenians could not send a large enough force needed to take the great city, nor would they be foolish enough to try.

Back in Corcyra, the Athenian's fleet now swelled to 134 triremes, and 2 Rhodian *penteconters*. Of these, 100 triremes were their own, comprised of 60 of their customary, fast combat ships, and 40 of the standard Greek design which the Athenians used for troop transport.[6] The land forces had also increased slightly, with a further 100 men joining the 5,000 men set out by Nicias. This large force included 700 of Athens' poorer citizens, the *thetes*, who had volunteered as marines.[7] When they were ready, the fleet sailed to Rhegium, on the south eastern tip of Italy. On arrival, they sent word to Egesta for the support which had been promised and began proceedings to attract local support to their cause. It did not go well.

To Nicias' great dismay, news came back from Egesta that they could only offer thirty *talents* to help fund the Athenian fleet – a far cry from the full funding that had originally been offered. It transpired that the Egestaeans had deceived the Athenian scrutineers and borrowed the treasures which they had displayed, to create the impression of wealth. To add to the disappointment, the Rhegians refused to offer any support to the expedition, financial or otherwise. As they were the first town approached by the Athenian commanders for support, this came as a major blow to the morale of the men. A decision needed to be made quickly, so Nicias proposed that, to save face, they should sail to Selinus and make a show of force in an attempt to settle their conflict with Egesta, before returning to Athens without wasting any resources. Alcibiades disagreed; he thought they should push on by reaching out to all of the Sicilian cities as allies. The third commander, Lamachus, argued even more strongly, proposing that they attack Syracuse immediately. He eventually sided with Alcibiades and Nicias was forced to agree with them, so Alcibiades went to the island in the hope of garnering support from Messana. They would not even let him inside the walls.

Alcibiades' humble return to Rhegium brought a change of plan from the three commanders. Sixty of their ships were sent to Naxos, far north of Syracuse, as a form of intimidation, and it worked. The Naxians immediately received them, allowing the fleet to rest for a short period before they moved south to the pro-Syracusan town of Catane. Understandably, they were refused entry, so they pushed further south towards Syracuse. Ten ships were sent ahead of the fleet to enter the Great Harbour. Their job was to reconnoitre to see if the Syracusans were about to launch a fleet against them, but they were not. After observing the city and its harbour, the fleet sailed back along the coast to Catane, where they were once again refused entry. However, the town did agree to meet the commanders to at least hear the demands.

Alcibiades began his speech in the middle of the Catanian assembly, but it was merely a distraction. For outside the city, his men were breaking down a poorly constructed postern gate and flooding the marketplace inside the town walls. Syracusan forces inside Catane saw what was happening and quickly fled, their number was too small to oppose the Athenians here. With the loss of their ally's men, and the successful infiltration made by the Athenians, the Catanian assembly had no choice but to vote for an Athenian alliance and they subsequently 'invited' the rest of Alcibiades' men inside. Alcibiades had finally secured a foothold on Sicily, so he went to Rhegium and returned to Catane with the remainder of the fleet and built a camp from which to wage war on Syracuse.

The winter of 415/4 BC saw the beginning of the two-year siege of Syracuse, but Alcibiades was not allowed to be a part of it. The young commander was recalled to Athens to answer accusations of blasphemy. At the time of the fleet's original departure, many of the *herms*, statues of Hermes, had been dismembered, and Alcibiades was considered the key suspect for being the ringleader of the vandalism. Alcibiades had no intention of answering these charges and fled to the Peloponnese, while back in Athens he was condemned to death in absentia.

For the Syracusans, the winter brought with it a stark realization: the Athenians were not bluffing. Following the first full battle of the conflict at the Anapus River, to the south of the city, the Syracusans sent word to the Peloponnese for help. While the Corinthians were more than happy to offer their assistance, the Spartans were not so forthcoming. After initially refusing the request, the Spartans were eventually convinced to take action by none other than the exiled Alcibiades himself. But even then, they did not commit any real strength; they sent a commander called Gylippus, and two ships.

The summer of 414 BC saw both the Syracusans and the Athenians construct great walls. For the Syracusans their aim was to extend the defences, for the Athenians they intended to circumvallate the city. The encircling wall was intended to extend from the north of the city, over the Epipolae plateau, and then split into two as it went round to join the coast of the Great Harbour. This made the harbour itself a key tactical position that needed to be secured.

Forces

The battle for the Great Harbour spanned two years, during the course of which both sides underwent many changes of personnel. The Athenian force remained fundamentally the same as the one which set out from Corcyra. Their fleet was large and predominantly made up of fast Athenian triremes that had yet to be bested in a fair fight. However, the toll of such a long period of time at sea struck the fleet hard. Their ships lost many of its crew members to death or desertion, and the constant threat of attack from the Syracusans made it very difficult to maintain the ships at a high standard.

The Syracusans invested in their navy at the behest of Gylippus, and began to intensively train it. They also adapted their ship designs based on those which brought the Corinthians success at Erineus in the early summer of 413 BC. The Syracusan fleet was strongest when it could hit the Athenian triremes head on, in confined spaces, whereas the Athenians relied on space and an ability to move fast to secure their victories, two things that were not available in the Great Harbour. Tactically, the Syracusans held the advantage, but in terms of morale, reputation and experience, the Athenians held the upper hand.

Battle   (Thucydides VI. 99–VII.72; Diodorus, XIII.7-17; Plutarch, *Life of Nicias*, 17-24)

Nicias smartly orchestrated his attack. He had refrained from taking the harbour until it was truly necessary and – as the wall's construction was continuing at a fast pace, it was extending further and further south – the time had come. The Athenians intended to engage the Syracusans in a skirmish around the walls, to distract the enemy from the events on the water. The Athenian army descended into the plains to capture one of Syracuse's extending counter-walls, and was, in turn, attacked by the Syracusans. As this battle began to rage, a Syracusan detachment noticed the main Athenian fort on the Epipolae was lightly guarded and attacked it. Nicias was unexpectedly forced to defend the main circle fort with the army's slaves, which amazingly he succeeded in doing. Before the Syracusans could regroup they saw that the Athenian army had gained the advantage down on the plain and was heading their way. They also saw in the distance, to the south, the foreboding movement of Athenian ships as they entered into the Great Harbour without opposition. Nicas' plan had worked, the distractions around the walls had allowed his fleet to move unnoticed and take control of the Great Harbour.

With the harbour secured, Nicias was able to further extend his control to the south of Syracuse. He ordered the fortification of Plemmyrium, a promontory directly south of the city that narrowed the mouth of the Great Harbour. This position allowed Nicias to have a base of operations from which to manage the naval blockade, it also allowed for a naval force to be positioned that could quickly react to Syracusan naval movements from the Small Harbour, where their fleet was moored.[8] Furthermore, the impending arrival of Gylippus had dashed Nicias' presumptions of success on the land. The Syracusan forces were strong and willing, but thus far poorly commanded. The introduction of a Spartan general would quickly rectify that problem, so Nicias turned his thoughts to the war at sea. He moved men and the majority of his ships to Plemmyrium, where he had ordered the construction of three forts. But the region had no fresh water supply, nor was it abundant in woodland, forcing the men to go long distances for the most basic of supplies. But any foraging venture was almost certain death for the men, as the Syracusan cavalry patrolled the area and cut them down on sight.

Nicias assigned twenty of his ships to try and intercept some Peloponnesian reinforcements from Corinth before they arrived, but they failed in their duties.[9] The Syracusans received more men and felt a greater impetus. Nicias knew that the Athenian position was becoming untenable, he either needed more help or else to be allowed to pack up and return with his army back to Athens. He sent a letter to Athens demanding this, and requesting permission to resign his post due to a disease of the kidneys.[10] His resignation was refused, but the Athenian assembly did agree to send another army to support him. They would arrive in the following summer.

Nicias did not have the luxury of time. In early 413 BC, the Syracusans were beginning to unite under the leadership of Gylippus, and the Spartan had an audacious plan. He intended to challenge the Athenian control of the sea. On receiving the reinforcements from Corinth, Gylippus toured Sicily, garnering more troops and ships from his allies, and attempting to convince any neutrals to join the resistance against Athens. While he was away, he left the Syracusans with strict instructions, to man a fleet as large as the Athenian one, and to begin a rigorous training plan. For Nicias, the sight of a new fleet being put through its tactical paces brought nothing but terror. While his own fleet was more experienced, it was also straining under a long battle of attrition. Many sailors were being killed whilst on foraging expeditions, many slaves were deserting the fleet as they no longer perceived the Athenians to be the superior force, and allies were defecting to Syracuse for the promise of greater pay. But worst of all, the fleet had been on active duty for too long and it was no longer safe to beach their ships so that they could dry out: the Athenian triremes were beginning to rot.

When the Syracusan fleet was ready, Gylippus planned a joint operations attack on the Athenian position. He would personally lead a Syracusan army south to attack the fortified positions at Plemmyrium, while he sent two fleets against the Great Harbour to engage with the Athenian navy. The first naval assault was made by thirty-five Sicilian triremes, as the remaining forty-five sailed round from the Small Harbour. The Athenians quickly manned sixty triremes, sending twenty-five of them to head off the Syracusans' initial push, while the remaining thirty-five left the harbour in the hope of cutting off the remainder of the enemy flotilla. The battle for the harbour was tenacious, with neither side able to press home an advantage. The shores of Plemmyrium were covered with Athenian hoplites assisting their fleet in whatever way they could. All Athenian eyes were on the harbour, if the battle was lost then their position would become an impossible one. But the distraction on the sea concealed the movements of Gylippus who had managed to march his army all the way to the Athenian forts. His attack was swift and devastating.

It was still early morning when the first call to attack was made. Gylippus' men quickly took the first and largest of the forts, killing the garrison before they had the chance to flee. On witnessing the speed of the attack, and the capitulation of its guard, the garrisons of the remaining forts chose not to stay. They ran to the shoreline and found refuge in the remaining ships and merchant boats, but they were no safer on the water. The Syracusans were beginning to find some success in the harbour, pushing the Athenian ships further and further back. The Athenian hoplites in the boats tried to head for the main Athenian camp on the western shore of the harbour, but were chased the entire way by a Syracusan trireme tasked with stopping them. By the time Gylippus had taken the remaining two forts, the sea battle had changed course. After the Syracusan vessels had broken through the Athenian line at the mouth of the harbour they lost their order. This disorder descended into chaos as the Syracusan ships began to obstruct one another, gifting the Athenians a victory when they had faced certain defeat only an hour before. Notwithstanding the Syracusan dominance, the Athenians only lost three triremes, while claiming eleven enemy ships. They raised a trophy on an islet in front of Plemmyrium and retired to their main camp.

For Gylippus, the venture had not been a disaster, in fact he raised three trophies of his own, and with good reason. He had destroyed one of the two smaller forts, and refortified and garrisoned the remaining two. Unfortunately for Nicias, these were not merely forts, but had served as warehouses filled with grain, personal belongings and the masts and equipment for forty triremes. Furthermore, the entrance of the Great Harbour had been compromised and was not longer a safe route for the Athenians to receive provisions. According to Thucydides, the capture of Plemmyrium was the beginning of the end for the Athenian expedition.[11]

The Syracusans intended to capitalize on their momentum and sent out twelve ships. One was dispatched to the Peloponnese to encourage their allies on the Greek mainland to send further support. The remaining eleven were sent to Italy to cut off an Athenian fleet full of supplies that was heading for Nicias' army. The Syracusans fell upon the supply fleet off the southern coast of Italy and destroyed most of the ships, along with a timber stockpile that had been put aside for the Athenians around Caulonia. The Athenians in Sicily received word of the loss and posted twenty triremes to intercept the returning Syracusan fleet, but they only managed to take one ship, the remainder making it safely back to Syracuse.

Throughout this time, the Great Harbour was a scene of small engagements and skirmishes. The focus of these were the large wooden piles that the Syracusans had driven into the sea bed, outside the old docks, to allow their ships to anchor in relative safety from the Athenians. The Athenians brought against them an enormous ship weighing 10,000 *talents*, roughly 3-400 tons, fitted with wooden turrets and screens to protect against projectiles. From this ship they fastened ropes around the largest piles, wrenched them out and broke them; those which they could not move were sawn in two by divers. The ship came under a barrage of arrows and javelins, which the Athenians returned in kind, until most of the piles had been removed. Of equal concern were parts of the pile stockade which the Syracusans intentionally constructed to lie beneath the water line, causing considerable damage to any Athenian vessels that sailed too close. Athenian divers were specifically rewarded for going down and cutting these away, but it was a continuous battle because the Syracusans merely drove in more piles to replace those they had lost.

Gylippus knew that time was no longer on his side. Word had reached Syracuse of the reinforcements that Athens was sending Nicias, a force as large as the original expedition. The Spartan commander knew that his best chance of success was to eliminate the Athenian threat in the harbour before the fresh troops arrived. He had held on for as long as possible to allow for his ships to be appropriately modified. The debrief that had followed the Corinthian victory at Erineus, earlier that same summer, had brought with it a better design of trireme with which to fight the Athenians. The Syracusan triremes had their prows shortened and strengthened, placed strong timbers across the bows, taking brackets from these to the ships' sides, both internally and externally, reinforcing the structure for head-on collisions. The Athenians were cordoned in the harbour and had no space to move; as long as the Syracusans could hold their nerve they could exploit the narrow seascape and ram the Athenians into defeat.

Gylippus repeated his strategy from the earlier sea battle, leading an army out of the city to attack the Athenian siege walls, while the Syracusan fleet prepared to sail out into the harbour. It was the attack on land which distracted the Athenians this time, so they were scrambling to their ships when they realized the enemy fleet had begun to advance. They were able to get seventy-five triremes out just in time to face the eighty coming against them. The first day of battle was a tentative affair. Both sides advanced and retreated without ever gaining a distinct advantage, although the Syracusans did claim one or two Athenian vessels. On the second day the Syracusans did not move from their dock early, but Nicias did not presume to have won the battle. He used his time carefully, mending any ships that had been damaged in the fighting, and also setting up a substitute enclosed harbour. He utilized the piles that had already been driven into the sea bed when they first made camp in the area. In front of this marine stockade he moored the merchant vessels, roughly 200 feet away from each other, which would allow any troubled Athenian trireme to retreat to the protected enclosure without being hard pressed. With these preparations complete, Nicias saw the day's light fade away without any assault from the enemy.

On the third day, the Syracusans repeated their original tactics, coordinating an attack by land and sea early in the morning. In the harbour the fighting took a similar course to the first day, with neither side making any headway. However, a Corinthian helmsman called Ariston persuaded the Syracusan commanders to implement a surprising move. He asked that they send word to the city and for a market to be quickly moved down to the sea so that the crews could dine near to their vessels. When the Syracusan fleet backed water and returned to the city to eat, the Athenians had presumed this was the end of the day's fighting and returned to camp at a leisurely pace. But, before many of the Athenians had even begun to disembark and start eating, the Syracusans had returned to their ships and rowed out once more.

The two lines faced off against one another in a stand-off, with neither side wishing to overcommit to an assault. But the Athenians could not maintain this status quo for long, with many of their crew getting hungrier and hungrier. The call went up and the Athenian triremes advanced straight in to the reinforced prows of their Syracusan enemy. The Syracusans rammed them head on, prow-against-prow, smashing the light, hollow noses of the Athenian ships and ripping the outriggers from them. Javelinmen on the trireme decks were raining their darts down on the Athenian crews to damaging effect, but worse still were those crewing the small boats which were able to race in between the Athenian oars, sail up next to the sides of the ships and throw their javelins at the sailors. The fighting was hard and the sea was becoming scattered with floating bodies as the mêlée took its toll. The Athenian ships could not find the space to move as they wanted to. They could not encircle the enemy, nor feign a retreat; there was simply no room. In the cramped conditions, the Athenian ships began to obstruct one another, and the unrelenting Syracusan fleet seemed unstoppable. It was time for the Athenian fleet to retreat from battle and find safety in the makeshift enclosed harbour at their camp.

The retreat was chased down by the fastest of the Syracusan ships, with a handful making it to the defensive line of merchant ships, but Nicias had planned for such a possibility. Those enemy ships that did try to cross the line were met by 'dolphins', heavy lead weights held out from the merchant ships by the long spars which normally suspended the sail. Two ships that passed by had a 'dolphin' dropped on them, neutralizing one and destroying the other, along with its crew. Back in the main harbour, the Syracusans took control over the disabled vessels. They had sunk seven Athenian triremes and disabled many more besides. They took some of the crews as prisoners, but the rest they killed on sight. When they retired back to their docks they erected their trophies, one for the victory at sea, and the other for their advancements on land. Gylippus now had what he desired. The Syracusans had control of the Great Harbour and, more importantly, they held superiority on the sea.

When the Athenian reinforcements finally arrived they caused panic in Syracuse. Led by the seasoned commander Demosthenes, the Athenian force was as strong as Nicias' original, and with him came seventy-three new, battle-ready triremes. But neither he nor the Athenians were able to take control of the situation. On realizing the precarious nature of the Athenian position, Demosthenes decided that they must either secure success immediately, or else plan an extraction back home. He planned on audacious assault on the Epipolae, which he conducted with great vigour. The fighting took place in the depth of night, with only the moon to light their way. The attack began well, but Gylippus was able to regain control of his frightened troops and mount a serious defence.

By the time the Spartan had won victory, Athenian morale had hit an all-time low. Demosthenes demanded that they abandon their position immediately, while they were still strong enough at sea to make it home. Nicias, however, was fed false information and believed the Syracusans were suffering just as badly. When he was finally convinced to order the evacuation it was too late. The Syracusans launched another joint-force assault, with seventy-six triremes going up against eighty-six Athenian. The battle was closely fought, but Syracusan superiority continued to reign. They soon broke through the Athenian centre, and also caught Eurymedon, the Athenian commander on the right wing, who was attempting to encircle their position in the recess of the harbour. After killing him and sinking the ships closest to him, the entire Syracusan fleet chased the Athenians and drove them ashore.

Gylippus did not dwell on his mounting victories, but decided to block the harbour's entrance with merchant ships, to permanently deny the sea to the Athenians. He positioned merchant ships, rowing boats, and even triremes across the entrance; the Athenian commanders, seeing their only means of escape closing before their eyes, made a quick decision. They reduced their defensive lines back to the fort in the harbour and manned every available ship, even those not deemed seaworthy. The plan was to force an opening and make their way to Italy; if they failed, the men were ordered to land within the harbour, burn their ships, and march in line toward the nearest friendly town they could reach.

The Syracusans split their force, part of which went to guard the harbour's entrance, while the remainder lined the inside of the harbour, so as to attack the Athenians from all sides. The Athenian strategy was a simple one, they needed to ram through the floating wall before the Syracusans could encircle them. Their first wave of assault against the barrier was powerful and effective. By the time the second wave arrived, the initial blow had overpowered the Syracusan resistance and they began untying the blockading ships. As this was happening, the Syracusan ships bore down on the Athenian line from all directions, spreading the fight away from the barrier and throughout the harbour. Nearly two hundred ships fought in the small space, allowing no room for manoeuvre. Ships could not even repeatedly ram because backing water was barely possible. This was a battle of grit and determination. Rowers stuck rigidly to the calls of their boatswains, and the helmsmen expertly threaded through the narrow spaces until they could ram into an enemy ship. But once contact was made it was now only the marines that could affect the outcome. The air became filled with arrows and stones being thrown from the decks, while ears rang with the screams of dying men mixed with the loud cracks of splintering wood.

Marines fought marines as the immobile triremes became just platforms for hand-to-hand combat. Yet the close-quarter fighting also meant the helmsmen had to contend with being in an offensive position on one side, but being rammed from the other, such was the close proximity of both fleets. The screaming of orders descended into the screaming of appeals. For the Athenians the call was to force the passage by any means. For the Syracusans, the cry was for the glory of victory. But still the battle continued, much to the consternation of the men

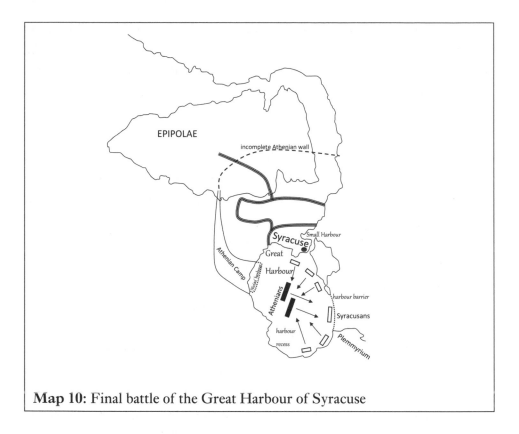

Map 10: Final battle of the Great Harbour of Syracuse

left ashore, watching it without any ability to influence it. That was, until the Athenian fleet could not take any more. They were finally forced back and into a retreat to the shore, chased incessantly by the Syracusan victors. When they landed, the Athenians ran back to their camp in a panic that Thucydides says had never been surpassed at the time of his writing of it.

Aftermath

The loss of life and of ships for both sides was substantial. So shocking and categorical was this defeat that the Athenians even forgot to request the return of their war dead, breaking all military and religious protocol. Numerically, the Athenian fleet still held the advantage. Demosthenes pointed this out to Nicias, they had sixty triremes to the Syracusan's fifty, and could try to contest the harbour once again. Nicias agreed and ordered a new assault, but the crews refused. They were so overcome with their defeat they did not believe success could ever be possible.

The Athenian commanders had to plan a different escape, this time over land. But Gylippus was prepared and left road blocks and ambushes to cut off the Athenians. The orderly retreat turned into a panicked rout and massacre. The Athenian army could not escape the Syracusan pursuit and, having lost more men in this single action than they had in the entire expedition to date, they were forced to surrender. The captives were taken to the quarries outside of Syracuse and held as prisoners, but Nicias and Demosthenes, as the Athenian commanders, were butchered, against the will of Gylippus.

For Athens, the defeat in Sicily was an unmitigated disaster. They had lost over 10,000 men, and hundreds of ships, as well as two of their best commanders. The defeat had revealed an innate weakness in Athenian naval tactics, one that could now be exploited by anybody. Back at home, they had dwindling resources, and no fleet capable of defending them indefinitely. To make matters even worse, the expedition had given rise to a renewed war with Sparta, who now held a fortified position in Attica. They did not have time to mourn their losses, they had a war that they needed to win, or at least try to survive.

Chapter 9

Battles of the Ionian Coast (412-411 BC)

Background (Thucydides VIII.1-103; Diodorus XIII.37-38)

Athens became a hive of industry and change in the winter of 413 BC. News of the Sicilian disaster had caused abject panic; not solely because of the loss of soldiers and brethren, but more so the loss of ships. The beating heart of the Athenian navy, the Piraeus, had fallen quiet and the threat of an imminent Peloponnesian attack was a stark reality. But Athenian pragmatism won over the assembly. Having established a list of prioritized policies – the consolidation of their allies, the reformation of their internal economic policies, and the building of a new fleet – the Athenians decided to resist against Peloponnesian aggression.

Athenian fears were not unfounded, for when news reached the Peloponnese from Sicily it ignited an intent to subdue Athens once and for all. The Peloponnesian *poleis* wanted to capitalize on a weakened Athens, yet they themselves had struggled to recover from the previous war and they needed extra help.[1] In the first instance this came from many of Athens' subject-states, who wanted to use this hiatus in Athenian strength to revolt and re-establish their own autonomy.[2] The Spartans also seized the opportunity and renewed their raids from the fort of Decelea in Attica, as well as ordering their allies to produce a newly-built fleet of 100 ships.[3] The original intent of these preparations was to support revolts in Euboea, but that winter saw many different *poleis* come to the Spartans for aid. One of the Spartan kings, Agis, was based at Decelea and it was he who was orchestrating the action in Euboea. But before he sent over the Peloponnesian forces, he received a delegation from the Ionian island of Lesbos who wanted support for their own revolt. Agis agreed to divert his attention to Lesbos, unaware that back in Sparta a different delegation had arrived.

In Sparta, envoys from the islands of Chios and Erythrae arrived, bringing with them an ambassador from the Persian commander, Tissaphernes. The

Persian satrap held authority over the 'maritime districts', which included the Ionian Greeks, but was struggling to collect his tribute from the *poleis* due to the demands made on them by the Athenians. Tissaphernes' offer was a beguiling one, he wanted the Peloponnesians to assist the revolt, and in exchange he would fund their costs. But Tissaphernes was not the only Persian satrap who sent representatives to Sparta. Pharnabazus was in control of the Hellespont region of the Persian Empire and a longstanding rival to Tissaphernes. He wanted the Peloponnesians to send him a fleet and in exchange he offered a lump sum of twenty-five *talents*. Pharnabazus' aim was achieve the same outcome as Tissaphernes, but be able to claim the tribute himself, and bring the Spartans into alliance with the Great King.

After much internal debate, the Spartans finally decided to support the Chian uprising and take the funds of Tissaphernes. Thus, in early summer, three *Spartiates* were sent to Corinth to assist in the hauling of the Peloponnesian fleet from the Corinthian Gulf across the Isthmus. This fleet was under strength and needed to incorporate those ships that Agis was equipping for his campaign to Lesbos, but even then it only numbered thirty-nine. When the Peloponnesian allies met again in Corinth, the plans for aiding Chios were finalized and, thanks to Tissaphernes' promise of more money, the Corinthians pledged to build a further twenty-one triremes. However, there were concerns from the Chians that Athens might discover the plot early and punish their 'ally', even though Athens did not yet have any great naval force to speak of. To that end, twenty-one ships were quickly dragged across the Corinthian Isthmus to go to Chios first, before further support followed later. Unfortunately for the Chians, the Corinthians had no intention of departing for Ionia before they had celebrated their Isthmian festival, a Panhellenic Games like the more famous Olympic Games, which brought with it a sacred truce between all Greeks that this expedition would break.

The Athenians caught wind of the Chians' plans and sent one of their generals to the island to challenge their loyalty. He demanded they send seven ships to aid the new Athenian fleet, which they quickly agreed to. Back at the Games, the Athenians present heard rumours of the Peloponnesian fleet crossing the Isthmus so that, by the time the festival was over and they had returned home, the Athenian fleet was prepared for action. The Peloponnesian fleet, under the command of Alcamenes, set off from Cenchreae only to find their route obstructed by twenty-one triremes under the command of the Athenians. It was a show of intent, but the Athenians could not trust the seven Chian ships in their number, so they shortly turned back after seeing Alcamenes retreat and regroup from the shock of seeing such a strong opposition. The Athenians soon returned with thirty-seven ships and chased Alcamenes' fleet along the Peloponnesian coast, forcing him into anchor at the deserted port of Spiraeum. Here the Athenians disembarked some of their men and assaulted the moored fleet by land and sea, disabling most of the enemy ships and killing Alcamenes in the process.

After this victory, the Athenian fleet maintained a blockade of the remaining Peloponnesian ships, while hauling up the rest of their own ships on a small island opposite and sending a request to Athens for reinforcements. The Corinthians arrived the following day, to support the surviving Peloponnesian fleet, but the situation looked so dire that they contemplated simply burning their fleet just to ensure the Athenians would not capture them. This extreme plan was overturned, most likely by more experienced commanders, and the ships were pulled onto the shore line to be guarded.[4] They would wait until the opportunity arose for them to safely set sail once more.

When news reach Sparta of this set back they became reluctant to send out the meagre five ships they had prepared to dispatch. Were it not for the intervention of the Athenian exile Alcibiades, the Spartans would have abandoned the whole venture. He persuaded the *ephor* Endius to persevere with the original plan and, in turn, be able to claim responsibility for the forthcoming alliance with Persia. Alcibiades sailed with the Spartan commander Chalcideus to Chios, without announcing their imminent arrival. On their arrival, the Chians were shocked and in awe of the sudden apparition of Spartan ships. Chalcideus and Alcibiades spoke to the Chian assembly and informed them that more Spartan support would arrive. They conveniently omitted the news of the Peloponnesian fleet besieged at Spiraeum. The people of Chios had little choice, they voted for rebellion.

This development caused panic and furore within Athens itself. They could not afford to lose such an important ally, and this rebellion could quickly spread throughout Asia Minor, which would devastate the Athenian Empire. The assembly voted for drastic action: they removed a ban that had restricted the ability for anybody to suggest the expenditure of an emergency fund of

1,000 *talents*, which had been set aside since the outbreak of the Archidamian War.[5] The decision was a clear one, Athens needed to react quickly and with a strong force, this injection of funds would enable them to rebuild their navy and put down the insurrections. But this would take time, so they sent eight ships that had just returned from chasing after the fleet of Chalcideus straight back to Ionia. They would be followed by twelve more triremes, taken from the blockading force at Spiraeum. Furthermore, they recalled the seven Chian ships from their blockade and freed the slaves, while imprisoning the Chian citizens. The Athenians sent 10 more ships back to the blockade to make up the numbers, and voted to man a further 30 ships as a matter of urgency.

From the very beginning the Athenians were on the back foot. Rebellion spread like wildfire, with Miletus in particular being a major loss for Athens. To exacerbate matters further, the Spartans succeeded in forming an alliance with the Persians. But, as the Athenians were able to establish their presence in the region the Ionian coast became a scene of utter chaos. Small *poleis* became the battle grounds for a large-scale political conflict for which they were not prepared. The small town of Teos had its walls destroyed by a Persian army led by Tissaphernes, before then having to admit ten Athenian triremes for resupply before they moved on. This left Teos devastated and at the whim of all sides in the conflict.

Even though the revolts spread further, the Athenians were able to start turning the tide. They encouraged a popular uprising in Samos, which overthrew the oligarchy in power and became autonomous allies of Athens. But the real effort for the Athenians needed to be the reassertion of control over Lesbos, which included the city of Mytilene. A fleet of 25 triremes, under the command of the Athenians Diomedon and Leon, took the Mytilenians by surprise. They brazenly sailed into the main harbour and defeated the Chian ships there, before disembarking their troops and defeating the weak defence put up against them. With Mytilene under their control, it did not take long for the Athenians to take the rest of Lesbos and re-establish pro–Athenian governance on the island.

The Athenians did not rest there; they refocussed on the mainland city of Miletus, which they had under blockade from their base at Lade. In the skirmishes and confrontations, the Athenians were able to kill the Spartan commander Chalcideus, but they could not capitalise and take the city.

With the end of summer fast encroaching, the Athenians sent out 1,000 hoplites alongside a further 1,500 Argive warriors on 48 vessels to Miletus. The Milesians came out from their walls with 800 of their own hoplites, supported by Peloponnesian hoplites, foreign mercenaries under the control of Tissaphernes, as well as the *satrap* himself and his cavalry. The Athenian army won the battle, but the Milesians were able to retreat back inside their city walls and continue their stoic defence. They did not have to resist for much longer, as a combined Peloponnesians and Syracusan fleet of 55 ships soon arrived to offer their assistance, leaving the Athenian commander no choice but to lift the blockade and retreat to Samos.

As winter came, Miletus was back under the control of the Peloponnesians and Tissaphernes was using their fleet to pursue his own campaign against a Persian traitor in Iasus, in the south of Asia Minor. Yet Athens was growing from strength to strength. Their fleet was reinforced once more from Athens, allowing it to dominate the Ionian coastline with 104 ships based at Samos. The war soon took the shape of a game of chess, and the Athenians were taking control of the board. They resumed their blockade of Miletus and attacked Chios, and any time the Peloponnesians attempted a counter-move they had to attempt to avoid a direct conflict on the open waters. The Athenians caught an enemy squadron near Cnidus, six ships in total, yet chose to push on and try to take Cnidus itself, which they only just failed to do.

For the Peloponnesians, the winter of 412 had a mixed effect on their situation. On the one hand they created a new treaty with Persia, one which made the Great King financially responsible for any force he requested and was brought into his lands. They also saw a further 27 ships arrive from the Peloponnese, funded by the Persians, commanded by Clearchus the Spartan. But on the other hand, Athenian successes were causing discontent and Chios in particular was struggling under Athenian aggression. The Chians called on the Spartan commander at Miletus, Astyochus, to help them, but he refused; it was an act which would see him accused of being a traitor back in Sparta. His concerns lay with securing the arrival of Clearchus' fleet which had made it to Caunus on the mainland north of Rhodes. His concerns were well founded, as 20 Athenian ships under the command of Charminus were based at Rhodes and the surrounding area, lying in wait.

Astyochus sailed his fleet round the Ionian coast toward the island of Syme, but they were plagued by rain and foggy weather, causing his fleet to lose sight of one another and get disordered in the dark. As morning broke, they had reached Syme in such disarray that when the Athenians spotted the left wing, they thought it to be a small detachment from Clearchus's fleet on the mainland and sent only a small proportion of their own fleet against them. The Athenian detachment succeeded in sinking three ships, and disabling a few more, but their advantage soon paled in significance when the rest of Astyochus' fleet came into view. The Peloponnesians moved to surround the Athenians from all sides, and forced them into a hasty retreat. Astyochus took six of the Athenian vessels, and drove the remainder north to the mainland shoreline. It was a moral victory for Astyochus, and a humiliating defeat for the Athenian, Charminus – one for which he would become the butt of many a joke on the Athenian stage.[6]

Astyochus sailed his fleet back to Cnidus, where he put it under repair. At the same time, the Spartans re-entered negotiations with the Persians, unhappy by the original terms which gave Persia control over many free Greek states. The discussions did not go well, and Tissaphernes, as the Great King's representative, stormed out without signing a treaty. While the Peloponnesian cause did not immediately falter, and they succeeded in enticing Rhodes to revolt against Athens, they had more problems brewing. Astyochus received word from Sparta: his second in command, the Athenian exile Alcibiades, was to be put to death with immediate effect. Alcibiades was a personal enemy of one of the Spartan kings, Agis, a status that was not aided by Alcibiades' seduction of Agis' wife and, allegedly, his fathering of a child by her.[7] Alcibiades fled to the court of Tissaphernes and became his advisor. From this new position, he began to undermine the Spartan cause by advising Tissaphernes to reduce the pay of the Spartan sailors and begin to refuse to aid the cities which had revolted from Athens. Alcibiades' main aim was to prolong the Ionian War and weaken both sides for as long as possible. But Alcibiades was not finished there, his final intention was to convince the Athenian people to abandon its democracy and instate an oligarchy. By doing this, it was argued, the Athenians could accept Alcibiades back into the fold and with him would follow the power and finances of the Persians.

Alcibiades' plan did not work how he had planned; Tissaphernes was non-committal to Athenian overtures and the assembly did not trust Alcibiades as a result. However, by the early summer of 411 a pro-oligarchy mob rose up and took control of Athens, causing chaos for the Athenian war effort. As the city went to war against itself, its fleet and forces still stationed at Samos chose to ignore the change in government, deciding instead to fight for democracy both in Athens and in Ionia. The oligarchs, for their part, preferred to lose the Athenian Empire, and even the city's own autonomy, to the Spartans in place of a return to democracy. These internal machinations left Athens vulnerable to Peloponnesian attack, and it was not long until word came of a Spartan led fleet, commanded by Agesandridas, which was heading towards the Piraeus. The Athenians put their own issues aside to launch a defence of the harbour, forcing Agesandridas to continue round the Attic coast and anchor at Oropus, which lay opposite the Euboean city of Eretria. When the Athenians finally sent out a fleet to protect their interests in Euboea, a region they relied on for much of their supplies, they were forced into an early battle.

The thirty-six Athenian triremes were moored by Eretria when they saw the Peloponnesians leave their position and take up their battle lines. The Athenians were caught off guard, for the Eretrians had ensured that there was no food in the agora, forcing the sailors to go further afield for their provisions. The Athenian force was therefore poorly manned, and hastily set out against an organised Peloponnesian enemy. To their credit, the Athenians fought hard but they had little to no chance of surviving the contest, let alone winning it. They were soon broken and many fled back to Eretria, only to find the city had betrayed them and the Eretrians killed any Athenian who sought refuge there. Agesandridas' victory was absolute. After taking twenty-two Athenian ships, and killing or imprisoning the crews, he set up his trophy before inciting the majority of Euboea to revolt against Athens.

The situation in Athens was dire. A Peloponnesian attack was imminent, the bulk of their fleet was in Samos and at war with itself over the new oligarchy, and they had just lost control of Euboea. An emergency assembly was called in which it was decided that the oligarchs in charge, the so called Four Hundred, would be replaced by the Five Thousand, a larger group of citizens whose membership criteria was the ownership of a full hoplite panoply.[8] One of their first points of business was to recall many of the exiles, including Alcibiades. They sent him word, along with the fleet at Samos, to continue the war in the region with a renewed vigour. The Peloponnesian counterpart in Miletus was having less fortune. His crews had still received no pay from Tissaphernes, nor had he received a promised reinforcement of Phoenician ships.[9] The Spartan commander Mindarus decided to take his fleet to the other powerful satrap, Pharnabazus, who had at least promised to pay his fleet. He weighed anchor and set off from Miletus with seventy-three ships, towards the Hellespont where he would meet up with a further sixteen Peloponnesian ships that had already arrived in the region earlier in the summer and had begun to cause havoc throughout the Chersonese region.

The Athenians, led by Thrasylus, set sail from Samos with fifty-five ships and hoped to cut Mindarus off around Lesbos. While he waited by the island, he lost focus and attempted to take one of the Lesbian cities which had recently revolted. Thrasylus was joined by Thrasybulus with five more ships, and was joined by some Lesbian allies, swelling the Athenian fleet to sixty-seven vessels. But, due to the distraction, the Athenians did not observe Mindarus' fleet's departure and he was able to pass unobserved all the way to the Hellespont. He briefly encountered a small Athenian fleet stationed in the region, but made short work of them, neutralizing four of their number. As soon as the Athenian commanders received the news that the Peloponnesian fleet had passed them by, they rushed toward the Hellespont as fast as they could, making camp at Elaeus at the entrance of the channel. For five days Thrasylus waited and prepared his forces for a decisive battle, one which he hoped would turn the tide of the war well and truly in the favour of Athens.

Forces

The Athenian fleet, commanded by the capable admiral Thrasybulus, numbered seventy-six ships.[10] They lined up within the Hellespont channel, with their sterns to the European coastline. Thrasybulus took his position on the right wing, toward the entrance of the Aegean Sea, and his second in command, Thrassylus, took the left wing.[11] The Athenians were outnumbered, and due to their position round the sharp Point Cynossema, they were unable to see their own line in its entirety. However, their great strength lay in their skilled and experienced helmsmen. If they could find a way to use their superior mobility and their skills of manoeuvre, inside the narrow straits, then they should be able to overcome their numerical weakness.

The Peloponnesian fleet, commanded by the Spartan *nauarch* Mindarus, numbered eighty-six ships. It was a conglomerate fleet, drawn from the many allies of the Peloponnesians, including some from as far afield as Sicily. Mindarus drew up his fleet opposite the Athenian position, with their sterns to the Asian coast of the Hellespont. He took his own personal position on the left flank, opposite Thrasybulus, along with the best sailors in his fleet. The right flank was held by the Syracusans. The historian Diodorus informs us that the Peloponnesians had braver and better marines than their Athenian counterparts, which may explain Mindarus' position on the left wing.[12] He intended to take the fight to the Athenians, and force them to engage in a mêlée-based form of combat. By taking the left wing, which also originally led the column, he held responsibility for cutting off the Athenian escape route into the Aegean, which would force the Athenians to face up to the confrontation.

Battle   (Thucydides, VIII. 104–106; Diodorus, XIII.39–40)

From his base in Elaeus, Thrasybulus formed his fleet in column and sailed through the Hellespont, keeping close to the northern, European shore, toward Sestos. The Athenian movements were soon noticed by the Peloponnesians, based at Abydos, and so Mindarus ordered his fleet out to meet them in battle. When both sides became aware of the imminence of combat, they extended their flanks and turned to line abreast. The Athenian line projected forwards in the centre, like a chevron, as it moulded its battle-line to Point Cynossema. The Peloponnesians mirrored it precisely, creating two near-perfect parallel lines.

Mindarus was eager to have his fleet take hold of the early momentum. He knew that if he could take control of this battle early, it could be fought entirely on his terms. Wishing to prevent the Athenian's exit from the narrow channel, the Spartan commander endeavoured to cut them off by outflanking them with his left wing. At the same time, the rest of his fleet pressed home their numerical advantage by engaging the Athenians frontally. The Peloponnesians began by sailing swiftly forwards as a compact group, trying to utilize their greater mass and smash the Athenians into oblivion by simply ramming them head-on.[13] But the Athenian helmsmen could move expertly so that the enemy were unable to strike them. When the Peloponnesians saw that this was not

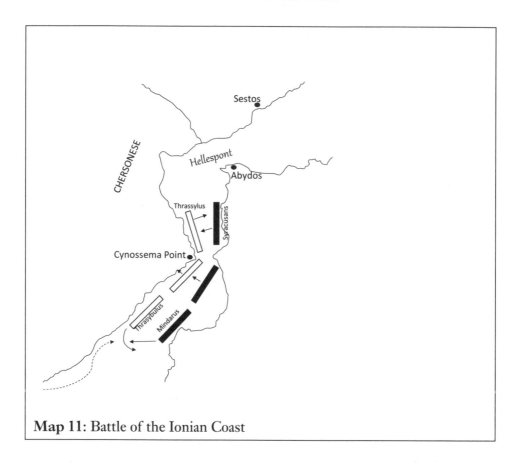

Map 11: Battle of the Ionian Coast

working, they changed their tactics. Orders were given for their ships to engage in small groups, or even as individual vessels, but this merely made matters worse. The Athenians were able to continue their counter-manoeuvres and were now able to ram the Peloponnesian ships in their sides, due to the space available to them.

The nature of the fighting did not concern Thrasybulus, his greatest problem was Mindarus' flanking movement. He moved fast to counteract the manoeuvre; he extended his own right wing and succeeded in out-sailing the enemy. Unfortunately for him, this countermeasure thinned the centre of his main lines, leaving it vulnerable to attack. The Athenian centre bore the brunt of the Peloponnesian aggression. Its position around the Point worked against it in two distinct ways. The first was that Thrasyllus, on the Athenian left, could not see what was happening on the right, and the impact that Thrasybulus was having on the centre. This in turn meant that he could not react in any way to support the thinning lines. The second problem was that the Point was in the narrowest part of the strait, where the tide had become slack, and the ships were unaffected by any strong currents.[14] This meant that the advantages that the Athenians had on their flanks, by exploiting their superiority as helmsmen and taking the optimum positions so that the currents were always against the enemy, could not be used in the centre. So when the Peloponnesians attacked the Athenian centre, it soon capitulated and was driven ashore. The Peloponnesian centre, looking to build upon its glory, began to disembark on the European shore to press home their victory.

On the Athenian left, Thrassylus was fighting hard against the Syracusans. Their numbers were equal, and neither force could gain any meaningful tactical advantage. The tenacity with which each side fought reduced the elegant naval movements of war into a tangled mess, ship got caught up with ship, and the marines fought it out on the decks. The titanic effort in the mêlée was matched only by the muscular exertion of the helmsmen who fought against the currents to keep control of their ships. The struggle continued on, aided by Thrasylus' unawareness of what was happening elsewhere in the battle.

Back on the Athenian right, Thrasybulus had won his race and watched as the battle unfolded. When he saw the remnants of his centre driven back to the shore, he noticed that the Peloponnesians had become overly confident in their victory, and their lines were becoming scattered. For the Athenian commander, this was not an opportunity he could ignore. He gave the orders for his contingent to turn back and launch an aggressive attack against Mindarus' flank which had continued to follow him. Due to the more open waters, the Athenians were able to exploit their speed and mobility to greater effect. The Peloponnesian wing could not hold out for long and were soon routed.[15] This left Thrasybulus free to drive his ships home against the disorganized Peloponnesian centre. Most of the enemy fled before a blow could be struck. When the Syracusans caught sight of their fleeing allies they soon disengaged from Thrassylus' wing and turned in flight as well.[16]

With the rout complete, most of the Peloponnesians fled to Abydos. Thrasybulus brought his scattered forces back together and erected a trophy on Point Cynossema. Due to the narrow waters and the close proximity of the Peloponnesian haven, the Athenians were unable to capture many Peloponnesian ships. They managed to take twenty-one ships, eight of which were from Chios, and five from Corinth; however, the Athenians did lose fifteen of their own.

Aftermath

Thrasybulus had orchestrated an important Athenian victory, one which reasserted its authority on the sea. In all likelihood, a heavy defeat would have seen an end to Athenian resistance in the war as a whole. However, in this position of power, the Athenians moved to consolidate in the region. A mere four days after the battle the Athenians, who had moored in Sestos, had refitted their ships and sailed against a city beyond the Hellespont, on the Asiatic coast of the Sea of Marmara. Cyzicus had revolted against Athens and needed to be brought back into line. The Athenian fleet sailed up to the unfortified city and quickly subdued it, levying yet more money from its citizens, but they then left soon thereafter.

The Peloponnesians, meanwhile, had sailed from the base at Abydos to Elaeus and were able to recapture many of the ships they had lost in the battle. However, they could not take all twenty-one because the Eleausians had begun to burn them. Mindarus knew that the balance of power was shifting towards the Athenians in the region, so he sent for the reinforcements which were anchored in Euboea to join him.

By the early summer of 410 BC, the town of Cyzicus became a focal point once more. Alcibiades, returned from his exile of Athens, brought together a fleet of eighty-six allied ships with the intention of attacking Cyzicus and a Peloponnesian fleet that was moored there. The fleet was split into three, with Alcibiades given the one squadron whose role was to goad the Peloponnesians into battle. Alcibiades led his contingent toward Cyzicus, and the ruse worked. The Peloponnesians thought that Alcibiades had come alone, with only twenty ships, and sailed boldly out to confront him.[17] Alcibiades began to withdraw, drawing the enemy further toward him and biding his time. When the Peloponnesian fleet was far enough away from the land, Alcibiades raised the signal and his ships turned quickly. At the same time, the two hidden Athenian squadrons moved towards the city and cut off the enemy's retreat. When the Peloponnesian commander finally realized what had happened, he swiftly beached his vessels to force the matter onto the land.[18] It was a long and bloody battle. The Athenians won the day and then marched on Cyzicus itself. The people inside the city received their army without resistance, and after twenty days Alcibiades returned to the Hellespont where he had been based, having restored Athenian dominance in the region.

Chapter 10

The Battle of Arginusae (406 BC)

Background   (Xenophon, *Hellenica*, I.4.10–I.6.26; Plutarch,
Life of Alcibiades, 29–36; Diodorus, XIII.76.1–79.7)

Following the Athenian victory at Cyzicus, the Peloponnesian fleet in the Hellespont was all but destroyed. As a letter that was bound for Sparta, but intercepted by Alcibiades' men, declared: 'The ships are gone. Mindarus [the *nauarch*] is dead, the men are starving; we don't know what to do.'[1] Fortunately for the Spartans, and their allies, they still held the support of the Persian satrap for the region, Pharnabazus. He took the remaining Peloponnesian soldiers and crewmen into his protection, putting them to work and paying them two months' worth of rations in advance. He also began rebuilding their fleet, paying for the cost himself and supplying the wood from his own lands as well.

In mainland Greece, the Spartan King Agis was based with an army at the fort of Decelea, from where he was launching raids and assaults on Athenian lands. After one attack was made close to the great walls of Athens itself, and was successfully repulsed by the mere presence of an organized Athenian resistance, Agis experienced an important realization. As he watched the Piraeus harbour receive convoy after convoy of ships carrying grain from the Black Sea region, Agis became aware that his campaign to stop the Athenians tilling their own lands was futile because they could still receive grain from overseas. This shift in focus brought the Athenian need to control the Hellespontine region into clear view for the Spartans, as it was the gateway to their grain lifeline. Agis sent a commander with experience of the region, a man named Clearchus, with fifteen ships to base himself in Byzantium, in the hope of loosening the Athenians' firm grasp.

By 408 BC, Clearchus' presence had caused enough of a disturbance that Alcibiades conducted direct operations against both Byzantium and

Chalcedon, a city which sat opposite on the Asian side of the Bosporus. Luckily for Alcibiades, the reign of Clearchus in Byzantium was not a happy one.[2] By the time the Athenians had placed the city under siege, Clearchus had left in search of more pay for his men, and to procure more ships with which to attack Athenian allies in the region and draw Alcibiades away from his siege. What Clearchus had not anticipated was that the Byzantine people had grown to hate him, due to his tyrannical reign: one of the main complaints was that he had given all of the food in the city to his troops, so causing a small scale famine that affected women and children especially.[3] It did not take long for the people of Byzantium to turn against their absent ruler, and Alcibiades was soon admitted.

The loss of Byzantium was a major blow to Peloponnesian strategy, but it was not the most pivotal event of that year. While the Spartans had lost personal control of the Bosporus, a group of Spartan envoys were heading home in the winter of 408/7 BC with something far more valuable: they had secured the full support of the Great King. Darius II would provide the much needed financial backing that neither the Peloponnesians nor the Athenians were capable of producing any more. Furthermore, and perhaps as importantly, Darius sent a new man to take control of the chaotic situation in Asia Minor, his son Cyrus the Younger. Cyrus was given the title of *karanon* (commander-in-chief) over Lydia, Phrygia and Cappadocia, this bestowed on him an authority that superseded two very powerful *satraps* (Pharnabazus and the now-demoted Tissaphernes).[4] Cyrus' role was to stop the Greek manipulation of Persian rivalries, and to give proactive and decisive support to the Peloponnesians. To that end Cyrus was given command of all of the Persian forces in Asia Minor, and a war chest of 500 *talents*, plus any extra coming from his personal funds. When the Athenians discovered this development they urgently sent envoys to Darius, but they were kept away from his court and refused access. The Persians had finally settled on their choice of who to support.

News of Alcibiades' successes in Asia Minor had long reached Athens and, even though he had not returned to Athens since his original exile in 415 BC, he was elected as one of the generals by the Assembly. For Alcibiades this was a final sign that he would be safe to return home after eight years of absence, so he sailed homeward. As his ship entered the Piraeus, he was greeted with large crowds of people who had flocked to catch a glimpse of their notorious hero. Once on dry land, he had to stand up before the

Assembly and defend himself against his original accusations of impiety, and possibly of supporting the Spartan cause. But no opposition was heard to his defence, the Assembly had already decided that he would be acquitted, and gave him supreme power over all of the other elected generals for that year. A mere two months after his homecoming, Alcibiades enrolled a new army and sailed forth in 100 ships to the rebellious island of Andros, the most northern of the Cycladic Islands. After winning a quick victory in battle he besieged the Andrians in their main city, but without success. So, after raising his trophy of victory, he sailed off to the island of Samos which would form his future base of operations.

The Spartans had similarly chosen a new *nauarch*; a charismatic and pragmatic man called Lysander. Lysander arrived in Asia by way of Rhodes, before he collected the fleet available in the region and moored at Ephesus in Ionia where he waited for the arrival of Cyrus. Cyrus travelled from Sardis to meet the new Spartan commander, and to plan their next course of action. The Spartans and Peloponnesians urged Cyrus to use his financial clout to undermine the Athenian fleet. They claimed that if he offered to pay Athenian crews the cost of one drachma a day each, then the enemy crew would desert to his fleet, thus he would save money by bringing the war to an earlier conclusion.[5] The argument was compelling but Cyrus was not convinced. While he had full authority in the region, he was still a young commander and his trusted advisor Tissaphernes had himself been reluctant to offer such support to one side in the war. Cyrus reiterated what his father had already promised the Peloponnesians: 30 *minae* per month per ship (the equivalent of 3,000 drachmas, or half a *talent*), which meant three *obols* (half a drachma) per person per day. Lysander stayed quiet through these proceedings, but when he feasted with Cyrus and was asked by the prince what he could do to please the Spartan, Lysander answered that he could add one obol to the pay of each sailor. Cyrus agreed and, further to this, back paid all of the outstanding wages to the crews.

The Athenians attempted diplomacy to stem the tide of Persian support, but Cyrus would not see them. They sent envoys to Tissaphernes but even his pleas to the prince were not enough to change his mind. The old Persian counselled against allowing one Greek side to become strong in any way, something that was being prevented by their long-standing state of internal warfare.[6] Cyrus was going to upset this balance with his large injection of funds, but he did not care. His orders from his father were clear.

Lysander was now content to amass his fleet. Beaching ninety of his triremes at Ephesus, he had them repaired and dried out, so that they were in the best condition possible. However, Lysander had no intention of actually initiating a battle against the Athenians anchored opposite him at Samos. Alcibiades, similarly, had no intention of forcing an issue that was not yet needed. So confident in the status quo, Alcibiades actually left Samos when he heard that a friend of his had arrived further north to fortify the town of Phocaea.[7] Before departing, Alcibiades nominated his helmsmen, Antiochus, to take charge of the fleet, but gave him definite instructions: under no circumstances should he attack Lysander's position. Yet Antiochus was evidently an impetuous man who wanted to win some glory for himself, so he disobeyed his orders.[8]

Antiochus wanted a victory of his own, but he wanted an easy one. He did not want to fight the entire Peloponnesian fleet, so he prepared an ambush that would give him his win without any perceptible danger.[9] He moved the entire fleet to Notium, just north of Ephesus, and personally took charge of ten triremes, sailing them toward Lysander's position. Antiochus had already noticed that Lysander had a habit of sending small squadrons, usually three ships in total, out on some duty or other on a daily basis. The Athenian intended to entice one of these squadrons into facing him, revealing only two of his own ships, before the remaining eight would launch a surprise attack. What Antiochus did not know was that Lysander had already heard of Alcibiades' absence, news brought to him by deserters from Samos. Lysander intended to capitalize on this good fortune by attacking the leaderless fleet, and Antiochus provided such an opportunity.

Antiochus, completely unaware, continued on his way to Ephesus and set his ambush. While still far out to sea, he split off from his squadron and ordered them to wait until the Peloponnesian ships had come far enough away from their harbour before attacking. He then continued on his journey all the way into the harbour of Ephesus with his two ships, goading the enemy into action. Lysander reacted immediately, sending out a small squadron of ships, the fastest to mobilize, to engage with Antiochus. To all intents and purposes, Antiochus' plan was working, he led this enemy squadron away from Ephesus toward his trap and, when far enough out at sea, the remaining eight Athenian ships attacked. However, Lysander had not stood by idly, he had continued the preparation of his fleet. When they were ready, the entire Peloponnesian flotilla sailed out in search of a morale–boosting victory.

The first ship they encountered was that of the hapless helmsman himself, which was quickly sunk and Antiochus himself killed. The remaining Athenian ships fled in a state of sheer panic, they had never intended to fight a full–scale battle like this. The main bulk of the Athenian fleet was still moored at Notium, but they only became aware of events when the Athenian ships came into view being chased by the enemy. By this point it was all too late. The main fleet attempted to mobilize and assist their comrades, but they were disorganized and caught unawares. The Athenians were only able to launch their ships in dribs and drabs, giving Lysander's orderly fleet an easy target to attack. The main body of Athenian ships had barely begun to exit the harbour before the Athenian vanguard was hit head–on and scattered. The battle became a rout before the Athenians could even launch their first counteroffensive. Most of the Athenian crews were able to escape to the mainland and return to Notium, but, in the chaos, Lysander destroyed a good number of Athenian ships and captured a further twenty-two.[10] This victory was the making of Lysander, and it was nothing but an unmitigated disaster for Athens.[11]

The Athenian fleet regrouped in Notium for three days, before returning to their main base on Samos. When Alcibiades returned, and had been fully informed of the calamity, he mobilized his fleet and sailed straight to the Ephesian harbour. But Lysander did not need to fight. He had won his victory, raised his trophy, and claimed his glory. Alcibiades' indignant posturing was not going to draw the Spartan into a foolish battle since Alcibiades still held the numerical advantage. The Athenians finally resigned themselves to their defeat and returned to Samos, where the popular opinion of the crew began to turn on their commander. It was a change in opinion that was mirrored back in Athens itself. When news of the defeat at Notium arrived, the Athenian Assembly blamed Alcibiades for it. It was thought that he had neglected his duties and lost control of his subordinates. In response, the Assembly elected a new set of ten generals and sent one of that number, Conon, to take Alcibiades' position in command of the fleet.[12]

Conon sailed to join with the fleet at Samos, taking with him an extra twenty triremes. What he found at Samos did not fill him with any great joy. The crews were despondent, and the ships not maintained well enough to be fit for purpose. But Conon was a dynamic man. He decided to cut his losses and fit out 70 triremes to form the basis of his fleet, in place of over 100 ships which had been accumulated at Samos. Conon then began a systematic campaign of raids and assaults in enemy territory throughout Asia Minor.

With the summer of 406 BC came news from Sparta, a new campaign season meant a new *nauarch*. The Spartans sent Callicratidas to replace Lysander, a decision that was not popular in the Peloponnesian fleet. The new *nauarch* had no naval experience, and the transfer of power was not a seamless one. Lysander promised to not interfere with the new commander, and handed over his fleet that now numbered 90 triremes, to which Callicratidas ordered the addition of 50 more, giving him 140 ships in all. But this was not the only thing Lysander handed over. He also transferred all the Persian money, which was still unspent, back to Cyrus, leaving the new *nauarch* bereft of money. Callicratidas was forced to go to Cyrus himself to request money, but after being left for two days without an answer he became enraged that the Spartans had been reduced to begging the barbarians for money. Instead he left empty handed and sailed to Miletus, from where he sent messages to Sparta calling for extra funds. Additionally, he spoke before an assembly of the Milesians and convinced them to supply money for the upkeep of the fleet.

Callicratidas took the money and, after securing similar payment from the people of Chios, and he sailed to Methymna, a pro-Athenian town on the north side of Lesbos. The people of Methymna refused to support the Peloponnesians, not least because the town had an Athenian garrison present, so the Peloponnesians launched an assault and took the town by force. Of those captured, only the Athenians were sold into slavery; Callicratidas wanted to send a message that he was here to free the Greeks from Athenian oppression. He also sent a direct and forthright message to Conon; he would not allow Conon to continue 'fucking' his sea (he uses the Greek verb used to describe another man having sex with one's wife).[13]

Conon was at this time based on one of the Hundred Isles, around Lesbos, and set off at daybreak to get far away from the Peloponnesian fleet. Callicratidas anticipated this movement and set off in pursuit, hoping to cut off the Athenian route south to Samos. Conon knew he could not outrace the enemy, his crew were mostly inexperienced, and he was forced to move his best rowers onto the same triremes to give him at least one arm of his fleet that was equal to the Peloponnesians. The Athenian commander decided to create a flash point by Mytilene, where he would instigate a skirmish which would either buy his fleet time to escape, or else allow them to retreat into an ally's harbour. Conon ordered his fleet to slow right down and allow the fastest of the Peloponnesian fleet to catch up. As the enemy wore out their rowers in the hot pursuit, Conon's fleet slowly continued to withdraw, separating the Peloponnesian's most advanced squadron from the rest of their fleet. When enough of a gap had appeared, Conon ordered a red banner flown from his ship. At this signal, all of the Athenian ships turned around in unison and raised the *paean*.

The cries of song and the blaring of the trumpets filled the ears of the Peloponnesian crews as the cold reality finally dawned on them. They tried to withdraw and regroup to repel the imminent attack, but they were in utter disarray. Conon exploited this disorder and pressed down on them hard, stopping them from being able to form any real defence. But the inexperience of the Athenians showed, and they could not force the Peloponnesians back from their position. By the time the rest of Callicratidas' fleet arrived, only the Athenian left wing had routed their opposing ships. Conon knew that his plan had not worked, so he withdrew with forty triremes into the harbour of Mytilene. The remaining Athenian ships which had broken through the enemy lines were caught during their own pursuit. The Peloponnesian fleet swarmed around them, cutting them off from entering the harbour with Conon. They were forced aground and the crews had to flee over land to Mytilene, abandoning their ships in the process. The Athenians lost thirty ships on this day, nearly half of Conon's fleet, and Callicratidas truly had mastery over the coastline of Asia Minor.

Conon was at a loss as to what to do. He was trapped in Mytilene and the Peloponnesians had blockaded the harbour, while simultaneously besieging the town by land. He decided that news of the siege must not have reached Athens, so he devised a ploy to try and get a message to them. He picked two triremes and manned them with his best crewmen. He also packed the holds of both ships with marines, and spread screens over each side, to prevent the Peloponnesians from seeing them. For five days he would have his men board the ships in the water, only to disembark again at nightfall. This seemingly meaningless repetition created apathy on the part of the enemy in the blockade, so on the fifth day, when the same thing happened, the Peloponnesians in charge of the blockade thought nothing of it and continued to have their meal on land. However this time it was different, the two Athenian triremes sailed out of the open harbour, with one heading north toward the Hellespont and the other south to open waters.

The Peloponnesians tried to get aboard their ships as fast as possible, cutting their anchor cables and setting off in pursuit. They chose to pursue the ship heading south, and by sunset they had overtaken it, defeated it in battle and towed it back to their camp outside of Mytilene. But the Athenian ship that headed north had escaped and was able to make the journey to Athens, where the *trierarch* informed the assembly of the siege. The Assembly acted quickly to try to protect their presence in Asia Minor. They voted to send a fleet of 110 ships, manned by every available man, slave and freeman; even the richer classes were called for duty on the ships. Within thirty days the new fleet was manned and departed for Samos where they collected more ships from their allies. The Athenians were preparing themselves for a final showdown of epic proportions; they were going to force a battle which could decide the war there and then..

Forces

The Peloponnesians, led by Callicratidas, numbered 120 triremes. Their crews, many of which were paid handsomely for their experience and expertise, were hardened by their time at sea. Peloponnesian morale was understandably high, having bested the Athenians at Notium and again at Mytilene. They had shown themselves to be the superior naval force, having overthrown a longstanding status quo of Athenian dominance. Although the Spartan fleet was outnumbered, they held the faster ships and thus the tactical advantage. They could face the Athenians at their own game, and use speed and mobility to cut through and isolate the Athenians ships.

The Athenian fleet was very inexperienced, and the ships had been built in a great hurry. In total, 150 triremes were led by 8 of the 10 elected generals, all with equal responsibility. The fleet was split into 10 smaller squadrons numbering 10–15 ships each: one for each general, one led by various lower officers in the very centre of their battle line, and a final squadron of Samians led by their own commander. The Athenians' only advantage was numerical, and they knew that the Spartans would attempt to use the *diekplous* manoeuvre to break up the lines, so their best chance lay in forming a dense formation and forcing the combat to be between the marines rather than the helmsmen.

Battle   Xenophon, *Hellenica*, I.6.26–35; Diodorus, XIII.97.4–100.4[14]

When Callicratidas first received word of the Athenian relief force, it had already reached Samos and was *en route* to the Arginusae islands by the Asian mainland, opposite Cape Malea on Lesbos. The Spartan commander decided to leave 50 of his ships to maintain the blockade of Mytilene, while he sailed 120 triremes around the Lesbian coast to Cape Malea, where he made camp. On the same day that he arrived and fed his crew their midday meal, the Athenians had arrived on the Arginusae islands. The Peloponnesians spent the night *in situ*; from there they could see the Athenian camp fires, little more than 9 miles (14.5km) away. In his confidence, Callicratidas planned an audacious night attack, hoping to catch the Athenians while they were resting. But his hopes were dashed by heavy rain and a lightning storm. He would have to wait for the storm to pass.

The following day it was the Athenians who wanted to begin the battle early, in spite of the bad omens.[15] The Athenian seer had interpreted the dream of one of the generals to mean that a great number of the generals would die as a result of the battle, but that the Athenians would win the day. The generals agreed to continue with their plan, and to keep this prophecy from their men. It was a similar problem facing Callicratidas, whose seer had watched as the traditional sacrificial victim's head lay on the beach and was lost from view when the waves lapped over it. He declared that it foretold the *nauarch*'s own death, but similarly to the Athenians, Callicratidas would not be put off by the omen.

The Athenians sailed out first. Their left wing extended out towards the open sea to the south, led by Aristocrates and his squadron of fifteen ships, formed probably in three lines, five deep, just as the other eight generals had with their squadrons.[16] Behind him, in support, was Pericles. Next to Aristocrates was Diomedon, with Erastinides in support. Beside these were the ten Samian ships, in single file extending back towards the islands, and alongside the Samians were ten Athenian ships also in single file. Behind these lines were three more Athenian ships led by experienced naval men and seven allied ships. To the right was a squadron led by Thrassylus, with Aristogenes in support, while the right wing was led by Protomachos, supported by Lysias. This formation gave the Athenian fleet both depth, which could defend against a *diekplous* more successfully, and mobility in the form of the autonomous subgroups.

Callicratidas sailed out to meet the Athenians, taking the right wing for himself and posting the Thebans on the left wing, with Cape Malea directly behind them. The Peloponnesians were set up for the *diekplous*, that is single-filed squadrons, maybe as many as eight of them, fifteen ships deep.[17] When his lines were set, the Spartan gave the orders to sound the trumpet; a loud call which soon doubled in volume as it was joined by the opposite trumpeters from the Athenian fleet. The sound soon gave way to the two sides making their cries of war. The rowers pulled with every sinew, every muscle they could call upon, each side wishing to be the first to make contact and start the largest sea battle ever fought between the Greeks.

While the Athenians lacked experience on the sea, each side had much experience in war, so this quickly became a stubborn and brutal fight for both survival and glory. Callicratidas acted like a man freed from the concerns of fate. He knew he was going to die, and wanted to go out in the most glorious way imaginable. He urged his ship forwards and his was the first from either side to strike a blow. His trireme was aimed at that of Aristocrates, and at first contact his ram smashed into its timbers and disabled the ship.[18] Without delay he continued on his suicidal mission, ramming and disabling as many ships as he could, before his own vessel had passed through the first squadron and began to engage with the second. Callicratidas was not deterred, and ordered his helmsmen to aim directly at the ship of Pericles, his ram boring a great hole in the enemy trireme. However, the force of the strike was so great that the ram became lodged, as did the bows of the ships, and they became stuck.

Pericles did not wait to find out what Callicratidas was going to do, he ordered his men to throw over an 'iron hand', a grappling iron, to the enemy ship and fasten it tight. With the ship secured, the Athenian crew poured onto the opponent's deck, supported by crew from other triremes in the squadron. The scene became a chaotic mêlèe, with the Peloponnesians fighting for their lives. Callicratidas fought valiantly and led a staunch resistance, but he was

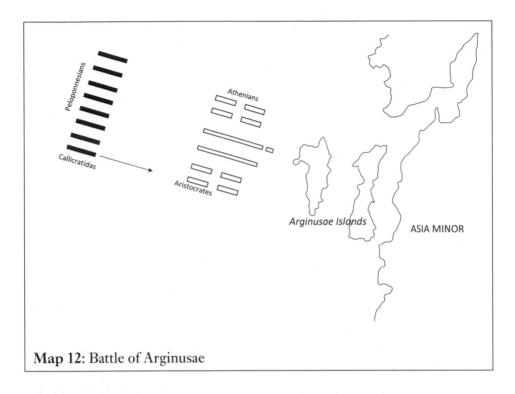

Map 12: Battle of Arginusae

finally overwhelmed by the numbers and he was struck down from all sides before falling into the sea, dead.[19]

The right side of the Peloponnesian fleet saw the *nauarch*'s ship overwhelmed, and news soon spread of Callicratidas' death, causing panic in the other ships. The right wing soon began to give way, but the Thebans and Euboeans on the left were still unaware. They were fighting a ferocious battle, driven by the fear of defeat more than most, due to the Thebans' longstanding rivalry with Athens and the Euboeans' revolt against Athenian rule. But when they finally saw their right wing in full flight, they too had to pull back and flee south to Phocaea.

The Athenians, having won the day, returned to the Arginusae islands. They took stock of their losses, twenty-five of their ships had been disabled, but in turn they had neutralized nine Spartan ships and a further sixty from the Peloponnesian fleet. The victory was resounding, but there was still work to do. The generals decided to send forty-seven ships to help their stranded comrades from the battle, scattered all over as they were, while the remainder of the fleet would raise the blockade on Mytilene and free Conon. Unfortunately, these plans were scuppered by an inbound storm, which made the expedition too dangerous, so they set up a trophy and pitched camp instead.

When the Spartans at Mytilene heard of the defeat, the commander kept the news quiet, except for the death of Callicratidas who was suitably mourned. But, without delay, the Spartan ordered his fleet to sail to Chios, while he burned their camp and marched his land forces north to Methymna. When Conon realised that the siege and blockade had disappeared, he sailed his fleet to the Argiunsae Islands and informed them that Mytilene was now free, their mission was complete.

Aftermath

The strategic impact of this victory for Athens should have been astronomical. They had successfully broken a giant Peloponnesian fleet, reasserted their naval reputation and lifted the blockade of Mytilene. The Peloponnesians had been shown to be poorly led, due to the Spartan practice of giving their *nauarch* a limited time of service, regardless of their capabilities or successes. But, rather than capitalize on their momentum, the Athenians focussed on one particular element of the battle reports that came into the city. It was not the victory that concerned them, nor the securing of Mytilene. No, Athens went into a furore over the news that after the battle, a storm had prevented the generals from collecting the Athenian dead, and the survivors.

Only six of the eight generals actually returned to Athens, and they walked straight into one of the most notorious legal cases known from classical Athens. To not collect the dead was a grave sacrilege, but it is not certain whether this was actually what the generals were accused of. It is described by the much later historian Diodorus, but our contemporary source, Xenophon, says the crime was that they did not immediately collect the survivors. [20] The generals put forward their defence, that the storm was too fierce to allow the ships to collect the survivors straight away. But the defence was shouted down. By the second meeting of the Assembly, the mood of the Athenians had turned to sheer anger, and that anger was going to dictate the fate of the generals. After two votes on the issue, they refused to hold individual trials for each man, and instead condemned them all to death. [21] Interestingly, in contrast to the leaders of the victory, all of the slaves who took part in the battle were freed and given citizenship as Plataeans [22]

For the Peloponnesians, their fate after the battle was the complete opposite to that of their enemy. Having witnessed such an unexpected turnover of power in the region, the Spartans realized the grave error in their judgement. They reinstated Lysander as a vice-*nauarch*, giving their fleet the much needed charisma and expertise that it had so sorely missed. Thanks to previous Persian support, the loss of ships was not a long-term problem, and Lysander's reinstatement implied one thing: the Peloponnesians did not intend to take this defeat lying down.

Chapter 11

The Battle of Aegospotami (405 BC)

Background   (Xenophon, *Hellenica*, II.1.1-21; Diodorus,
                   XIII.104-105.2; Plutarch, *Life of Lysander*, 7.1-11.5)

In the spring of 405 BC, the arrival of Lysander brought a new vigour and direction to the faltering Peloponnesian fleet. Following the defeat at Arginusae, the allies sent desperate word to Sparta asking for Lysander to be reinstated as commander. However, there was still in place a Spartan law that meant Lysander could not be the *nauarch*, as no man was allowed take the position twice.[1] Times were desperate, and the original command to remove Lysander from his post had resulted in the loss of finance from the Persians, since Cyrus the younger had a close relationship with him. This loss of finance meant that the Peloponnesians were on the verge of total disaster. If the Athenians could muster another attack, then the fleet could have been all but lost, and with it the war.[2]

The Spartans were a traditional people, but they were not foolish. They understood what was at stake and they created a position for a superior commander, as they had done on earlier occasions, without breaking their own laws.[3]A different *nauarch* was announced, but he would have Lysander as his vice-*nauarch* who, for all intents and purposes, would have real command of the fleet. So Lysander sped his way to Ephesus where he intended to gather together all of the Peloponnesian ships from the region. Once this was achieved, the main body of ships were given much needed repairs, and Lysander ordered even more to be built.

For his part, Lysander went to see his old friend Cyrus in search of some much-needed financial contribution. The response he got was not a promising one, for Cyrus had begun to lose the favour of his father, Darius II. Cyrus had grown increasingly arrogant in his position of power, and in 406 BC he had executed outlying members of the royal family who had refused to place their arms inside their long sleeves in his presence – a mark of respect reserved only for the king.[4] On hearing of his son's antics, Darius was left with no choice but to bring him into line. He feigned an illness and sent word for his son to join him in Media. It was during the preparations for this departure that Lysander met the Persian prince.[5]

Cyrus was forced to admit to his friend that all of the money from the king had already been spent. In fact, spending had long since outrun the amount provided by his father and Cyrus had already had to pay from his own resources. However, out of loyalty to their friendship, Cyrus offered to procure more funds from Darius. If that was not successful, he jokingly offered to cut up his own throne, made from gold and silver, to give to the Spartan. Cyrus did not want Lysander to leave empty handed, so he offered him an extraordinary concession. While Cyrus was travelling to see his father, he gave Lysander access to all of the tribute from the cities under his control, which was considered Cyrus' personal property. So Cyrus gave Lysander access to a continuous stream of funds, with which he could expand the Peloponnesian fleet without fear of the funds running dry prematurely. Cyrus, for all of his generosity, did make one demand of Lysander. He ordered Lysander to not attack the Athenian fleet before he had a larger fleet under his own command.

The Spartan *nauarch* knew that Cyrus' command was as much wise counsel as it was an order. His fleet was not ready to take on the Athenians, but Lysander was not one to sit idly while he held so much power in his hands. So, when Cyrus finally left to visit his father, Lysander distributed the first of his funds to pay his forces and then set out to hurt the Athenians indirectly by attacking their allies. The Peloponnesian fleet headed south from Ephesus toward Caria, and landed by the Athenian-allied town of Cedreiae. After a two day siege, Lysander's force entered the city and enslaved all its people before boarding his ships and sailing off once more to Rhodes. His plan was simple, but effective. Knowing that he could not face a full-scale battle at the present, he raided numerous allies of his enemy as he moved from Rhodes north to the Hellespont. In effect, weakening the Athenians without ever fighting them.

The Athenian fleet were not idle during these assaults. From their base on the island of Samos they raided the Asiatic coast, focusing their attentions on the lands of the Great King. They then sailed against Chios to the north of their base, and nearby Ephesus, all in the hope of forcing Lysander to commit to a great sea battle, but to no avail. Lysander's plan was working, he was hurting his enemy without putting his forces in any immediate danger.

But Lysander's plans were not the ultimate solution to his problem. If he wanted to cause permanent damage to the Athenians, he needed to strike where they were most vulnerable. Athens' greatest strength lay in its ability to become a land based island, due to the great walls that surrounded the city and joined it to the walled harbour, the Piraeus. In the Piraeus, the Athenians received hundreds of merchant ships transporting the vital grain supplies coming from the Hellespont. If this grain route could not be disrupted, then all the raiding of Attica and the destruction of harvests that King Agis was achieving in Decelea would have no real impact on Athenian food supplies.[6] Lysander intended to continue Spartan policy, attempting to turn this great strength of Athens into its weakness by directly challenging the grain route.

The Spartan-led fleet sailed north from Rhodes, up the Ionian coast, toward the Hellespont.[7] Lysander wanted to base himself in the region and watch over the merchant ships carrying the grain, but also he wanted to place himself in a region that was witnessing many cities revolting against the Spartan alliance. The Athenians, for their part, moved their camp to Chios, but sailed there by the unorthodox method of keeping to open water. Triremes were generally sailed near to the coastline, but the Athenian raids of the Ionian coast had turned most of Asia against them, making for a very hostile environment for them to move within.

Lysander found the Hellespont unprotected by Athenian ships and so sailed his fleet to Abydos. From here he planned an assault on the city of Lampsacus, an Athenian ally that lay further up the coast, over 30 miles inside the Hellespont. Lysander coordinated his naval attack with land forces made up of Spartan allies from Abydos and the surrounding area, led by a Spartiate called Thorax. The two pronged attack was too powerful for Lampsacus to withstand and it quickly fell, leading the way for Lysander's men to plunder the city of its rich wine and grain supplies. Yet Lysander did not let his men run riot. He released any captives who were freeborn, allowed the Athenian garrison in the city to leave under a truce, and left the city in the hands of its own citizens.[8] This victory was as much a symbol of his leniency as of his power.

News of the Spartan victory quickly travelled down the Hellespont to the Athenian fleet that had been slowly trailing Lysander's movements. While sat eating their morning meal in the mouth of the Hellespont, the Athenian sailors received word and immediately put their ships out to sea, 180 in number, and sailed to Sestos to restock. From here they continued toward Lampsacus and made camp on the European coastline opposite, right next to the Goat Rivers, Aegospotami.[9]

Forces

The Athenians had 180 of their light, nimble and speedy triremes that, if they were manned at maximum capacity of 200 men per ship, would have given them 36,000 rowers and marines. This fleet was led by a group of commanders who shared command on a daily rotation. The two most important for this battle were Conon, the overall commander originally sent to replace Alcibiades in the region, and Philocles who was in command on the day of the actual fighting.[10] Conon's importance is highlighted by his personal command of the state trireme, the *Paralos*, which was used for sacred embassies and other public missions of importance.

We do not know how strong the Peloponnesian fleet was, not one of our sources gives us a figure. We can presume, following the warnings that Cyrus gave to Lysander, that the fleet was smaller than the Athenians', but we do not know by how much. After the heavy losses that the Peloponnesian fleet faced at Arginusae the year before, the trireme-building regimen implemented by Lysander would have been hard pushed to expand beyond the original strength from the year before. A range between 125 and 150 ships is realistic as an estimate, but more likely at the lower end of this scale.[11] Unlike the Athenians, there was only one true commander of the Peloponnesians, Lysander. His plan was to utilize a land force in conjunction with his naval operation, so he appointed the trusted sub-commander who had helped him take Lampsacus, Thorax.

Battle[12]   (Xenophon, *Hellenica*, II.1.22–29;
Diodorus, XIII.105.3; Plutarch, *Life of Lysander*, 10–11)

The Athenian camp at Aegospotami was poorly chosen, it was a barren place with no access for resupply. Lysander would have realized this and that it meant one simple thing: the Athenians did not intend to spend any time there, they had come for a decisive battle and to resolve it quickly. So, as dawn rose on the first morning, Lysander decided to give the Athenians what they wanted. He signalled all of his men to take their morning meal and swiftly board their ships. The triremes themselves were fully prepared for battle, and even the screens were attached which protected the uppermost rower from missile attacks.

On the opposite side of the channel, the Athenians likewise prepared their ships. The men climbed aboard, the ships were kitted out for combat, and the fleet sailed out in front of their anchorage to await battle. But battle never came. Lysander had ordered his men to neither put out to sea, nor to form a battle line. The hours passed and, as it came toward dusk, the Athenians were ordered back to land. As they withdrew, Lysander ordered a few of his fastest ships to follow them and spy on the Athenian camp – paying particular attention to the behaviour of the crews as they disembarked. Only when these spy ships flashed a bronze shield in the sunlight, as a signal that the Athenians had disembarked, did the Spartan commander finally give the order for his men to disembark their own vessels and return to camp. On the following morning Lysander began this rigmarole once again, inciting the Athenians to take up their battle lines and, in frustration, return to their camps at the end of the day. For three more days he repeated this process, and each day the Athenians went out to meet him, expecting battle and running down their limited supplies in the pursuit of it, only to return to their camp, followed by the spy ships of Lysander, who observed their movements.

These five days of manoeuvring and posturing had been watched with interest by the disgraced Athenian, Alcibiades, from his castle in the Hellespont.[13] He went down to the Athenian camp and offered his own, unique, assistance. He proclaimed that two Thracian kings in the region were friends of his and, thanks to him, had promised to send a large army to fight the Spartans – at his personal command, of course. Alcibiades played his hand too hard; he offered to use this army to help the Athenians if they gave him a share in their command. His promise to the generals was that he could either compel the Peloponnesian fleet to engage, somehow, or else he would use the Thracian army to attack them on land.[14]

If this offer had come from anyone other than Alcibiades, it may have been one that the Athenians could have considered. But Alcibiades' stock had plummeted since his unsuccessful turn as commander of the fleet and the defeat at Notium. This was the same man who had caused all the problems before the Sicilian expedition, back in 415 BC, and the man who had fled to the Spartans in exile and assisted them through the latter parts of the war. The Athenian generals saw Alcibiades' offer for what it was; an attempt by the man to orchestrate a personal victory and enable him return to Athens as a hero.[15] Also, since the trial of the generals following the victory at Arginusae, these generals were particularly aware how they would collectively get the blame for a defeat (or even in the aftermath of a victory), but Alcibiades alone would get the glory of victory. So Alcibiades was promptly sent away from camp, and banned from ever returning.

Anger and frustration was reaching a fever pitch inside the Athenian camp, exacerbated by the presence then dismissal of Alcibiades. When day six arrived, it was the turn of Philocles to take charge. Philocles had decided his day was the day to act, to try and force something, anything, to happen. It began like every day beforehand, with Lysander preparing his ships and the Athenians forming up their lines, but no battle commencing. The Athenians withdrew back to land and disembarked, followed by the spy ships. Most of the Athenian crews disembarked and the Spartan spy ships flashed their bronze shields to Lysander. But Philocles was not going to allow this day to end like every other. He wanted to force a battle, and the only way this would be achieved was through making contact with a Peloponnesian ship, or squadron of ships, thus forcing Lysander to assist them. The only enemy ships that sailed close enough to Aegospotami were the spy ships, so they would have to do.

Philocles allowed his men to disembark and begin foraging, but he maintained thirty triremes under his direct command. Once he had lured Lysander's fleet to sea, then the remainder of the Athenian ships would be ordered to join the battle. So, when the flash of bronze was made from the spy ships, Philocles decided to act, sending his squadron out as fast as they could. What he did not anticipate was that the flashing of bronze was not just a signal to Lysander that the Athenians had disembarked, but that they were now vulnerable. Lysander had carefully waited for five days, lulling his enemy into a sense of security through monotony and routine, and practised his attack every day without the Athenians realizing. On this day, the signal that Lysander received did not follow with an order to disembark, but to set out to sea and attack.[16]

By the time Philocles' squadron reached the spy ships, the commander may have seen that his plan was working. But such elation at his own genius would have quickly subsided when he realized that Lysander's ships were not just setting out but were almost upon him, and the Athenian crews on the shore were still nowhere near their ships. Philocles had been out-thought and out-manoeuvred, and his thirty triremes were sitting ducks against the full strength of the Peloponnesian attack. Philocles was forced into a retreat and was pursued back to the rest of his beached fleet.

The Athenian triremes were empty targets, most of the crews were dispersed through the surrounding lands in the search for food and firewood. Lysander moved quickly to exploit the growing panic and confusion in the Athenian forces. He landed his trusted lieutenant Thorax with a strong force with which to hunt down the enemy crewmen, stopping them from taking to the boats. Lysander himself stayed with his fleet and, with the aid of grappling irons, began to pull the Athenian triremes away. On land, the Athenians watched in disbelief as their ships were dragged away. They soon gave up any remaining desire to fight and took flight in every direction available, all in the hope of finding safety.

Back on the sea, the Athenian commander Conon had been able to man nine or ten ships, including the state-ship *Paralos*. Conon quickly realized that the Athenian cause was lost, he could do nothing but watch as the rest of the fleet was hauled away, and the crewmen taken captive. His only chance was to use his small squadron and force their escape. Exploiting the speed of the Athenian ship design, Conon was able to cross the Hellespont and reach Lysander's empty camp, where he stole the Peloponnesians' mainsails for their ships. This gave him time to escape without fear of being immediately followed. Conon knew he could not return to Athens after such a disaster as this, so he took his ships south to Cyprus, and only the *Paralos* returned to the Piraeus and bore news of the battle.

Lysander had pulled off the greatest naval victory of his time. He had destroyed or captured the entire Athenian navy in one engagement, in a battle which resulted in the loss of very little Peloponnesian blood. When he finally completed his task of bringing together all of his gains, nearly 170 ships and every prisoner, Lysander sent a messenger to Sparta with news of what had happened. While he awaited any new orders from Sparta, Lysander had a separate issue to rectify. He had in his power all of the generals, minus Conon, and he needed to decide what he was going to do with them. Lysander took

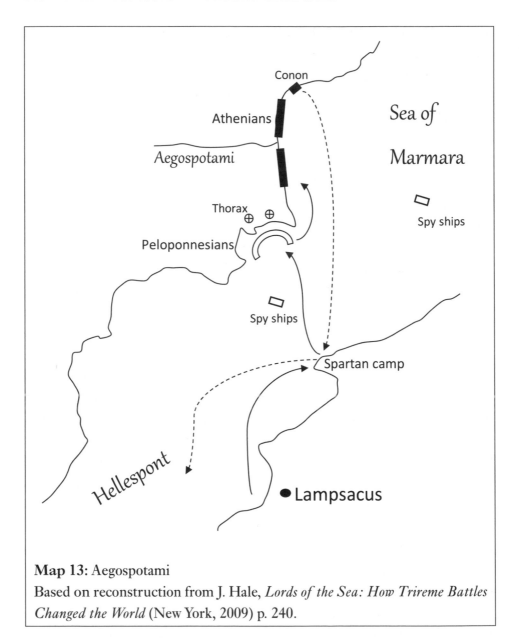

Map 13: Aegospotami
Based on reconstruction from J. Hale, *Lords of the Sea: How Trireme Battles Changed the World* (New York, 2009) p. 240.

this question to his allies, and the response he received was not a kind one. The Athenians had not long passed a law which permitted the mutilation of war captives by cutting off their right hands. Furthermore, there were rumours that Philocles had recently ordered the murder of two Peloponnesian crews by throwing them overboard. These actions went against the unwritten rules of Greek-on-Greek battle, so Lysander followed the vote of his allies and had all but one of the generals put to death, the survivor was chosen because he opposed the Athenian decree to chop off the hands of captives.

Aftermath

The aftermath of Aegospotami was cataclysmic for the Athenians. Lysander took control of the Hellespont and moved north to take hold of Byzantium and the entrance to the Black Sea. With control of the region in his hands, Lysander was now able to cut off the Athenian lifeline, the grain route that kept its citizens fed. Further still, Lysander stopped taking Athenian prisoners; so each time he took a city with an Athenian garrison he allowed them to return to Athens, thus putting extra strain on the limited food supplies in the city.

When the *Paralos* arrived in Athens with news of the battle, the city became consumed by fear and despair. They knew that the city of Athens would be next on the Spartans' hit list, so they voted to prepare for a siege and hold out as long as they possibly could. But Lysander was in no rush. He needed the influx of Athenian soldiers to the city to take its toll on supplies. He also had to complete his destruction of the Athenian empire, sailing around the Aegean islands and aligning their political affairs with the interests of Sparta.

When he was ready, Lysander's ships joined a huge land and sea force led by the Spartan king Pausanias. The army encamped in the Academy, just outside the north wall of Athens, while a fleet of 150 ships blockaded the Piraeus. Athens was cut off and the citizenry became frightened at the prospect of what might come. They sent messengers to Sparta and offered to become their direct ally, if it meant they could keep their Long Walls and the fortification of the Piraeus. But the Spartans refused their offer outright, and the siege continued for a further three months.

After all of the food had run out and the situation in Athens had become dire, they sent another ambassadorial mission to Sparta in the search for peace. Sparta's allies knew that Athens was on its knees, so they urged the Spartans to not make peace but, instead, destroy the city and wipe out the Athenian culture, without necessarily killing all of the Athenians; in essence, they suggested a rudimentary form of genocide. But the Spartans were a cautious people, they did not want to eradicate a major power in Greece, especially one which had done so much for the Greeks when it was under threat by the Persians. More pragmatically, it was in Sparta's interest to maintain a city with strong industrial and financial capabilities, and what is more incorporate it into an alliance which would allow Sparta to exploit these riches. So the Spartans ignored their allies and offered a peace with the Athenians, but on very strict terms: the Long Walls linking the city to the harbour would be destroyed, as would the defences of the Piraeus; Athens would hand over all of its remaining ships except for a paltry fleet of twelve which they could keep; the Athenians would allow all of their exiles to return to the city; they would share the same friends and enemies as Sparta; and they would follow the lead of Sparta in war, on both land and sea, on whatever campaign Sparta should order them.

The Athenians deliberated on the offer, but ultimately they had no choice. They voted to agree to the terms, and Lysander sailed into the Piraeus. To the sound of flute girls playing in the open air, the Peloponnesians dismantled the fortifications around the harbour and ripped down the Long Walls, believing that this day brought with it a new freedom for all Greek people.

Part 4

TURNING OF THE TIDE

The beginning of the fourth century BC sees a continuation of naval conflict between the Greek *poleis*, but for some reason does not provide any account of major battles which have survived. The reasons for this could be varied, the most obvious being there were not any major battles, but rather skirmishes between fleets. Another possibility is that our sources have chosen to not record them at any great length, or simply that the sources that may record them have not survived in full for us to read.

Yet the fourth century saw two interesting developments, both geopolitically and nautically, which are epitomized by two great battles. The first development was in the west. Following the Syracusan victory over Athens, the city grew from strength to strength. Its growing power and influence brought it into direct conflict with an unappreciated political presence in this period – the Carthaginians. A society more famous for its conflict with Rome in the third and second centuries BC, the Carthaginians were even at this early stage one of the biggest powers in the Mediterranean. Their conflict with Syracuse was reluctantly pursued by the North Africans, because many of their allies on Sicily were coming under increasing threat. But what the Carthaginians originally lacked in enthusiasm, the Syracusans had in abundance.

Syracuse was led by a tyrant, Dionysius I, and he was a man with drive and vision. He turned his city into a living and breathing factory of war. He became patron to innovative military designs which incorporated machinery and technology from the Carthaginians themselves. He also oversaw the creation of a newly designed set of warships, far larger and far more powerful than the trireme. His impertinence and overt aggression finally forced the Carthaginians to take his threat seriously, resulting in a large expedition being sent to Sicily in 397 BC. After a series of land battles, the Carthaginians gained the upper hand and moved on Syracuse itself.

In 396 BC, the North African fleet become isolated from the supporting land army near to Mount Etna, by the town of Catane, where it came under attack from the Syracusans. The battle ended in a Carthaginian victory, thanks in part to the poor decision making of the Syracusan commander on the day. The battle is the first time that the new form of ship, the Syracusan quinquereme, was used and it showed its worth, even if it was part of the defeated fleet.

The battle itself was not a pivotal moment in Sicilian history, but it sets the scene for a shift in power that would consume the next two centuries. Carthage had been forced to mobilize an enormous land force and giant fleet, and discovered itself to be very capable at warfare. What Dionysius could not have anticipated was that it would be with his newly designed quinquereme that the Carthaginians would go on to form the most feared navy in the Mediterranean, a navy which Carthage would use to become the next great superpower.

Interestingly, only two years later, in an almost completely unrelated series of events, the great superpower of the east, Persia, reached its highest level of success. The fourth century had brought with it Spartan dominance in Greece and the Aegean. Spartan attention soon turned to the Greek states under Persian rule, those in Ionia, and set about trying to liberate them. This attracted the anger of the Persian king and he sent his commanders to solve the Spartan problem. After various setbacks along the way, the Persians finally found a solution: they would turn the rest of the Greeks against the Spartans. Additionally, the Persian king financed the construction of a new, Greek–built fleet on Cyprus which would be commanded by an Athenian exile called Conon.

This large fleet was a major threat to Spartan dominance in the Aegean and could not be ignored for long. The two finally came to a head in 394 BC at the Battle of Cnidus. The battle was almost farcical; the Spartans attacked well but in poor order, yet the Persian fleet could not resist because they themselves were in even worse order. Only the intervention of a second Persian fleet ensured that Conon and Persia won the day and neutralized the Spartan fleet. However, the battle is pivotal because it was remembered in Athens as an Athenian victory. So it was a Persian fleet, destroying a Greek allied fleet led by Sparta, that was remembered as a victory for Athens. This was a long way from the Panhellenic sentiment of comradeship which characterized the Persian wars nearly a century earlier. The Persians had finally mastered a way to defeat the Greeks, and it was to let them defeat themselves.

Chapter 12

Battle of Catane (396 BC)

Background   (Diodorus, XIII.43-44, 54-63, 75-96,
                   114, XIV.7-9, 41-59.4)

In the early ninth century BC a band of Phoenicians from the city of Tyre, in modern Lebanon, traversed the North African coastline and arrived in what is now Tunisia. Supposedly led by the mythical princess Dido, the adventurers formed a new colony named Qart-hadasht ('New City'), which has been latinized to the more familiar name of Carthage. From these humble beginnings, the city of Carthage quickly grew, nourished as it was by a wide network of Phoenician colonies throughout the western Mediterranean. Unique amongst the colonies, Carthage maintained its autonomy from its mother city Tyre, giving it the freedom to expand and grow its own empire of influence.

A lack of contemporary written evidence makes it very difficult to reconstruct the rise of Carthage, but by the end of the sixth century BC Carthage had formed its first treaty with another growing power in the west, Rome. In this treaty, Carthage is described as already having control over 'Africa', Sardinia, and the western part of Sicily.[1] However, for now the Carthaginians were not as concerned with Rome as with the Western Greeks, a term given to those Greek colonists that settled in Italy or in the Western Mediterranean more generally. This concern soon grew into friction, and the source of this friction was the large island of Sicily. So perfectly placed between the city of Carthage and the southern tip of Italy, as well as being a very fertile land in its own right, the island of Sicily was a prize worth coveting.

The Phoenicians had already colonized much of Sicily by the eighth century BC, but when the Greeks arrived and colonized the eastern part of the island, the Phoenicians were pushed back to the western coast.[2] In the west, the major Phoenician cities like Motya, Soluntum and Palermo became allies of Carthage, while in the east the Corinthian colony of Syracuse was fast becoming one of the great cities of the Hellenic world. The Greek states on the island would often form alliance blocs in the face of what they considered the Carthaginian threat. By the turn of the fifth century BC one such bloc had been formed by a newly established tyrant of Syracuse, Gelon, with another local Greek tyrant. The bloc gained control of the Greek town of Himera, by the north coast, on the border of the Carthaginian territory. This seems to have upset a political status quo, because the Carthaginian response was immediate, with one source citing an army of 300,000 men being sent over in 480 BC, with a fleet of 3,200 ships, drawn from the vast Carthaginian empire.[3] While these numbers are clearly an exaggeration, the Carthaginian defeat that followed was not. The Carthaginian army marched on Himera and, after an initial victory in the field, the Greek allied force deceived the Carthaginian general and gained entry to their camp, killing thousands of unprepared warriors.

Following the defeat at Himera, Carthaginian interests focussed on Africa and the lands of Iberia. While they never abandoned their allies in Sicily during this time, neither did they launch any sort of assault on the ever-growing power of Syracuse. But by the end of the fifth century BC things were beginning to change. Two Greek-Sicilian towns, Segesta and Selinus, began to renew an old rivalry and each looked to a stronger power to support their cause. Segesta found its lands being raided by their rivals, who were by tradition allies of Syracuse, so the Segestans looked to Carthage for help. Their pleas were ignored, and they turned instead to Athens who, in 415 BC, sent the ill-fated Sicilian Expedition (see Chapter 8).

Following the great victory over Athens, Syracuse became complacent regarding its control over Sicily, and began to send more and more forces to their Peloponnesian allies to help in the Ionian War. But Segesta was still under threat from Selinus, and they once again implored Carthage to aid them. This time the Carthaginians did not refuse.[4] Responsibility for the operation was given to one Hannibal Mago, the grandson of the original general who was killed and defeated at Himera in 480 BC. Hannibal intended to manipulate Syracuse and force their hand; his actions would either cause war or else force Syracuse to allow a Carthaginian presence on Sicily, either way it would be Syracuse's decision. A small force of 5,800 Libyans and Campanians were first sent to Sicily, perhaps via the Phoenician city of Motya on the west coast. This army made its way to Segesta and aided the inhabitants in defeating the forces of Selinus. The Selinuntians predictably appealed to Syracuse for help, forcing Segesta to remind Carthage of its own promise of support. By the following spring, Hannibal had amassed a force large enough to achieve three primary aims: to defeat Selinus, to avenge his grandfather's death by destroying Himera, and to establish a proper Carthaginian presence on Sicily.

With a large army maybe 50,000 strong, made up of allies and mercenaries to supplement a citizen levy, Hannibal sailed across to Motya and landed in a small bay which would later become the site of the great Carthaginian city of Lilybaeum.[5] From there, Hannibal marched his army to Selinus and put it under siege. What neither Selinus nor Syracuse, which still resisted sending any substantial support to their ally, realized was that the Carthaginians did not wage war in the same way as the Greeks. To Syracuse, the prospect of a strong town like Selinus falling to anything except starvation or betrayal seemed unthinkable.[6] But the Greeks had not encountered the Carthaginian way of laying siege. Once Hannibal was ready, he ordered the advance of his metal-tipped battering rams, and missile troops were placed on giant mobile towers, from where they cleared the ramparts of defenders while the rams did their work. The city almost fell on the first day of assaults, as money-driven fanatical mercenaries forced their way through the breaches in the walls and threw themselves upon the desperate defenders. On the second day, Hannibal successfully broke into the city and, after nine days of street fighting, the city was finally taken.

In less than four weeks, Hannibal had achieved his primary aim in Sicily. Now he had time to exact his revenge on Himera. Hannibal invested the town, employing similar siege tactics as at Selinus, but with the additional use of fire on the walls, and utilizing an excavation team to undermine the fortifications. The defenders did not want to experience the same fate as Selinus, so they attempted a sortie from the city, 10,000 Greeks in all. But after initial success, the bulk of Hannibal's forces joined the fray and caught the Greek hoplites in a rout. Following this failed breakout, the city only lasted two more days of assaults before it inevitably fell. Hannibal showed no mercy, he slaughtered 3,000 Greek men on the traditional site of his grandfather's death, and the city itself was razed to the ground. Having now achieved two of his primary aims, Hannibal left garrisons in each of his allies' cities, forming a permanent

Carthaginian presence in Sicily, and returned with the rest of his forces back to Carthage. The speed of Hannibal's victory shocked the Greek cities, but his speedy departure created a false sense of ease. Believing Hannibal to have completed his limited aims in Sicily, they felt no need to exacerbate tensions with Carthage by retaliating in west Sicily. The only city with any sense of obligation to Selinus was Syracuse, but even it remained inactive.

Yet the inaction of Syracuse did not relate to one of their exiled citizens. Hermocrates, a former leader of the city, saw an opportunity to regain his power and position by inspiring direct action against the western cities in 409 BC. He amassed a force of mercenaries and refugees, and fortified part of the city of Selinus as his base. From here, his army of 6,000 men raided the Carthaginian allies, winning a morale-boosting victory against the forces at Motya. But Hermocrates' victories were not enough to convince the Syracusan people to let him return. In 408 BC, Hermocrates attempted one final act to convince his fellow citizens, he marched to Himera and collected the unburied bodies of the Greeks who had died there in 410 BC. But even this was not enough. Frustrations grew, and supporters of Hermocrates still living in the city planned a coup, inviting him and his army in to take power. The result was a brutal street fight involving thousands of men, ending in Hermocrates' own death.

The failed coup had two outcomes: the first was that the Greek raids on western Sicily abruptly stopped; the second was that the Carthaginians became fully aware of the situation in Sicily. After working under the false assumption of Syracusan superiority – in terms of military prowess and political stability – the senate of Carthage realized that Syracuse itself was in disarray, and that a mediocre force of 6,000 rogue men was capable of dominating much of the island. The senate decided that the easiest way to secure the trade routes in the Mediterranean, and in turn protect their allies, was to take control of the whole of Sicily. So in 407 BC, they took their first step by establishing a new colony. Provocatively placed near to the remains of Himera, the Carthaginians built the new town of Therma, pushing their area of influence further east. But the Carthaginians were not finished, they raised a large army and chose Hannibal Mago to lead it once again. He attempted to refuse the position on account of his advancing years, but he was persuaded after he was given a younger commander to assist him, his own cousin Himilco.

By the spring of 406 BC, Hannibal's army was ready, so an advance force of forty ships was sent over to Sicily to secure a landing position. This force was met by a Syracusan fleet of the same strength, which had been sent to intercept the invasion. During the sea battle, fifteen Carthaginian ships were sunk and the rest retreated to the safety of the open sea. News of the defeat did not deter Hannibal; he sailed out with his remaining fifty ships and combined it with those remaining from the advance force. The strength of seventy-five triremes was too much for the Syracusan fleet to oppose, so Hannibal was able to prepare two landing points for his army, one at Motya, the other at Panormus.[7] Once his forces were reunited he had to choose his first target. The decision was an easy one, the city of Acragas on the southern coast was simply too strong to ignore, and if Hannibal intended to attack Syracuse he could not afford such a powerful enemy at his rear.

Hannibal marched his army to Acragas without any opposition. He set up two camps on the eastern and southwestern sides of the city, before heralds were sent into the city to negotiate a treaty. The city refused straightaway, so the siege began in earnest. Hannibal brought up his siege engines, erected his siege towers, and built his siege mounds, but the Acragantini resisted with all their might. Before the city could fall, a plague struck the Carthaginian camps, slowing their progress exponentially. Among the dead was Hannibal himself, leaving full command of the army to Himilco.

As Himilco continued the siege, an allied force, led by Syracuse, arrived with enough men to nearly match those of the Carthaginians. Himilco ordered his eastern camp to descend into the plain and meet the approaching Greek army. The Greek hoplites won the day, killing 6,000 of the enemy, before driving the remainder back to their main camp in the southwest. With the Greeks occupying the second fort, and combining the reinforcements with the land forces of Acragas, the momentum had shifted, with the Carthaginians now cut off and blockaded in their camp. The searing heat of the Sicilian summer put a great strain on the Carthaginian resources and morale, with mutiny and desertion threatening. However, following the successful interception of a grain convoy being sent to Acragas, the city came under threat of starvation, and Himilco became the besieger once more. With the arrival of winter, the people of Acragas made the difficult decision to abandon the town, which became the winter base for Himilco's land forces.

In the summer of 405 BC, Himilco moved his army toward his next target, Gela. Having learned from the events at Acragas, the Carthaginians took greater precaution in planning his camp and siege tactics against the city. The forces of Gela held out, awaiting as they were the promised forces from their Syracusan allies. Syracuse did not disappoint and a strong army soon arrived, led by their new tyrant, Dionysius I.[8] His men began a three-week campaign, raiding the Carthaginians in their camp and attacking them as they foraged. But it had no impact on the enemy, who had large stores of food inside their camp. Dionysius needed to raise the siege quickly, so he planned an audacious attack on Himilco's camp. The battle was hard fought, but the Carthaginians were able to repulse the offensive and win the day. Dionysius' army was not nullified by the defeat and could have entered Gela to recuperate before trying again. But Dionysius could not afford to stay away from Syracuse any longer; his position of power had made him an unpopular man back home, and the longer he was away the longer his enemies could plan to overthrow him. Instead, he sent an envoy to Himilco to call a truce to collect the dead, which was agreed. But, instead of doing this, the Syracusans and the population of Gela left the city that same night. When daybreak came, Himilco marched his army into Gela and plundered it.

Himilco took his time following his success at Gela, and at a slow pace marched on Syracuse. He set up camp near to the city and remained inactive, to the great embarrassment of Dionysius. Yet Himilco knew that he did not have the manpower to besiege Syracuse right now, especially as many of the Peloponnesian allies of Syracuse were now free to support her, since the Ionian War had come to an end in 404 BC. Himilco had extended Carthaginian influence to its highest level in Sicily, and Syracuse was ostensibly too weak to form any serious threat to their claims on the island. So Himilco sent an offer of peace to Dionysius, a peace which confirmed Carthage's position of power on the island, and in turn Dionysius' tyranny of Syracuse was ratified. After peace was agreed, Himilco returned to North Africa with the majority of his army, but he also brought with him the plague that had cut through his forces in Sicily. The plague spread through Carthage and affected many of her allies as well, making her disinclined to commit to military activity for a few years.

Unfortunately for Carthage, Dionysius had no intention of maintaining the peace. Once he had subdued a revolt against his power in Syracuse, he broke the peace treaty with Carthage in 404 BC by attacking many of the Sicilian cities, absorbing them into his own growing domain. He also invested great funds in securing and improving the defences of Syracuse. Finally, purely in preparation for his coming war with Carthage, Dionysius aimed to arm his men with superior weaponry. He brought together some of the greatest craftsmen available, turning Syracuse into a giant workshop. He purposefully targeted craftsmen from different regions, including from Carthage, allowing him to sponsor the production of a truly international armoury. Because of this, Syracuse saw the reproduction of Carthaginian-style siege weapons, the production of a new form of siege weapon that fired large bolts (the original catapult, which looked more like a crossbow on a stand), and the invention of two new forms of ship: the *tetreres* and *penteres*, better known by their latinized names as the quadrireme and quinquereme respectively.[9]

The summer of 397 BC saw Dionysius' military preparations completed and his grand plan could begin. He considered the Carthaginians to be in a weakened state and, having learned from the lessons of Hannibal's and Himilco's attacks, Dionysius intended to invade the western half of Sicily. His main target was the richest and most powerful city in the west, Motya. A fortified city on an island in the middle of a lagoon, Motya was well placed to withstand a sustained siege. Dionysius threw everything he had at the city, he even began the construction of a great mole to cross the lagoon, but he was soon interrupted by naval forces coming from Carthage.

Regardless of the internal problems that Carthage had been facing in terms of manpower and a reduced militarism in the city, a direct assault on such an important ally as Motya could not be ignored. Himilco initially sent ten ships to raid the Great Harbour of Syracuse, in the hope of drawing Dionysius away from his siege. The raids were a tactical success, but Dionysius did not move. He wanted Motya to fall above all else. Himilco upped the ante by launching a fleet of 100 ships, having received information that the Syracusan fleet had been hauled ashore in a lagoon and were in a state of carelessness. He purposefully timed his arrival for daybreak, so as to amplify the element of surprise, but Dionysius had already received reports of the giant fleet's departure from Carthage. Dionysius moved a large portion of his infantry down to the camp, so that, when Himilco arrived, his ships were quickly forced back to the mouth of the lagoon, where they waited for the coming naval battle.

Dionysius, however, had no intention of fighting a sea battle on Himilco's terms. The mouth of the lagoon was a narrow strip, giving the Carthaginians a great advantage. Dionysius ordered his men to drag eighty ships across the small peninsula on rollers, and launch them in the open sea instead. Furthermore, he had purposefully manned his ships with a high proportion of missile troops so that, when Himilco launched his attack on the fleet, the Syracusans repelled the assault with relative ease. Himilco's fleet was further inundated with missiles from the shoreline. Dionysius had lined the coast with his new catapults which were firing arrows from a great distance, and with devastating effect.

The barrage forced Himilco to abandon his designs in the region and sail his fleet back home. This, in turn, gave Dionysius *carte blanche* to continue his siege works around Motya. Once the mole was complete, the Syracusans moved up their battering rams, their catapults and their new siege towers. The battle for the walls was bitter and brutal, and when the city finally fell, Dionysius' men exacted great vengeance on its inhabitants, protecting only the Greek inhabitants; many of those Motyans who were not killed were sold off into slavery. After this, and much to Dionysius' dismay, his forces returned home before the onset of winter.

The Syracusan forces returned to the west of the island in the new campaigning season of 496 BC, and began to ravage the lands of Carthage's allies once again. But Himilco had not been idle through the winter break. Alarmed by the size of the Syracusan forces that attacked Motya, the senate moved to mobilize a much-larger force and to resolve the Sicilian Problem once and for all. The army, possibly over 50,000 men, was transported to Sicily and landed at Panormus, after a quick skirmish with a crack force of 30 ships sent by Dionysius – possibly the first ever action of the new quinqueremes.[10] Himilco had avoided a full-on assault against his entire fleet by splitting his forces between troop transporters, which were attacked, and his fighting fleet, which took a different route.

With his forces now on Sicily, Himilco attracted allied reinforcements and went about systematically regaining control of western Sicily. His success was resounding, as he avoided any form of pitched battle. Himilco refrained from attacking outside of the Carthaginian sphere of influence, such as Segesta, or Syracuse itself. His concern was the reestablishment of the sea route between Carthage and Sicily which was once held by the city of Motya. Possibly under his own guidance, old inhabitants of Motya founded a new city on the other side of the lagoon, on the bay of Lilybaeum, Lilybaeum being the name given to the new city.[11] While Motya was not entirely abandoned at this point, it lost its position of importance to the Carthaginian cause.

To enable a successful blockade and siege of Syracuse, Himilco knew he needed to control the sea route to the east; cutting off aid from Italy and the Peloponnese. He marched his army along the north coast, shadowed by his fleet, and headed for the Straits of Messana, which separates the northeastern corner of Sicily from the toe of Italy. By the autumn, the Carthaginian force had entered the lands of Messana and set up camp. The Messanians had decided to remain loyal to Syracuse and, having sent the women and children away, they planned to resist Himilco's great army. They sent a small force of picked men to hold the narrow roads near the coastline, hoping to neutralize Himilco's vast numbers. But Himilco was a smart general and, rather than waste time and energy fighting a strong defensive position, he simply used his large fleet to transport thousands of his men directly to the city of Messana, bypassing the blockade entirely. The landing was uncontested and the city was swiftly taken, although most of the remaining population had already fled to the fortified villages in the surrounding hills.

Himilco, in characteristic fashion, did not rush. He spent some time trying to take many of the hill forts in the area, before giving his army a few days' rest. Once he was ready, he ordered the city to be razed to the ground, to prevent it being reoccupied, and then he began the long march south. As he neared Mount Etna, he found that the coastal path was out of action, due to a recent lava flow from the volcano, so he decided to send his fleet on ahead while he marched his men on a long detour. They would reconvene at Catane.

Forces

The Carthaginian fleet was led by Mago, a relative of Himilco. Under his command was a fleet consisting of no less than 500 vessels. Diodorus does not tell us how many of these were actually warships, but it is possible to ascertain a rough figure. Himilco's original force that arrived on Sicily in 496 BC was said to consist of 400 large ships of war (triremes) and 600 other vessels to carry troops, food and siege weapons.[12] We know that, by the time Himilco was targeting Messana, he specifically had eyes on their harbour, which was large enough to contain his entire fleet of 600 ships. It can be assumed that Himilco left 100 ships at Messana,[13] perhaps to control the strait, giving him 500 at Catane. After the Battle of Catane we are told that 250 warships entered the Great Harbour of Syracuse and, taking into account the losses of the battle, it can be assumed that Mago had around 300 triremes under his command. The remaining 200 ships would have been *penteconters* and, smaller still, *triaconters*, which were also built for combat with a ram, but were not as powerful as the trireme.[14]

Carthaginian naval tactics are hard to ascertain during this period because, amazingly for such a naval power, there is only a small selection of instances in which they fought a naval battle; two of which were against Syracuse in 406 BC and the summer of 496 BC, both of which they lost. Before these two, the next closest in date that we know of was the Battle of Alalia, which took place in the sixth century BC and may have been the first battle to witness the use of the ram in naval tactics –the Carthaginians were on the receiving end of that defeat as well.[15] Carthaginian fleets would later become famous for the skilful manoeuvring of their ships, but during this period they placed a greater emphasis on the superior marines. They would try to draw abreast of the enemy ships and fight it out on the decks, similarly to the Corinthians.[16]

The forces of Syracuse consisted of a land army and a naval fleet. Dionysius took control of the army, numbering 20,000 infantry and 3,000 cavalry, who were to hold the shoreline to give a safe haven for the fleet should they be defeated. Control of the fleet was given to his trusted admiral Leptines, who was in fact his own brother. Leptines had already shown himself a capable commander, having been in charge of the fleet since the siege of Motya, at the latest. Under his command were 180 war ships, the majority of which were triremes. Within his fleet he is said to have had thirty superior ships, a crack force of the same number which had confronted the Carthaginian armada at the beginning of their expedition. It seems extremely probable that these thirty ships, or at least a proportion of them, were of the new designs: quadriremes and quinqueremes. These ships were bigger and more powerful, propelled forward by four or five men to each oar (an attribute which most likely gave the ships their names).

All Leptines needed to do was maintain his fleet's unity and cohesion. If he could keep a tight formation, headed by his thirty great ships, he had a good chance of neutralizing the threat of Mago's numbers. Leptines could use the agile nature of Greek naval tactics to prevent the Carthaginians from being able to board his ships, and in turn win an astonishing victory.

Battle   (Diodorus, XIV.59.5-60.7)

Dionysius had been kept well informed of Himilco's actions. He knew that Mago's fleet had been forced to part company with Himilco's army. He also knew that Mago's journey down to Catane would only be a short one, leaving him isolated from any land support for a prolonged period of time. Furthermore, Dionysius would have been aware that his fighting strength on land was at a greater numerical disadvantage than his strength at sea. For Syracuse to survive, Dionysius needed to repulse Mago's fleet, if not destroy it.

Dionysius acted quickly. He ordered Leptines to take his entire fleet and attack the Carthaginians. Leptines was to maintain control of the battle, and his own ships, by keeping a tight formation and forcing the battle into close quarters. Simultaneously, Dionysius took his land forces and lined them up along the coast. If the Carthaginian ships tried to beach to escape Leptines' onslaught, then his forces would cut them down. However, if Leptines for whatever reason failed in his mission, the Syracusan fleet could beach themselves and have a strong land army ready to protect them.

As Mago's fleet approached Catane, the sight on the shoreline must have been overwhelming. Thousands of armed men formed a seemingly impenetrable mass where the Carthaginians believed they were going to land. What is worse, Mago saw in front of him the forbidding hulls of the Syracusan fleet in the distance, which were quickly bearing down on his positon. Initially, the Carthaginians panicked and headed straight for land, and certain destruction. It was not until Mago, overcoming the shock of the whole situation, took command of his senses that he realized his best chance of survival was to fight the Syracusans at sea. If nothing else, the sheer numerical advantage made it likely that the majority of his fleet could escape this trap. Mago turned his ships around and set up his battle lines ready to receive Leptines. The Syracusan commander duly obliged, but in doing so he ordered the one thing Dionysius had warned him not to: he split up his fleet.

Leptines' reasoning is impossible to fathom. Maybe he got overly excited at the prospect of his victory, or maybe he purposely decided to ignore the tactics of his brother as a way of reasserting his own authority. Whatever the case, Leptines ordered his thirty superior ships, his quadriremes and his quinqueremes, to lead the advance. Throwing caution to the wind, Leptines led the vanguard further and further ahead of his battle lines, driving them into the heart of Mago's fleet.

The power of the Syracusan juggernauts was immense and seemingly unstoppable. With the power of almost twice the number of rowers to the trireme, the quinqueremes would have ploughed into enemy ships, shattering the hulls that were unfortunate enough to be in their way. Mago could not confront these ships head on, he knew this. His best bet was to wait for the great strength of the enemy ships to lose its momentum. As the first triremes were sunk, the Syracusan ships began to slow down, becoming bogged in the cluttered seascape that its own devastation was creating. As the fighting became fiercer and more congested, the Carthaginian helmsmen began to manoeuvre towards the enemy, laying their ships alongside the Syracusans'.

Once Mago's ships were in position the shape of the battle changed. It began to resemble a land battle, fought on the decks of the ships. Marines jumped

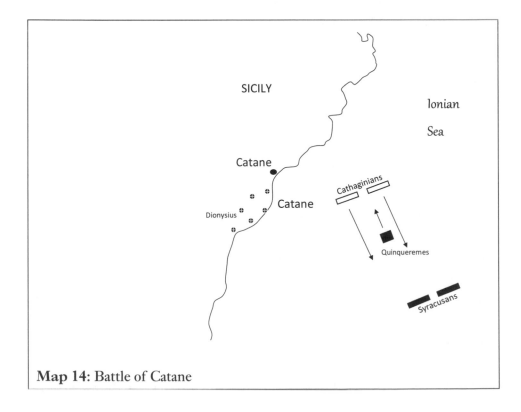

Map 14: Battle of Catane

from ship to ship, fighting with every muscle and sinew they had. The small gaps between the ships were quickly filled with fallen bodies. Many marines, in their excitement, tried jumping the gaps to board ships, only to miss and fall into the sea, either to be crushed by the ships as they hit one another, battered to death by the hundreds of oars, or else drowned in the tumultuous wash that the battle was creating.

The large Syracusan ships were overwhelmed by the swarms of Carthaginian marines. Leptines needed to conduct some form of damage limitation. He ordered his advance force to retreat back to the safety of his main battle lines. But as they turned they realized that the main bulk of the fleet had continued its advance and were, in total disarray, beginning to engage Mago's fleet. Leptines took his squadron out into the open sea in full retreat, leaving the rest of his fleet to fight it out for themselves.

Seeing their illustrious admiral in full flight, the Syracusans' morale dropped considerably. Conversely, for the Carthaginians, the sight of the enemy in flight buoyed their spirits and they fought even harder against the Syracusans in front of them. The lack of unity in the enemy fleet made the job of the Carthaginians that bit easier, but the fighting was still brutal and exhausting. The Syracusans could not resist for long, and the Carthaginian dominance soon won the day, forcing the Greek fleet into retreat.

In the rout that followed dozens of Syracusan ships were immobilized and captured. Mago also stationed many of his lighter ships, his *penteconters* and *triaconters*, near the shallows by the shoreline. Their job was to kill any sailors that had abandoned their ships in the search for safety on land. No one would be allowed to escape so easily. Thousands of Syracusans were being killed, while Dionysius could only watch helplessly from land. The entire coast was filling with corpses, the sand itself would have been turned red by the blood-tinted surf.

With the Syracusan fleet in full flight, and Dionysius abandoning his position to return to Syracuse, Mago could finally pull his ships into land. With the Carthaginian ships came many of the captured Greek vessels, which were then hauled onto the beaches and repaired, ready to be used if necessary in the coming battles for Syracuse. The body count for both sides was monumental. Mago had masterminded the defeat and capture of more than 100 Syracusan ships, over fifty per cent of Leptines' fleet. With them, the Carthaginians had killed over 20,000 men, but Mago's losses would not have been small. We are not given the figures of the Carthaginian casualties, but the impact of Syracusan ramming techniques would have surely taken their toll. Yet the sheer numbers of Mago's fleet meant that losses could easily be swallowed, and the reclamation of Greek ships allowed for a speedy replacement to take place.

Aftermath

Himilco arrived at Catane and reunited with this victorious fleet. The Carthaginians continued their move south and set up camp outside the walls of Syracuse itself, while their fleet made a great display of strength by entering the Great Harbour. But it all turned sour for Himilco. After initial success outside of the walls, the Syracusans were able to strike back with ever increasing effect.

Dionysius' forces raided the Carthaginian camps, and even set fire to part of their fleet. Himilco quickly realized that Syracuse would not fall as easily as the other Sicilian cities. Syracusan success bred more success, and many of the Carthaginian depots and camps set up around the Great Harbour were effectively targeted. Himilco was not going to endure the potential ignominy of defeat, so he commenced negotiations with Dionysius to permit him to evacuate his forces, before he had recreated his own Sicilian disaster, like that the Athenians had suffered so many years earlier.

Himilco was so intent on retreat he offered Dionysius 300 *talents*, the entire remainder of his war chest, as part of the agreement. Dionysius finally relented and announced a four-day truce, giving Himilco time to evacuate the citizen levy of his army by night as he left the rest to fend for themselves. For Dionysius, this result allowed him to accrue the political credit for such as strong victory over a powerful enemy, without having to shed any more Syracusan blood. In turn, he was able to reassert his faltering authority over the city and its population, sustaining his tyranny until his death in 367 BC

Himilco's return was one of a failed expedition, there was no glory or triumph to Carthage. Carthage began a process of political restructuring, so as to restrict the power that could be possessed by an individual. They created a new form of governance, headed not by kings but by two annually-elected leaders, and the armed forces would from then on be led by an elected general who was himself answerable to the court of 104 judges. Himilco, the last of the Magonid dynasty that had seen Carthage grow in influence and power through the sixth and fifth centuries BC, starved himself to death. Carthage chose a less expansionist foreign policy, preferring to consolidate their trade empire in the Mediterranean and subdue new uprisings in Libya. But the Punic–Syracusan conflict would rumble on until Carthage was finally able to stamp her authority on the island, only to be faced by a new rival on the scene, the Roman Republic.

Chapter 13

Battle of Cnidus (394 BC)

Background   (Xenophon, *Hellenica*, III.4.1–IV.3.9; Diodorus
                   XIV.39, 79.1–82.4; Plutarch, *Life of Artaxerxes*, 20–1)

At the turn of the fourth century BC, the political landscape of the
Mediterranean had shifted drastically from what the previous
century had witnessed. The Ionian War had been brought to an end
following Lysander's great naval victory at Aegospotami; Athens had been
forced to rescind most of its naval strength and remove the Great Walls that
protected the road from the city down to the Piraeus. Sparta, as the leader
of the Peloponnesians, had taken to its new position of power with much
gusto, forming a hegemony. But Sparta's position of authority resulted in
their interference with the governance of other Greek *poleis*, actions which
contradicted the Spartan rhetoric during the Ionian War that had claimed they
would liberate the Greek cities from the oppression of the Athenian Empire.

In 401 BC, the Spartans saw an opportunity to distract a growing discontent
in Greece, by uniting everyone against a common, external, enemy. This had
the added bonus of justifying Sparta's own position, by becoming a leader of
a joint military operation. That year saw the new king of Persia, Artaxerxes
II, under threat from his own brother, Cyrus the Younger. The Spartans
decided to support the cause of Cyrus, the same man who had given Sparta the
necessary funding to win the Ionian War, and sent forces to join his rebel army.
Cyrus' venture ended in defeat and his own death at the Battle of Cunaxa, and
Artaxerxes now considered the Spartans to be enemies of his empire.[1]

The Spartans lived up to this billing. In 400 BC they sent a force to Asia Minor
and declared their support for the Asiatic Greek cities against the Persians – in
essence establishing a protectorate over the coastal region.[2] With help from
their Greek allies, including Athens, and the very fleet that the Persians had
paid for, the Spartans spent two years detaching Greek *poleis* from Persian

control. For Artaxerxes, understandably, this was a serious problem, but he had greater concerns to manage. In 401 BC, the lands of Egypt had successfully revolted and were in the hands of a sole rebel leader. The rich lands of Egypt were of the utmost important for the Persian Empire as a whole, not least because of its vast supply of food. Egypt had often revolted against Persian rule, but never had a single rebel dynast established himself over such a vast swathe of the country. If Artaxerxes did not react, the situation could become unfixable.

Perhaps more concerning for Artaxerxes was that the geopolitical situation, as it stood, seemed very familiar. In the 450s BC, the Persian King Artaxerxes I had contended with a revolt in Egypt, and the Greek hegemon at the time, Athens, was working along the Ionian Coast to free Greek cities from Persian control. At that time, the Athenians decided to exploit the Egyptian revolt by siding with the rebels and sending considerable military support. For Artaxerxes II, the situation was actually worse, the Egyptian revolt had taken hold of the entire country, and the Spartans were achieving in two years what had taken the Athenians decades.[3]

In 398 BC, Artaxerxes took measures to constrain Sparta's activities in the east. Following a meeting with Pharnabazus, one of his satraps in the region, the Great King appointed the experienced commander and satrap Tissaphernes as *karanos* of Anatolia, in charge of all military operations in the region.[4] In addition, Artaxerxes funded the creation of a new fleet which was to be predominantly built by the kings on Cyprus. The demand made of the Cypriots was large, 100 triremes, but it was not beyond their means. It is also possible that this responsibility gave the Cypriots a means of leverage over the Great King, for Artaxerxes made an unprecedented move. The fleet was under the authority of Pharnabazus, but the king appointed an operational commander of the fleet, and what is more, he picked a Greek admiral.

The choice for operational command was an ex-Athenian commander called Conon. This was the same man who held command for the Athenians at Arginusae, and at the defeat at Aegospotami, where he escaped in the aftermath of the disaster (see Chapters 10 and 11). Since then, Conon had been in a self-imposed exile, taking refuge with one of the Cypriot kings, Evagoras. For Evagoras, Conon could be used as a form of tribute to the Persian king. By offering such an experienced and capable naval commander, Evagoras was demonstrating his loyalty to the Great King, while also asserting his own semi-autonomy by putting such a suggestion to Artaxerxes, something that no vassal state had any right to do. Artaxerxes accepted the recommendation, but in return he insisted on Evagoras' complete submission to his authority.

It transpired that Conon was, in fact, an inspired choice for Artaxerxes. The Athenian became a beacon, attracting to him masses of unemployed, but highly experienced, rowers and sailors from Athens.[5] He was, in turn, given complete freedom to choose his crews and subordinate commanders, giving this Persian fleet a very Athenian flavour from top to bottom. In reality, Conon's job was a simple one: he was to keep the Spartan fleet preoccupied. Artaxerxes' plans revolved around the securing of Egypt, and the Spartans were a threat to these Persian operations.

In 397/6 BC, the Spartan naval base of operations in the Aegean was at the city of Rhodes, on the island of the same name. For Conon to have the greatest impact, he needed to put Rhodes under threat as fast as possible. However, to complicate matters, Conon did not yet have the full Cypriot-built fleet available to him, so he would have to act with only a small squadron of forty ships. The wily Athenian picked his target perfectly. Knowing that he could not assault Rhodes itself, which housed some 120 Spartan triremes, he chose to sail his small fleet along the southern coast of Caria and take a position at the town of Caunus. An excellent choice, Caunus had two major advantages. Firstly, it was the same base which the Spartans, back in 412-1 BC, used to take control of Rhodes, so it caused a frantic reaction from the Spartan *nauarch*, Pharax.[6] Secondly, the town sat beside a river which connected the sea with an inland lake, giving Conon somewhere safe to anchor his ships if the position came under threat.[7]

Conon's gamble paid off. Pharax immediately mobilized all 120 ships based at Rhodes, his entire fleet, and put Caunus under siege and naval blockade. The siege lasted a few months, with Conon being able to avoid direct combat with the superior numbers of Pharax.[8] All that Conon needed was for time to pass and Caunus to hold out, something it achieved with great ease. The Persian response was perfectly timed, so when a further forty ships had been completed in Cyprus, it was time for the siege at Caunus to be lifted. Pharnabazus moved a large army overland to relieve the town, forcing Pharax to abandon the entire operation.

Once the Spartan fleet had departed, Conon waited for his forty new ships to join him before sailing out from the safety of Caunus, into the exposed position of Loryma, a small peninsula which is directly opposite the north side of Rhodes. From here Conon could see everything that the Spartan fleet was doing, and Pharax's base was under constant threat from this brand new Persian fleet, manned by experienced sailors, and led by a good Athenian commander. Pharax's actions were bold and decisive – he ordered the abandonment of Rhodes. With the Spartans now gone, Rhodes invited Conon in to use the city as his own base in the Aegean.[9]

In 396 BC, Artaxerxes must have felt ready to launch his campaign into Egypt, but some very disconcerting news soon arrived from Rhodes. Ships carrying a vast consignment of naval equipment and grain had arrived in the belief that the city was still in Spartan hands – the ships were Egyptian. This resulted from a Spartan misunderstanding. In 397 BC, word had reached Sparta that the Persians had begun the construction of a vast fleet in Phoenicia and, in classic Greek style, they presumed themselves to be the target, not realizing that this fleet was being built to deal with Egypt. In response, the Spartans mobilized 8,000 troops under the command of the great military strategist and Spartan king, Agesilaus. Once Agesilaus landed in Asia Minor he joined with the forces out there and had an army some 20,000 strong. To support such a large operation, the Spartans sent an envoy to Egypt to ask for support from the rebel dynast, who in turn agreed to send much-needed supplies to Rhodes.

For Artaxerxes, this was confirmation of his worst nightmare: the Spartans were in collusion with the Egyptians. The Persians had to completely change their plans to deal with this new threat. If Artaxerxes continued with his original plan to focus on Egypt then the Spartans could easily dominate the Aegean, liberate the Ionian Coast, and threaten the eastern Mediterranean. In case the Great King had any doubts, Agesilaus was now doing everything in his power to make his intentions clear. He set himself up as a new Agamemnon, the mythical Mycenaean king who took the city of Troy. Agesilaus intended to strike into the heart of Persian lands, taking the fight into the homeland of the enemy. And what is worse for Artaxerxes, Agesilaus was winning victory after victory, leaving him free to roam throughout Asia Minor without any fear of being defeated in battle.

Artaxerxes postponed his intentions in Egypt and focussed on unbalancing the Spartan hegemony in the Aegean. To achieve this he needed to first secure the Persians' own position in the western theatre. A further 90 ships from the Phoenician fleet were sent to Conon, bringing his strength to 170 triremes and thus outnumbering the Spartan fleet by almost 50 per cent. However, Conon was under orders not to go on the offensive, so Conon focussed on consolidating his power on Rhodes, unofficially supporting a democratic uprising in the city, and a government that was, at its core, anti-Spartan. But Artaxerxes was not finished; he sent a trusted official, Tithraustes, to the court of Tissaphernes, and saw to his arrest and execution. Tissaphernes was held responsible for the growing Spartan problem, having failed to contain their expansive growth in Ionia. Tithraustes was not given the same military responsibility as Tissaphernes, but was quite clearly given a very specific job by the Great King, one which he performed perfectly.

As the envoy of Artaxerxes, Tithraustes met with Agesilaus and arranged a truce, giving him time to sort out Persian affairs in the region. With a little breathing space he then used the vast funds in Tissaphernes' treasury to settle debts with the crews of Conon's fleet: a vast sum of 220 *talents* was given to the Athenian commander to prevent his men from mutinying.[10] Tithraustes also sent a messenger to mainland Greece with 50 talents of silver to entice disgruntled Greek cities to form a coalition and oppose the Spartan hegemony. But the effect of this plan would take time, and until then Agesilaus was still causing chaos in Asia Minor; while he had agreed in the truce to stop attacking the old lands of Tissaphernes, he had simply moved into the lands of Pharnabazus instead.

The Spartans held the advantage in the Aegean. Agesilaus held sole command of land and naval forces in Asia and intended to build a fleet that would rival that of Conon. Even if the Persians could convince some Greek states to revolt, Spartan control of the sea would make it very easy for them to subdue it. But Conon, the grizzled veteran of the Ionian War, saw the Persian strategy for what it would be, ineffective. So he took it upon himself to leave his fleet and travel to Babylon for an audience with the king. Conon stood before Artaxerxes and promised that, with full financial support and strategic autonomy, he could break the Spartan domination of the sea. What he specifically said to Artaxerxes is not recorded in history, however it must have been impressive for he convinced the Great King to honour him with personal gifts, and appointed him a paymaster to provide him funds reliably, and on a regular basis. Furthermore, he allowed Conon to appoint a Persian to be an associate leader with him. For Conon there was only one logical choice, Pharnabazus, the *satrap* who had suffered most at the hands of the Spartans.

The year 395 BC brought the news that Artaxerxes had been waiting for. The Greek cities of Thebes, Corinth, Argos and Athens formed an anti-Spartan alliance and swiftly prepared for war. The situation in Greece quickly escalated. Two Spartan armies headed to Heliartus in Boeotia, one led by the second Spartan king Pausanias, and the other led by the great Spartan commander who masterminded the victory of Aegospotami, Lysander. The Thebans sent an army to face them, but Pausanias failed to arrive in time and Lysander, in characteristic arrogance, decided to force the battle alone. The Spartans were defeated and, worse yet, Lysander himself was killed. When Pausanias did arrive the situation was on a knife edge, so when the offer came to call a truce, both sides leapt at the chance, and the Spartans then retreated from Boeotia. In Sparta, the authorities were furious with Pausanias. They blamed him for failing to meet Lysander, and for failing to commit to battle; he did not arrive in Sparta for his trial, so he was convicted *in absentia* and sentenced to death

Back in Asia Minor, Agesilaus was wreaking havoc in the lands of Pharnabazus, around the Hellespont. The situation became so dire that Pharnabazus was forced to arrange a face-to-face meeting with the Spartan king. In their meeting, Agesilaus tried to convince Pharnabazus to rebel against the Great King by joining the Spartans. Pharnabazus softly refused the offer, knowing full well how Artaxerxes' own plans were progressing, and somehow convinced Agesilaus to leave his territory alone. For Agesilaus, his opportunity had finally come. He had a truce with Pharnabazus, securing his northern frontier, and he had a truce with the old lands of Tissaphernes, securing his southern frontier. Now with the advantage of surprise, he could march into the lands of the Persian empire and take control of every territory he entered. However, as the campaigning season of 394 BC arrived, it brought with it a messenger from the Greek mainland. It had been sent by the Spartan authorities. The anti-Spartan alliance was becoming too serious a threat to ignore, Agesilaus needed to come home.

Agesilaus left garrisons to protect the Greek cities, and he left the majority of his naval force under the command of his brother-in-law, Peisander. Peisander had only been appointed as the commander of the Spartan fleet the year before, by Agesilaus himself. He was a strong personality, and certainly an ambitious man, but he was horrifically inexperienced and grossly out of his depth to be left alone to pit his wits against Conon. But Agesilaus had made his decision and, at this point, he felt that the threat of Persian aggression was minimal. For the Spartan king, his priority was to march his forces back into Greece over land, via the Hellespont.

The anti-Spartan coalition had no intention of waiting for the Spartans to prepare themselves for war. They mobilized early in the year and faced a hastily formed Spartan army at the Nemea River, to the west of Corinth. After a hard fought battle, the Greek allies were routed from the field and the Spartans won the day. But the threat of the allies was not yet dead. News of the victory reached Agesilaus as he was marching through Chalcidice, which buoyed the morale of his men. Their march continued through Thessaly, where his army came under attack from Theban allies in the region. The march became a hard-fought endeavour, but Agesilaus successfully led his men to the border of Boeotia. During the day of 14 August 394 BC, the sky ominously went completely dark but for a crescent sun, and on that same day further dramatic news came to Agesilaus. The Spartans had suffered a damaging defeat and a Spartan commander had been killed in action. But this information had not come from the Greek mainland, it had come from the east. Enquiring as to the commander who died, the name Peisander would have resounded in the king's mind as he realized his vast fleet had suffered a humiliating defeat.

Forces

The Persian fleet was led primarily by Conon, with a large Phoenician contingent led by Pharnabazus. In total they had ninety triremes, with the majority being of Cypriot construction and under the direct command of Conon. Taking into account that Conon had 170 ships in his entire fleet, we can assume that this was the special offensive squadron that Conon had convinced Artaxerxes to let him create. Presuming that this is the case, we can assume that these ships would have been Conon's best, manned by his most experienced crewmen. Conon himself was a seasoned naval commander, and he had surrounded himself with men with similar experience. He was not as much a Greek commander leading a foreign fleet, as he was a Greek commander leading a Greek fleet, given to him by a foreign backer. This meant that the language on the ships could be Greek, the tactics he used could be Greek, the way he dealt with his men could be Greek, all of which meant that everyone under his direct command knew what was expected of them at all times. The majority of the non-Greek force was under Pharnabazus, and their role would be to support Conon, not to lead.

The Spartan fleet was led by Peisander, a smart and dynamic leader who suffered with inexperience. He led a fleet of eighty-five triremes, some of which, if not all, were newly built under the orders of Agesilaus in 495 BC.[11] The crews were experienced men drawn from all over the Hellenic world, but not necessarily the best. Not only could Conon attract Athenian sailors, who were often considered the very best, Conon also had direct access to Persian funds, since Artaxerxes gave him his own paymaster. This large treasury would have enabled Conon to pay his men a slightly higher rate that the Spartans could afford, which would have allowed Conon to recruit the best, non-Athenian, sailors.[12]

Battle   (Diodorus XIV.83.4–7; Xenophon, *Hellenica*, IV.3.10–12)

Ever since Conon's victory at Caunus, and the taking of Rhodes, the Persians had held a definitive, defensive line: Caunus-Loryma-Rhodes.[13] This line gave the Persians the security of knowing that a Spartan-led fleet could not leave the Aegean without a major battle taking place. However, until 494 BC, Conon had been forced to remain relatively inactive, and certainly not aggressive in his actions. This led to the Spartans becoming somewhat complacent, and Peisander could be forgiven for thinking that Conon had no intention of changing his tactics any time soon. Unfortunately, he was wrong.

Peisander was no fool, he certainly realized that something was amiss when Conon received his Phoenician reinforcements, but he could not have anticipated the Athenian's plans. Ultimately, Conon was about to break a three-year hiatus of Persian inactivity in the Aegean, but where was he heading? There were two logical targets for a Persian fleet of this size. Either Conon was going to exploit the reduced Spartan presence in Asia Minor, by raiding the coasts and retaking the Greek cities; or he was aiming to cross the Aegean and support the anti-Spartan coalition by supplying such a formidable naval contingent.

Whichever one Conon had planned, Peisander only had one option, to strike first and to strike early.[14]

Peisander knew that the Persian fleet was still in and around Rhodes, so he moved his fleet south and anchored in Cnidus. Cnidus had become one of the primary naval bases for the Spartans since they lost control of Rhodes, and it positioned Peisander perfectly to operate in the southeastern Aegean. The Spartan commander needed to take the initiative if he were to stand any chance of eliminating the enemy fleet. Luckily for him, Conon took too long to recognize the imminent threat. His preparations for a battle were too slow, allowing Peisander to weight the odds heavily in his own favour.

The Spartan commander led his entire fleet out, moving east from Cnidus, towards a bay closer to the enemy who were now, predominantly, at Loryma. The exact position of this bay is not certain, but it must have been well concealed, because neither fleet had any real understanding of what the other was doing. After giving his final orders and letting his men take their last meal before the fight, Peisander ordered his fleet to take to the sea once again and sail around the remaining promontories to descend on the unwitting Persian ships.

Peisander had planned this to near perfection. The timing of the attack, the aggression of the offensive, and his understanding of the coastal geography, enabled him to catch Conon completely off guard. The Athenian had fortunately given the orders for his Greek ships to prepare for battle, possibly once he received notification that Peisander had moved from Cnidus. Yet he had only been able to get his own contingent to sea, but not yet in battle line, before Peisander's fleet appeared. If Conon could hold his position long enough, the battle would be decided by the arrival of Pharnabazus and the Phoenicians, but they were far away and in an even greater state of disorder than Conon himself.

Peisander saw that he held the advantage; his element of surprise greatly outweighed the minor numerical advantage held by Conon. Peisander led from the front, in stereotypical Spartan fashion. His ships quickly overwhelmed the most advanced of Conon's ships and pushed into the bulk of the enemy fleet. In stark contrast to Peisander's ordered lines and calm advance, Conon's fleet was in a panic. Trying hard to form a combative line capable of withstanding an attack that was already picking up momentum, the Greek fleet could do little more than resist with all of their might. The fighting took to the decks as the Greek marines fought it out.

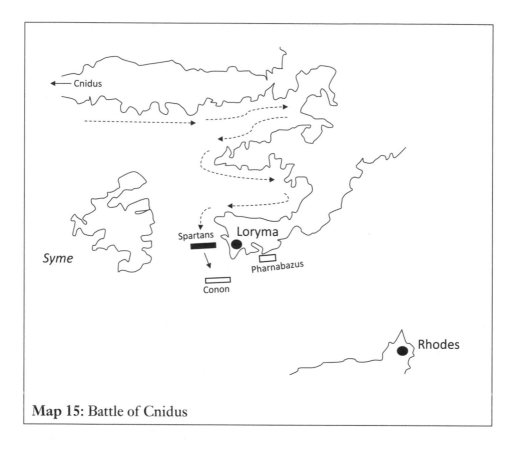

Map 15: Battle of Cnidus

Peisander's victory was there for the taking, but for an unwelcome sight heading toward his left wing. Pharnabazus had finally arrived, and his ships were now in battle formation, bearing down on the wing of Sparta's allies. The mere sight of a battle-ready fleet was enough for many of the allies to flee to land. Even in the face of such desertion, Peisander maintained his offensive by turning his attention towards Pharnabazus. He ploughed his trireme into the closely packed Phoenician ships and fought admirably. But he was too isolated, and the loss of his allies gave Conon time to regroup and re-engage in the battle. Peisander's ship was rammed hard and the *nauarch* died fighting, and with him went the rest of his fleet's will to fight. The battle quickly turned into a rout, and the Spartan fleet was aggressively pursued by Conon back to Cnidus. Conon and Pharnabazus had captured 50 triremes and 500 sailors from the enemy, destroying any chance Sparta had of maintaining its maritime hegemony over the Aegean.

Aftermath

Following Peisander's defeat, the Spartan autonomy over the sea had well and truly ended. While the Spartan hegemony period would continue until their defeat in the land battle at Leuctra in 471 BC, the later Greek historian Polybius considered the defeat at Cnidus to be the end of Sparta's period of power.[15]

The loss at Cnidus was so catastrophic for the Spartans, and so damaging to the morale of the Spartan allies, that Agesilaus actually hid the outcome from his men. When the messenger gave him notice of the defeat he asked that the message be given to his men that the Spartans had been victorious, but that Peisander had been valiantly killed. On the one hand, Agesilaus was controlling the morale of his men, like any good general, and censoring the information being given to them during a long march home. On the other hand, the Spartans were concerned that the revolt against them might gain traction if news arrived of such a military defeat. As it was, Agesiluas marched his army south into Boeotia and fought a large allied force of Greeks at Coronea in the same year, 394 BC. The Spartan king won the day but the war, known as the Corinthian War, would last for a further seven years.

For Conon, his victory brought with it a greater freedom to expand his influence in the Aegean. After touring many of the Spartan-controlled Greek cities in Ionia and the Aegean islands, bringing them over to his cause, he sailed his ship into the Piraeus of Athens. Conon rebuilt the fortifications of the city and its Long Walls; in doing so, he placed the Athenians into a position of strength once again.

Conclusion

The history of ancient Greek naval warfare is still much understudied. And yet, it was the phenomenon of the fleet which was the beating heart of Greek resistance to Persian aggression, which was the foundation of Athenian expansionism, and which was the ultimate cause of the Athenian defeat. Similarly it was the fleet which enabled many of the great land campaigns by which Greek warfare is most often characterized.

Much like Greek land warfare, naval battles were anything but static in their tactics and in their ingenuity. From the very first battle at Lade, it is clear that the Greeks were learning and honing the craft of naval warfare – in which they would excel for nearly a century. The Athenians were the first to truly depart from the status quo of trireme battle. They modified their designs early, gaining an advantage of speed and agility. The Corinthians soon adapted to this, not by changing how they fought, but by maximizing the power of their ships and the sophistication and efficiency of their tactics. In so doing, the Corinthians became capable of properly neutralizing the Athenian advantage. Heavier ships, reinforced to withstand head-on ramming, allowed the Corinthians to continue their direct style of combat, a style of combat to which the Athenians had no reply. This model was soon taken up by Corinth's allies and Athens was no longer the indomitable force it once was. However, not to be outdone, the Athenians adapted tactically and were able to neutralize the power and momentum of the Peloponnesian ships through deeper battle lines and clever tactics.

Naval tactics were varied during this period. The so-called 'old-fashioned' tactic of turning a sea battle into a land battle on the decks was always an option. It was efficient in its approach, utilizing the specialism of the marines that manned each of the triremes. The Corinthians and the Syracusans were the best at it, proving themselves capable of improving upon it with new ship designs and the use of smaller ships to aid the triremes by throwing missiles.

Tactics focussed more on mobility were perfected by the Athenians, but present throughout all Greek navies. The *diekplous* can be seen as early as Artemisium, and the *periplous* is explicitly described at the battle for the Corinthian Gulf. Defensive tactics are also varied, with the *kuklos* being the most prevalent within these battles. Yet the *kuklos* itself had a few different forms. The one formed at Artemisium was used as a basis for a counterattack in which the triremes struck out in all directions. The one formed in the Corinthian Gulf made the mistake of remaining static, hoping to hold out indefinitely, but instead succumbed to a modified *periplous*; while the one at Corcyra was used to stall an Athenian advance long enough for reinforcements to arrive and for the *kuklos* to then unfurl itself.

The battles also bear witness to the various strategies available to commanders, with many fleets feigning a retreat or a course to entice the enemy to attack without due consideration. Conversely, we have seen instances where this failed and ships have been left overly exposed to the counterattack. Battles such as Salamis and Erineus show how aware commanders were of the importance of geography in battle. And Phormio showed in the Battle of the Corinthian Gulf how valuable local weather knowledge could be to tactical decision making.

Tactics and strategy were, undoubtedly, influenced by the individual commanders. However, it is interesting that, unlike land battle which saw many a great commander, naval warfare only generates one or two names worthy of mention. Phormio was, understandably, renowned in Athens as possibly the greatest admiral they ever had. He is a shining example of what a naval commander was capable of doing, even with the limited technology available to him. It is interesting to note, however, that he never took command of a large fleet in battle. Perhaps the small compact fleets under his command were easier for him to control, using flag signals and chants for communication, giving him the ability to react to changes in battle faster than a commander of a larger fleet. Yet, Phormio aside, many of the naval commanders are fleeting in their appearances not because of a great drop in standards, but perhaps evidencing an acceptance of a universal competence throughout the rank. The instances in which this is not the case are, predominantly, when the Spartans are involved. Although the Spartans were not known for their naval prowess, men such as Gylippus and Lysander showed themselves to be very capable. However, the Spartan system of assigning a *nauarch* almost like a political reward, without much consideration for merit or experience, often left the Peloponnesian fleet unable to capitalize on progress that was being made during the Peloponnesian War. This was rectified at times, by the appointment of an experienced second-in-command or advisors, such as Brasidas and Lysander. But if Sparta had been able to maintain a level of consistency in its commanders, one wonders how much more they could have achieved.

The importance of the navy for activities on the land cannot be overstated. In one way, it was its vital role as a support mechanism for the land forces they were following, such as the fleets at Artemisium and Catane. But, perhaps more interestingly, the navy would often be used in conjunction with land forces in joint-force operations. During the siege of Syracuse, Gylippus repeatedly used the two in tandem, mimicking the Athenian commander Nicias, who used his land troops to distract the enemy enough so that his fleet could take the Great Harbour without detection. Similarly, at Aegospotami, Lysander lands a pre-selected land force to work simultaneously with his fleet to exploit the poor situation the Athenians were in, to devastating effect.

The fourth century BC saw a definite turn in the tide, even if it did not result in any overt destruction of Greek independence. The victory at Cnidus revealed a crack in Greek politics that would persist indefinitely. The Greeks could be split apart and turned on one another, and they would then look for a strong ally to assist them. It worked for Persia, and it would work again in the latter half of the century for Philip II of Macedon. But this is to place too much emphasis on the Greek side of the Mediterranean. Over in the west, Syracuse would continue its rise in power, only to be subdued by an even greater power in Carthage. Interestingly, the new quinqueremes were not really utilized by the Greeks, raising the question of whether they did not appreciate the breakthrough that had occurred, or was it that they just could not capitalize on it? To man a quinquereme took an extraordinary number of men, and to man a fleet of them was simply beyond the capability of the Greek *poleis*. By the time we see quinqueremes being adopted by the Greeks in the 320s BC, Greece was under the control of Macedon, and a naval arms race was under way throughout the Mediterranean, in the next century producing ships of mammoth proportions, with twice the capacity for rowers and marines. While the quinqueremes would become the dominant ship of the sea, the Greeks were no longer able to stay at the cutting edge of naval innovation.

Endnotes

Introduction

1. Plato, *Laws* 4.706c.

Chapter 1: The Battle of Lade (494 BC)

1. Tyrant, in its modern usage, is tainted with negative connotations, but to the ancient Greeks it simply denoted a single ruler who achieved authority without any due process. It did not stand that a tyrant was automatically a bad person, nor that his rule was violent or oppressive.
2. For an interesting take on the Ionian situation under Persian rule see P George, 'Persian Ionia under Darius: The Revolt Reconsidered', *Historia*, 49:1, (2000), pp1-39.
3. As will be revealed, Aristagoras was not the official tyrant of Miletus, but it was the capacity within which he acted so it is the title that I have chosen to give him.
4. Herodotus does not actually use the term hoplite in the narrative but instead describes 8,000 armed with shields (*aspides*). The term 'long boats' has been maintained, although warship is a more common translation, because it emphasises the point that these were not described as triremes.
5. Darius was always fond of Histiaeus, but would always naturally give preference to the word of a fellow Persian. A Keaveney, 'The Attack on Naxos: a "Forgotten Cause" of the Ionian Revolt', *The Classical Quarterly*, 38:1(1988), pp 77-9.
6. Guest-friendship (*xenia*) was a ritualized friendship between powerful men, or cities. It secured certain privileges, hospitality and, in this case, assistance, between the two parties.
7. The lack of reasoning behind Artaphernes' figure has led some scholars to speculate on it. Wallinga argues that 100 triremes were more than enough to take Naxos, so he argues that Artaphernes intended to immediately expand from

the island, or conversely that he was afraid of Ionian interference. Ultimately, we do not know, and the idea of Ionian interference in the expedition is purely theoretical because we do not know how much of the fleet consisted of Ionians; Wallinga is assuming that the Ionians would man 100 vessels, which may have been the case, but may in part contradict Aristagoras point that he would turn to Artaphernes because of his large army and many ships (Herodotus, *Histories*, V.30.4). H T Wallinga, 'The Ionian Revolt', *Mnemosyne*, 37:3/4 (1984), pp 427-9.

8. Herodotus switches his terminology from 'ships' to specifically 'triremes' once Artaphernes gets permission from Darius.

9. Keaveney argues that an underlying Persian disdain for the Greeks may also play an important role in Megabates' reaction during this episode: A Keaveney, 'The Attack on Naxos: a "Forgotten Cause" of the Ionian Revolt', *The Classical Quarterly*, 38:1(1988), pp 80-1.

10. This entire element of the narrative which Herodotus (V. 33) gives us is generally disputed by historians. It seems unlikely that a Persian commander would sabotage his own mission because the blame would fall upon him. However, there is no counter narrative from another source to challenge Herodotus' own, so that is the one I have followed. For an overview of the debate and a few of the opposing views in scholarship see D Fink, *The Battle of Marathon in Scholarship: Research, Theories and Controversies since 1850* (Jefferson, 2014), pp 83-5.

11. Another reason to question this element of Herodotus' story is that the travel between Chios and Naxos would have been quite short – definitely not long enough for a completely unprepared island to get ready for a siege.

12. Histiaeus did not know of Aristagoras' own plans. He wanted the revolt so that Darius may be forced to send Histiaeus to quell an uprising, thus freeing him from his luxurious imprisonment in Susa.

13. Hecataeus of Miletus was a literary predecessor to Herodotus. He wrote many works which have since been lost, one of which was on the geography of the ancient world that Herodotus drew much of his own information from. His role in this debate, as the voice of reason, whether true or not, is a sign of Herodotus' admiration for the man. S West, 'Herodotus Portrait of Hecataeus', *The Journal of Hellenic Studies*, 111 (1991), pp 155-7.

14. Once again, Herodotus does not use the term for trireme here but the more general terms for ships.

15. This episode in Herodotus is an interesting one because it raises many questions: were the Persians weak in Europe, and is that why the Paeonians were able to march such a long distance home? Why were the Paeonians sent home in the first place, what possible benefit was there to the cause of Miletus? And many more besides. For a recent attempt at answering some of these riddles see M I Vasilev, *The Policy of Darius and Xerxes towards Thrace and Macedonia* (Leiden, 2015), pp 127-30.

16. Eretria definitely sent triremes, and the research by van Wees suggests that this was a contingent of a publically funded trireme fleet. As an aside, this is the earliest source we have for a trireme force outside of the Persian sphere of influence. Hans van Wees, *Ships and Silver, Taxes and Tribute: A Fiscal History of Archaic Athens* (London, 2013), p 36; also 'Those Who Sail are to Receive a Wage: Naval Warfare and Finance in Archaic Erteria', in Garrett Fagan and Matthew Trundle (eds), *New Perspectives on Ancient Warfare* (Leiden, 2010), p 218.

17. The important temple of Cybele, mother of Phyrgian and Lydian gods, was burned to the ground. This event was later used by the Persians as a pretext for burning Greek temples.

18. Herodotus is very clear that these were all triremes. However, it cannot be assumed that these were uniform in build because we know, for instance, that the Chian triremes held forty marines (VI.15.1), which would have needed a wider and sturdier ship which was less adept at ramming (see below).

19. Frustratingly, 600 ships appears to have been a stock phrase of Herodotus to describe a large fleet from Persia, whose actual numbers were unknown to him. He uses the exact same number of ships in his description of the earlier Persian invasion of Scythia (IV.87.1), and again in the later campaign of Marathon (VI.95.2). C Hignett, *Xerxes' Invasion of Greece* (Oxford, 1963), p 348; D Fink, *The Battle of Marathon in Scholarship: Research, Theories and Controversies since 1850* (Jefferson, 2014), pp 97; cf J S Morrison, J F Coates and N B Rankov, *The Athenian Trireme: The History and Reconstruction of an Ancient Greek Warship*, 2nd ed, (Cambridge, 2000), p 44, note 17.

20. This follows the model by Lazenby who convincingly argues the case that the line-ahead formation was used when a fleet was on the move, but was very rarely used as a fighting formation, citing only a tiny handful of exceptions to the contrary. J Lazenby, 'The Diekplous', *Greece & Rome*, 34:2 (1987), pp 170-72.

21. J Lazenby, 'The Diekplous', *Greece & Rome*, 34:2 (1987), p 172.
22. The Greeks, like most ancient navies, did not fight with the aid of their sails; they were solely powered by the oars.
23. These eleven were awarded a pillar in the agora of Samos with their names, and their fathers' names, inscribed upon it. It was proclaimed that these were the bravest and most valiant of men in Samos (Herodotus, VI.14.3).
24. We have no information about the Milesian contingent. It cannot be assumed that they stayed to fight the battle, but on the same token they had the most to fight for so may well have fought to the bitter end.
25. The *Thesmophoria* was an all-female ritual conducted at night in honour of Demeter.

Chapter 2: The Battle of Artemisium (480 BC)

1. Xerxes was not the customary eldest son and heir to the king but he managed to convince Darius that he was the right choice due to his status as the first born after Darius himself had taken the throne – thus making him the first son of the king (Herodotus, *Histories*, VII.3.1-4). In Xerxes' commissioned inscription found at Persepolis he claimed that Darius 'made me the greatest after himself' (XPf §4), but Herodotus describes Xerxes actually taking his case to his father and convincing him, with the aid of the Spartan Demaratus.
2. The revolts in Babylonia are not attested in Herodotus at all. There is a clear reference to some sort of revolt in Ctesias (fr 26), and there is some evidence to be drawn from a few Babylonian economic documents which name two short-lived kingships in Babylon. There is a debate surrounding the dating of the revolt(s) but I have aligned this narrative with the work of Kurht who convincingly argues for a date of 484 BC. For a brief, accessible, summary of the debate, and further references, see A Kurht, *The Persian Empire: A Corpus of Sources from the Achaemenid Period* (New York, 2010), p 248-9, especially note 4. See also M Dandamaev, *A Political History of the Achaemenid Empire* (Leiden, 1989), p 183; M. Waters, *Ancient Persia: a Concise History of the Achaemenid Empire, 550-330 BCE* (Cambridge, 2014), pp 116-7.
3. A new king needed to receive his crown from the hands of Marduk at the New Year festival. Xerxes had already been through this ceremony himself and, by removing it from the city, he was ultimately destroying any Babylonian's claim to kingship.

4. Xerxes was petitioned by a powerful family from Thessaly, and exiles from Athens (Herodotus, VII.6.2-4), both pledging their support to an invasion by the king.

5. The king had been advised by the experienced *satrap* Mardonius to prioritize the troubles in Egypt before continuing Darius' plans to invade Greece (Herodotus, VII.5.2). For the Athenian involvement in the Ionian revolt see Chapter 1.

6. Retribution is unlikely to have been the sole, or even the main, motivating factor behind Xerxes' plans. While this notion of power and retribution does fit into Persian royal ideology, and is likely to have been an important factor that he himself may have emphasized, the invasion does fit within the larger Persian expansion that had been occurring under Darius. In other words, the invasion was a logical step for the Persian ruler as he looked to expand his borders and increase his power. M Waters, *Ancient Persia: a Concise History of the Achaemenid Empire, 550-330 BCE* (Cambridge, 2014), p 121.

7. While no specific types of food are offered by Herodotus, the advanced time scale implies that this would be predominantly preserved foods such as salted fish and meat. The later historian Xenophon describes the characteristics of ideal meat for soldiers to consume: 'For meats, we must pack up and take along only such as are sharp, pungent, salty; for these not only stimulate the appetite but also afford the most lasting nourishment'. (*Cyropaedia*, VI.2.31)

8. These losses were incurred under the command of Xerxes' aide and advisor Mardonius, so it is likely that the dangers of the region were in some part raised by the experienced *satrap*. For the loss of the fleet see Herodotus (VI.44)

9. This was a project that Herodotus derided as unnecessary and just a show of power (*Histories*, 7.24). However, his own idea that the ships called have been simply beached and dragged across the peninsula shows the only alternative available to Xerxes. With time on the king's side, and the manpower to achieve it, why would Xerxes not want to take a pragmatic approach and build the canal? Herodotus' view prevailed, however, and the canal became part of an ancient literary construct to portray arrogance and ostentation. E Bridges, *Imagining Xerxes: Ancient Perspectives on a Persian King* (London, 2014), pp 52, 173.

10. The Royal Road was a vast highway which connected the two major cities of Susa, to the east of Babylonia, and Sardis on the west coast of Asia Minor. For a full, yet controversial, description see Herodotus (*Histories*, V.52-53).

11. Athens cast the Persian herald into a pit to collect his earth, while the Spartans threw their herald down a well to collect his water. (Herodotus, VII.133.1).

12. This astronomical number should be taken with a large pinch of salt. We know that it is a highly suspicious set of figures, the number of triremes is seven more than the fleet which was taken to Troy in Homer's *Iliad*; however, any refinement of the figure by historians is based upon little more than supposition and guess work. Cf H T Wallinga, *Xerxes' Greek Adventure: A Naval Perspective* (Leiden, 2005), pp 32–46.

13. Herodotus (VII.132) gives the (most likely highly edited) list which includes two very important regions: Thessaly, the Greek lands that Xerxes would march through next; and Thebes which was a major Greek power that held great sway in Boeotia and, therefore, central Greece.

14. This occurred before Xerxes had even left Sardis (Herodotus, VII.146).

15. Such a large increase in the Athenian naval capacity, from having no triremes to send to Ionia in 491 BC to 200 by the end of the 480s, was only possible due to the newly established silver mines in Laureion, southern Attica.

16. See Herodotus (VII.148-171) for a breakdown of various Greek contingents, their responses to the Persian threat and the attempts to unify a Greek response. These include powerful Hellenic *poleis* such as Argos and Syracuse.

17. Herodotus (VII.173.4) claims this is the main reason that the Greeks retired from their position, not because of the Persian weight of numbers. Which of these is true is contentious, Herodotus may be adding a strong element of hindsight because Xerxes did in fact take the second pass and not travel through Tempe.

18. Artemisium describes the cape on the northernmost point of the island, and the temple of Artemis which is found on land in that same area.

19. Herodotus, VII.89.1-99.3. See note 12. The extra 120 triremes can be found in VII.185.1.

20. J S Morrison, J F Coates and N B Rankov, *The Athenian Trireme: The History and Reconstruction of an Ancient Greek Warship*, 2nd ed (Cambridge, 2000), p 51.

21. It may also be due to the land army also being led by a Spartan, Leonidas.

22. Herodotus VIII.42.2. The notion that Themistocles adapted the design to result in faster, more agile, triremes comes from a possible tradition preserved in Plutarch, *Life of Cimon*, 12.2.

23. A talent was a unit of weight equal to 60 minae or 6,000 drachmae, an astronomical amount of money.

24. Although Plutarch relates this story, via Herodotus, in his *Life of Themistocles*, 7.4-5, he elsewhere attacks Herodotus for this version of events, describing it as malicious and untrue (*On the Malice of Herodotus*, 34). As he offers no alternative, and his reasoning is based simply on Hellenic pride, Herodotus' intrigue has been maintained in this narrative.

25. We are told by Herodotus (VIII.13) that this storm resulted in the Persian fleet being roughly equal in strength to the Greeks.

26. The battle was fought within such a narrow space that one source compared the fighting to that experienced at Thermopylae, which was fought in a very narrow passage along the coast. Diodorus, XI.13.2.

Chapter 3: The Battle of Salamis (480 BC)

1. The exact dates for the battles of Thermopylae and Artemisium (which were fought over the same three-day period) are contested, due in part to Herodotus' honest use of language when he does not know the exact time frames involved (using phrases equivalent to 'a few days', 'a long time', etc). Some scholars place them at the end of June, others at the end of August. For the evidence that is available start with K Sacks, 'Herodotus and the Dating of the Battle of Thermopylae', *The Classical Quarterly*, 26:2 (1976), pp 232-48.

2. For the controversy behind Herodotus' numbers for the buried Persians see J Lazenby, *The Defence of Greece, 490-479 B.C.* (Warminster, 1993), p 148.

3. Herodotus (VIII. 36-39) gives a detailed account of what his sources told him, but he marks his narrative with a hint of scepticism as to the tale's veracity. It has since been argued that this story may have been an invention, either by or with the full support of the Delphians, to give Delphi an active and heroic role in the Persian Wars. M Scott, *Delphi: A History of the Centre of the Ancient World* (Princeton, 2014), p 116, referencing: H Bowden, *Classical Athens and the Delphic Oracle: Divination and Democracy* (Cambridge, 2005), p 35.

4. Herodotus VIII.41.2, referring to the two oracles given at VII.140-141. See R Sealey, 'Again the Siege of the Acropolis, 480 B.C.', *California Studies in Classical Antiquity*, 5 (1972), pp 185-6.

5. Plutarch, *Life of Themistocles*, 10.1.

6. The garrison is not mentioned by Herodotus (VIII.51.2), who only mentions the treasurers and an unnumbered group of indignant people who did not believe in the power of the fleet, and those too poor, or infirm, to leave

(whatever that may mean). The placement of the garrison here follows the argument made by J B Bury, 'Aristides at Salamis', *Classical Review*, 10 (1896), pp 414–18, and defended by R Sealey, 'Again the Siege of the Acropolis, 480 B C', *California Studies in Classical Antiquity*, 5 (1972), pp 187–94. For a more traditional account of the siege, which argues for the defensive strength of the Acropolis allowing a misfit group of several hundred men to hold the Persian army at bay, see B. Strauss, *Salamis: The Greatest Naval Battle of the Ancient World, 480 B.C.* (London, 2005), pp 85–7; 'Flames over Athens', *Arion: A Journal of Humanities and the Classics*, 12:1 (2004), pp 113–15.

7. Herodotus (VIII.53.1) claims that the Persians found a path that took them up the back of the Acropolis, which may well be true. But the story is quite similar in form to the sudden discovery of the path at Thermopylae which allowed them to win the day there (VII.213–214). This raises a question as to whether the Persians were not thorough in their reconnaissance, which is unlikely for such a powerful and successful armed force, or that Herodotus is choosing to portray them as such – the narrative here follows the latter.

8. Herodotus (VIII.68α.1–68γ) also claims that Artemisia argued that the Persian fleet would be mauled in a battle, and that the Greek fleet was superior. This is suspect to say the least, as the Phoenicians were considered to have the greatest ships and sailors, and Themistocles himself conceded that the Greek ships were too heavy, too slow, and too few to beat the Persians in a fair battle (VIII.60α).

9. Herodotus, VIII.66.1–2.

10. Aeschylus, *Persians*, 341–43.

11. Pausanias, I.36.2.

12. Aeschylus, *Persians*, 338–40. J Lazenby, 'Aischylos and Salamis', *Hermes*, 116:2 (1988), pp 168–169.

13. Ctesias, *Persica*, fr.30.

14. For this supposition in full see the demonstrably cautious approach by J Lazenby, 'Aischylos and Salamis', *Hermes*, 116:2 (1988), pp 168–9. Another suggestion has been offered by Hammond that these seventy ships may account for the mysterious role of the Corinthian ships, but he is forced to acknowledge that Herodotus' tells us that Corinth supplied the same number of ships at Salamis as they did at Artemisium, forty. Hammond's subsequent attempt to fill out the numbers with Spartan ships is clever but unconvincing: N G L

Hammond, 'The Battle of Salamis', *The Journal of Hellenic Studies*, 76 (1956), p 40 & 49, note 66.

15. Ctesias, *Persica*, fr 30.

16. Diodorus, XI.17.2. Cf Strauss who does not believe Diodorus' statement and places the Egyptians within the main Persian battle line; B Strauss, *Salamis: The Greatest Naval Battle of the Ancient World, 480 B.C.* (London, 2005), pp 161-2. I have sided with Diodorus because Aeschylus (*Persians*, 366) similarly describes only three out of the four contingents of the Persian fleet being in the main battle, meaning that one major 'ethnic group' was missing for this mission, as per N G L Hammond, 'The Battle of Salamis', *The Journal of Hellenic Studies*, 76 (1956), p 44. Also, Strauss' observation that Egyptian casualties are accounted for in the sources does not negate their position on the other side of the island; it just raises the question as to who they were fighting.

17. There is a later tradition that Xerxes picked a spot and sat on a throne, overlooking the battle. However, this implies that Xerxes already knew where the battle would take pace, which is unlikely. The myth has been succinctly ridiculed in F Frost, 'A Note on Xerxes at Salamis', *Historia: Zeitschrift für Alte Geschichte*, 22:1 (1973), pp 118-19.

18. Plutarch, *Life of Themistocles*, 13.2. Plutarch relates this story as he read it in the otherwise-unknown work of Phanias of Lesbos, who was a disciple of Aristotle. On the surface of it, this story of human sacrifice is fanciful, but Plutarch stresses the reliability of Phanias as a historical source (13.3); so it is at least possible that there was a tradition of this sacrifice which Phanias may have heard or read himself and then relayed. Possible, but unlikely. Either way it is interesting enough to warrant discussion and, therefore, inclusion here.

19. The role of the Corinthians in the battle is one of the great puzzles of Salamis. Herodotus (VIII.94.1-4) records an Athenian tale that the Corinthians fled north and only returned when most of the fighting had ended, but the historian himself is suspicious of this and qualifies it by saying that no other *polis* agrees with this version. Plutarch offers numerous epigraphs and testimony that show the Corinthians to have had a very active role in the battle, so I have followed Labarbe's argument that they most likely fought the Egyptians to the north, as opposed to Hammond who speculates that they may have joined the battle from their position in the north. J Labarbe, 'Chiffres et modes de répartition de la flotte grecque à l'Artémision et à Salamine', *Bulletin de correspondance*

hellénique, 76:1 (1952), pp 433-4; cf N G L Hammond, 'The Battle of Salamis', *The Journal of Hellenic Studies*, 76 (1956), p 49 and note 66. See also Strauss who presents the Corinthian movements north as a clever feign to encourage the Persians to advance at the sight of them fleeing, B Strauss, *Salamis: The Greatest Naval Battle of the Ancient World, 480 B.C.* (London, 2005), pp 244-7.

20. The main Persian advantage was that each of their ships carried more marines than their Greek counterparts. N G L Hammond, 'The Battle of Salamis', *The Journal of Hellenic Studies*, 76 (1956), p 48 referencing: Herodotus, VIII.90.2; Plutarch, *Life of Themistocles*, 14.

21. The fighting on Psyttaleia is mentioned in passing by Herodotus (VIII.95), but a graphic account is given by Aeschylus (*Persians*, 447-71) who did fight at the battle, but not necessarily on the island.

Chapter 4: The Battle of Sybota (433 BC)

1. The main concern that would plague Sparta for the remaining classical period was the large population of Helots, a serf nation of sorts, who were responsible for the farming of Spartan lands, freeing the Spartan citizens to become what is often described as a professional army, or perhaps more accurately to become what Ducat describes as almost professional citizens. J Ducat, 'La société spartiate et la guerre', in F Prost (ed) *Armées et Sociétés de la Grèce classique: Aspects sociaux et politiques de la guerre aux Ve et Ive s. av. J.-C.* (Paris, 1999), p 44.

2. A siege is not described by Thucydides, but is so by Diodorus (XII.30.3). The presence of a siege is perfectly plausible, and gives greater credence to Thucydides' report that the Epidamnians were concerned about perishing – which is not something we would expect to occur due to plundering raids, but is a distinct likelihood in the aftermath of a failed siege defence.

3. One of the great mysteries surrounding the outbreak of the Peloponnesian War is why did the Corcyraeans refuse the plea for help? Thucydides (I.26.3) does later state that the exiles had also made contact with Corcyra; so I have inserted the episode where I think it makes the best chronological sense. It has also been argued that the exiles came after the Epidamnians, and Corcyra accepted their plea as a reaction to later events, but this then reopens the question of why did the Epidamnians get refused in the first place? N McKenzie (unpublished MA thesis), *Thucydides' Corinthians: an examination of Corinth in Thucydides'*

account of the outbreak of the Peloponnesian War (University of Otago, New Zealand: 2010), p 8, note 5; H-P Stahl, 'Narrative Unity and Consistency of Thought: Composition of Event Sequences in Thucydides', in A Rengakos and A Tsakmakis (eds), *Brill's Companion to Thucydides* (Leiden: 2006), p 303-4.

4. E F Bloedow, 'Athens' Treaty with Corcyra: a Study in Athenian Foreign Policy', *Athenaeum*, 79 (1991), pp 193-4.

5. Thucydides makes a big point of describing the Corinthians as being afraid to go to sea, in fear of the 'superior' naval force of Corcyra (I.26.2, 1.27.1), however this does not seem to be the most plausible explanation. For Thucydides' inherent bias against Corinth, and Corinthian naval power in particular, see N McKenzie and P Hannah, 'Thucydides' Take on the Corinthian Navy. Οἵ τε γὰρ Κορίνθιοι ἡγήσαντο κρατεῖν εἰ μὴ καὶ πολὺ ἐκρατοῦντο, "The Corinthians believed they were victors if they were only just defeated"', *Mnemosyne*, 66 (2013), pp 206-27. McKenzie and Hannah's article is a strong influence in the reconstructions of all Corinthian naval battles within this book.

6. As noted by Gomme, Sparta's decision to support Corcyra in this case is not expressly given. Maybe it reflects Spartan concerns that the fighting could escalate into a war they were trying hard to avoid. A W Gomme. *A Historical Commentary on Thucydides: Volume I, Introduction and Commentary on Book I* (Oxford, 1945), p 162.

7. Corcyra had an entire fleet 120 strong, but 40 of these triremes were still involved in the siege at Epidamnus. Cf J S Morrison, J F Coates and N B Rankov, *The Athenian Trireme: The History and Reconstruction of an Ancient Greek Warship*, 2nd ed. (Cambridge, 2000), p 63.

8. For the Corcyraeans being overtaken as the second greatest navy by Corinth, and this as a possible explanation for Thucydides' (Athenian) animosity towards the Corinthian navy see N McKenzie and P Hannah, 'Thucydides' Take on the Corinthian Navy. Οἵ τε γὰρ Κορίνθιοι ἡγήσαντο κρατεῖν εἰ μὴ καὶ πολὺ ἐκρατοῦντο, "The Corinthians believed they were victors if they were only just defeated"', *Mnemosyne*, 66 (2013), p. 222.

9. An adopted principle that Thucydides (I.32.5) has them observe, in their pleas, to be the consequence of an error of judgement.

10. The Greek *poleis* were often at great pains to emphasize that they were not the cause of war – Corinth's own appeal to Athens is a good example of this (Thucydides, I-37-39). Regularly, war meant the breaking of sanctified treaties

and therefore, in effect, a sacrilegious act. For a military culture that expended so much energy trying to win the favour of the gods, it was vital that the gods were not insulted from the very beginning.

11. As Hammond speculates, the Corcyraeans could not have been pleased with this outcome. It was a poor commitment by Athens that left Corcyra open to Corithinian intervention by other means. Specifically the presence of the Corinthian fleet could incite a possible uprising on the island, as it was as factional as many Greek *poleis*, or more simply it would allow the Corinthians to manoeuvre around Corcyra and choose an area for battle more advantageous to themselves. N G L Hammond, 'Naval Operations in the South Channel of Corcyra 435-433 B. C.', *The Journal of Hellenic Studies*, 65 (1945), p 31.

12. The predominance of slave rowers is a fair supposition made by Hammond, based upon the ratio of slaves to freemen given in the figures of prisoners after the battle. N G L Hammond, 'Naval Operations in the South Channel of Corcyra 435-433 B.C.', *The Journal of Hellenic Studies*, 65 (1945), p 32.

13. Thucydides, I.49.1. For evidence that this was an invasion force also note in the coming narrative: the three-day rations held by the soldiers (a normal requirement for a land force, but not expected of marines). Finally, remember that the Athenians were under strict orders not to engage unless the Corinthians were trying to land on Corcyra. N McKenzie and P Hannah, 'Thucydides' Take on the Corinthian Navy. Οἵ τε γὰρ Κορίνθιοι ἡγήσαντο κρατεῖν εἰ μὴ καὶ πολὺ ἐκρατοῦντο, "The Corinthians believed they were victors if they were only just defeated"', *Mnemosyne*, 66 (2013) p. 223; J S Morrison, J F Coates and N B Rankov, *The Athenian Trireme: The History and Reconstruction of an Ancient Greek Warship*, 2nd ed (Cambridge, 2000), p 67-8; N G L Hammond, 'Naval Operations in the South Channel of Corcyra 435-433 B.C.', *The Journal of Hellenic Studies*, 65 (1945), p 33.

14. The timings involved are estimates given by Hammond who had a personal and in depth knowledge of the area's (modern) geography. N G L Hammond, 'Naval Operations in the South Channel of Corcyra 435-433 B.C.', *The Journal of Hellenic Studies*, 65 (1945), p 32.

15. See note 13. For the three-day provisions as a normal feature of hoplite service see, for example, Aristophanes, *Acharnians*, 197.

16. Thucydides (I.49) was grossly unfair in his assessment of Corinthian tactics as old-fashioned and 'not remarkable for its science'. This was not an old-fashioned

style of battle but an invasion that was blocked, something the Corinthians had prepared for and had adapted the (now-established) method of fighting at sea.

17. The arrival of these twenty new ships has caused much confusion for historians, as we are not told when they were sent. Were they part of the original agreement, but Thucydides neglected to tell us for some reason? Were they the result of a reconsideration in Athens, as Thucydides (I.50.5) claims rather abruptly? Hornblower may be right in his claim of a third assembly that has not been mentioned by Thucydides. S Hornblower, *A Commentary on Thucydides: Volume I Books I-III* (Oxford, 1991) p 90, 94. For an interesting analysis of this episode arguing that Thucydides is purposefully building tension for added drama see N McKenzie (unpublished MA thesis), *Thucydides' Corinthians: an examination of Corinth in Thucydides' account of the outbreak of the Peloponnesian War* (University of Otago, New Zealand: 2010), pp 31-3.

18. It could have been similar to the shock that resonated after the Spartans famously surrendered on the island of Pylos in 425 BC (eg Thucydides, IV.40.1).

19. Naval protocol copied that of land battles; the victors were those who controlled the battlefield and, therefore, the bodies of the dead.

20. See note 19. The difference between land and sea battles is, of course, that the sea moves dead bodies. So, in this case, the Corcyraeans were aided by a strong wind during the night which beached many of their own dead, giving them control of their bodies and, in essence, holding certain claims to victory.

21. Thuc. I.55.2.

Chapter 5: The Battle of the Corinthian Gulf (429 BC)

1. Thucydides, II.13.3, II.70.2; Diodorus, XII.40.2. This was an astronomical amount of money lost in a very short amount of time. Interestingly, Thucydides' obsession with these costs – he mentions them again at III.17.4 – gives the modern historian an idea of how much a siege cost an attacking army: 6,000 drachmae per day (approximately 1 talent).

2. For Pericles' strategy of sea-borne raids, and Pericles' emphasis on naval power combined with financial strength, see especially H D Westlake, 'Seaborne Raids in Periclean Strategy', *The Classical Quarterly*, 39: ¾, (1945), pp 75-84.

3. For the relocation of helots to Naupactus see Thucydides I.103.1-3, and for Naupactus' resulting commitment to Athens see especially Pausanias, IV.25.

4. The prospect for success with this plan, as outlined by Thucydides, is debated by historians. How realistic it was to expect such an impact within the region by the capturing of Acarnania is hard to establish; however, there is no reason to suspect that the Spartans had been purposefully lied to by their allies. It is possible that the Ambracians, living on the periphery of the Greek mainland, did not have a firm grasp on the entire military situation this early in the war, and truly believed that Spartan intervention was enough to win dominance in the entire northwestern sphere. D Kagan, *Archidamian War*, (New York: 1974) p 107; cf J B Salmon, *Wealthy Corinth: a History of the City to 338 B.C.* (Oxford: 1984).

5. Thucydides does not actually state where Cnemus landed, and my placement in the Ambracian gulf contradicts my preferred translation of the text (Strassler) which claims he disembarked in the Corinthian gulf. However, Cnemus' subsequent march only makes sense if he is marching from the northern gulf in a southward direction as opposed to marching from the southern gulf, northward. It is also relevant to note that all of his named allies that had joined him live north of the Corinthian gulf, further suggesting a northern starting point.

6. Patrae is the most common name given by historians to the first battle, but Diodorus (XII.48.1) describes it as taking place off the coast by Rhium (on the opposite side of the gulf), which is also where the trophy was set up after the victory. Ultimately this is the difficulty of naming battles that occur at sea, and either name is perfectly valid.

7. The experience of the Corinthian commanders is implied by the fact that Thucydides chooses to name them. In addition to this, Corinth had been an experienced naval power longer than Athens (see introduction); to assume anything other than that the Corinthians utilized experienced naval commanders belies an anti-Corinthian bias that seemingly stems from Thucydides himself. N McKenzie & P Hannah, 'Thucydides' Take on the Corinthian Navy. Οἵ τε γὰρ Κορίνθιοι ἡγήσαντο κρατεῖν εἰ μὴ καὶ πολὺ ἐκρατοῦντο, "The Corinthians believed they were victors if they were only just defeated"', *Mnemosyne*, 66 (2013), pp 210-11.

8. There is a strong historical tradition that has Phormio plan all of the events in this battle, and the change in weather was part of these plans. The tradition, stemming from Thucydides, is so strong that Hornblower postulates that

Phormio may well have been a primary source for Thucydides' narrative, while one modern historian has gone a step further and claimed that Thucydides (by way of Phormio?) converted Athenian *responses* to events into purposeful *causes*. The reasoning behind this is that Thucydides is emphasizing his own prejudiced belief that the Corinthians were inexperienced and poor sailors – which we know was not true. Hornblower, *A Commentary on Thucydides, 1: Books I–III* (Oxford: 1991) p 365; Hunter, *Thucydides: The Artful Reporter* (Toronto: 1973), p 45; N McKenzie and P Hannah 'Thucydides' Take on the Corinthian Navy. Οἵ τε γὰρ Κορίνθιοι ἡγήσαντο κρατεῖν εἰ μὴ καὶ πολὺ ἐκρατοῦντο, "The Corinthians believed they were victors if they were only just defeated"', *Mnemosyne*, 66 (2013), p 210.

9. This 'seaport' is often translated as 'arsenal', which is a less literal translation of the Greek, but perhaps more informative about the nature of this specific port. The term only appears twice in Thucydides, both times in reference to the port at Cyllene, and in both situations it appears to have been a point from which ships of war departed for active duty. This makes it likely that the rendezvous was not merely one of convenience but one chosen to optimize the fighting capabilities of the Peloponnesian fleet, a port experienced in preparing ships for battle.

10. The exact role of these advisors is not entirely clear. Cnemus still held the office of *nauarch*, and thus held control of the tactical decisions. Sparta did have a precedent within their army of commanders being given advisors to help them in their decision making, so it is likely that their presence was in a similar capacity. Cf M Roberts, *Two Deaths in Amphipolis: Cleon vs Brasidas in the Peloponnesian War* (Barnsley: 2015), pp 61-2.

11. For an incisive analysis on this unfathomable decision to go to Crete first, see D Kagan, *The Archidamian War* (New York: 1974), pp 111-13.

12. This small group of triremes seems to have been a mixed selection from more than one *polis*. We are not told of its actual make up but Thucydides (II.91.2) does tell us that one was from Leucas, and this is only worth telling the reader if they were not all Leucadian.

13. The garrison formed a land force to support the fleet, so that if the ships needed to ground themselves due to being overwhelmed they had greater support to resist by land. The land force would also be responsible for guarding the equipment that was shed from the vessels before battle.

14. It is easy to ignore just how outmanoeuvred the Athenians were in this opening battle, and how Phormio had been tactically defeated. For an example of how overlooked this element of the battle has come to be, see, for instance, the single sentence given by Kagan in the relevant section of his masterpiece on the Peloponnesian War. D Kagan, *The Archidamian War* (New York: 1974), p 114.

Chapter 6: The Battle of Corcyra (427 BC)

1. The position of Lesbos, which was so close to the Hellespont and the grain route which was so vital to Athens, made any Spartan interaction with the island a political quagmire. If Sparta pledged support it not only opposed Athenian authority, but threatened the food supply line to the city and would have forced an immediate and unrestrained response from the Athenians.

2. Thucydides (III.2.1) claims that the Lesbians were rushed into their revolt by the Spartans, but these extensive preparations appear to suggest otherwise. Thucydides seems to be trying to portray the Spartans as bad allies; refusing help initially, and then making unreasonable demands when it suited them.

3. Note again that Thucydides' suggestion that the Lesbians were rushed into revolt does not seem to be the case.

4. Thucydides (III.4.2) again reiterates how the Mytilenians were forced into action early. While it must be acknowledged that they had not expected the Athenians to act this early into the campaign season, they were by no means unprepared, nor did they have reason to believe they would fail in their venture. They were in a strong position at Lesbos, with much of the island on their side (Thucydides, III.4.3), while their allies in Boeotia and Sparta could be called upon for their support if necessary.

5. For the geography of Mytilene and its two harbours see Strabo, *Geography*, XIII.2.2.

6. Sparta was habitually making its allies invade Attica, but to no real end (because the Athenians would not meet them in battle). Morale was particularly hit by the prospect of this expedition because it would be the second one made in the year.

7. The information was a fair estimate of Athenian manpower, especially as the plague had ripped into its population with ruthless efficiency. However, the Athenians always found a way to man their fleet, even in the direst of emergencies.

8. It came at a great cost, however. If Thucydides (III.17.3) is correct in its costings, then a trireme of 200 men would cost 1 talent a month (based on 1 drachma a day per man) to be at sea. Thus 30 triremes would cost 1 talent a day and the fleet of 250 triremes would therefore cost over 8 talents a day. To put it in context, the Athenian treasury at the beginning of the war could afford to have this fleet out at sea for 750 days, just over 2 years (based on Thucydides' assertion that the treasury started the war with 6,000 talents). This seems like a long time, however this would mean no other force could be mustered, or at least paid for. Also it does not take into account that the siege of Potidaea, on its own, cost the treasury around 2,000 talents (Thucydides, II.70.2), so expenses were liable to increase at any given moment.

9. Thucydides (III.16.3) states that the allies of Sparta would supply 40 ships, later on (III.26.1) he declares Alcidas' fleet to be forty-two ships strong when it was sent to Mytilene. There is no error here; logically the Spartans supplied two ships of their own. Diodorus (XII.55.6) gives a similar figure of forty-five ships.

10. The concern of the Spartan here is a little strange, and out of keeping with the portrayal of the Spartan military ethos we normally see. It is possible that Thucydides has omitted information about the siege, namely the number of assaults on the walls and the harbour (Diodorus, XII.55.5), which might explain the otherwise suspect level of concern from an experienced Spartan commander.

11. This interesting point is made by Thucydides without a moment's reflection, frustratingly. He says that the citizens that were armed were more accustomed to light armed equipment. This would mean that they were the poorer citizens of the city who would normally form lightly armed military duties, or possibly man the fleet. Presumably the city's hoplites were already in service defending the walls.

12. For a good account of the civil war on Corcyra see I. Bruce, 'The Corcyraean Civil War of 427 B.C.', *Phoenix*, 25:2 (1971), pp 108-17.

13. While this is conjecture, it is based on the aftermath of the battle in which Brasidas is said to demand an assault on the city of Corcyra (Thucydides, III.79.3), something that would require a large number of fighting men.

14. The Peloponnesians had learned from their experiences in the Corinthian Gulf and knew that the Athenians would eventually break the formation.

The forming of a circle needs some explanation, especially as Brasidas knew from first-hand experience that it was a doomed tactical decision. The reason may lie in the number of marines on the ships, and the main aim of the fleet's expedition. If, as postulated here, the triremes were carrying more marines than the Athenians', then their lack of speed would be a great disadvantage if the Athenians had managed to outflank the Peloponnesian line. Thucydides is seemingly being unfair in his claim that the twenty extra triremes acted on their own volition, out of fear for their main fleet, it seems more probable that this was a planned counter move.

15. This means in real terms that the Corcyraeans lost thirty ships in the battle, either through desertion or from damage incurred. The thirteen ships previously mentioned as being captured were simply that, those which were captured.

16. To harm someone who was a suppliant to an altar was a grievous and impious offence. For a man to die in a temple was similarly sacrilegious, so to actually kill inside these sacred spaces was a disgusting affront to Greek sensibilities and indicative of the complete degradation of order and personal control.

Chapter 7: The Battle of Erineus (413 BC)

1. The departure scene for this expedition is without precedent in the histories. The costs involved, and the size of the crowds, are dwelled on by Thucydides for some time. This was a huge event for the Athenians, as it was the first major military venture since the city had recovered from its great plague of the 420s.

2. For a full account of the Sicilian expedition see Chapter 8. This chapter follows the events in Athens during that same period.

3. Thucydides VI.95.1.

4. Alcibiades was recalled from the Sicilian expedition and sent into exile for impious actions. For more see Chapter 8.

5. Nicias had been struggling with ill-health and, having lost his joint commanders, he felt unable to continue to command effectively.

6. For the importance of this position and the Athenian hold on it see Chapter 5.

7. Sparta had supported the Theban assault on Plataea which not only broke the peace that was in place in Greece at that time (431 BC), but also violated an oath made to protect Plataea after its role in the successful repulse of the Persian invasion 479 BC.

8. Thucydides VI.105.

9. Thucydides overplays Alcibiades' role in the decision to fortify Decelea, something that is copied and elaborated on by authors such as Diodorus (XIII.9.2). The Peloponnesians had originally considered the idea of a fortified point in enemy land back in 431 BC at the outbreak of the Archidamian War (Thuc. I.122.1), and by 422/1 BC had even begun preparations to do so (Thuc. V.17.2) but peace was agreed before this plan was executed. So, if Alcibiades did suggest the fortification of Decelea, perhaps he was at most influential in suggesting a set location rather than responsible for the plan in its entirety. P A Brunt, 'Spartan Policy and Strategy in the Archidamian War', *Phoenix*, Vol 19, No 4 (Winter, 1965), pp 267-9.

10. Thebes, especially, profited from the Athenian slaves and Attic resources more generally. We are also told that, due to the close proximity between Decelea and Thebes, the Thebans took large quantities of timber and house tiles back with them. (*Hell. Oxy.* , XVII.3-4).

11. The terminology used to describe both commanders is identical (*archē*, leader, or commander in a literal sense). So perhaps the simplest answer is the correct one: Conon had served his year-long tour and had been replaced.

12. N McKenzie and P Hannah, 'Thucydides' Take on the Corinthian Navy. Οἵ τε γὰρ Κορίνθιοι ἡγήσαντο κρατεῖν εἰ μὴ καὶ πολὺ ἐκρατοῦντο, "The Corinthians believed they were victors if they were only just defeated"', *Mnemosyne*, 66 (2013), p 216. It has been a long-held historical view that the Athenians did not have their best ships and crews at the Battle of Erineus, as they would have been sent to Sicily. A W Gomme, A Andrewes and K J Dover, *A Historical Commentary on Thucydides, 4: Books V.25-VII* (Oxford, 1970) p 411; D Kagan, *The Peace of Nicias and the Sicilian Expedition* (London, 1981), pp 296-7; J B Salmon, *Wealthy Corinth: A History of the City to 338 B.C.* (Oxford, 1984), p 334. This is, of course, plausible and makes perfect sense; however, the importance of the Corinthian Gulf to Athenian strategy over the previous fifteen or so years, makes it unlikely that they would man the position with a weakened fleet. For this reason, this reconstruction is based upon the presence of a highly capable and experienced Athenian fleet.

13. This description is based on that of J S Morrison, J F Coates and N B Rankov, *The Athenian Trireme: The History and Reconstruction of an Ancient Greek Warship* (Cambridge, 2000), p 165.

Chapter 8: The Battle for the Great Harbour of Syracuse (413 BC)

1. The Peace of Nicias brought an end to the Archidamian War, but it was not a simple treaty. The divisions between *poleis* resulted in various treaties being drawn up between different groups of allies. The way Thucydides describes it (V.46–48), the peace between Athens and Sparta, as the two largest protagonists in the war, was almost accidental. A treaty was agreed by the orchestration of the Athenian statesman Nicias, but the Athenian Assembly did not like it at all and arranged new ones with their allies, but they never nullified the original, so it was left to stand.

2. Thucydides V.66–75; Diodorus XII.79. J Lazenby, *The Spartan Army* (Barnsley, 2012), pp 141-60; L Tritle, *A New History of the Peloponnesian War* (Oxford, 2010), pp 123-7; O Rees, *Great Battles of the Classical Greek World* (Barnsley, 2016), p 123-8.

3. A phenomenally large sum of money, equating to one talent per ship, per month. This is in keeping with Thucydides' calculations, mentioned in Chapter 6, note 8. It means that the sixty ships would be costing two talents a day.

4. Thucydides V.116.

5. Thucydides makes this quite clear (VI.32) when he points this out, raising the question why would he need to tell his readers this? He never normally mentions departure rituals, and in the one instance he does it seems to be for its unique nature.

6. Thucydides (VI.43) uses the terminology of triremes, and then differentiates between the two Athenian types by the terms 'fast' (which I have referred to as the combat ships) and a Greek term *stratiōtis* which just means 'martial' but when it refers to ships is often translated as troopship.

7. Thucydides' description of these marines as *thetes* has caused some problems with interpretation, because marines were an extension of hoplites, and the *thetes* are often considered too poor to afford this role (although it is not unheard of).

8. Syracuse had two harbours: the Great Harbour, which rested in the northern edge of the whole 'Great Harbour', and the Small Harbour, which sat on the northern side of the city. The Syracusan naval arsenal was kept in the Small Harbour (Thuc. VII.22.1). For the topography in question see H Gerding, 'Syracuse', in David Blackman et al (eds), *Shipsheds of the Ancient Mediterranean* (Cambridge, 2013), pp 535-6.

9. For the actions on the Greek mainland during this period see Chapter 7 Erineus

10. Plutarch, *Nicias*, 17.

11. Thucydides VII.24.3.

Chapter 9: Battles of the Ionian Coast (412–411 BC)

1. Thucydides VIII.3.2 describes a Peloponnesian fleet being built in which the usually dominant numbers from Corinth are reduced to a mere 15 per cent. The Corinthian navy had been stretched thin during the Archidamian War, and had been very active in the interlude period (see chapters 5 and 7). The reduced expectation on Corinth, compared to the 25 per cent to be provided by both Thebes and Sparta, may suggest a financial repercussion to their exploits that Thucydides leaves unstated. Cf J B Salmon, *Wealthy Corinth: A History of the City to 338 B.C.* (Oxford, 1984), pp 338-9, who argues that this figure relates to new-builds, and when added to the Corinthian fleet already in action it amounted to roughly fifty ships. What Salmon does not consider is that this is still a marked reduction from the seventy-five triremes Corinth was able to launch back in 435 BC (Thucydides I.29.1)

2. Athenian allies had been required to pay tribute and were generally treated as client states of an Athenian empire, hence the desire for autonomy.

3. Sparta would contribute twenty-five, as would Thebes, Corinth would supply fifteen, as would the combined economies of Phocis and Locris, while the Arcadians, Pellenians and Sicyonians would band together to make a further ten, as would the Megarians, Troezenians, Epidaurians and Hermonians.

4. This detail by Thucydides is somewhat suspect, and his disdain for the Corinthians has been highlighted by N McKenzie and P Hannah, 'Thucydides' Take on the Corinthian Navy. Οἵ τε γὰρ Κορίνθιοι ἡγήσαντο κρατεῖν εἰ μὴ καὶ πολὺ ἐκρατοῦντο, "The Corinthians believed they were victors if they were only just defeated"', *Mnemosyne*, 66 (2013) pp 206-27. It seems more logical that an experienced naval power such as Corinth would only decide to wait for the remainder of their fleet to join them, most of which had yet to be pulled across the Isthmus, rather than decide to destroy their important, and very expensive, ships.

5. See Thucydides II.24.1.

6. Aristophanes, *Thesmophoriazusae*, 804-5.

7. Plutarch, *Alcibiades*, 23.7–8.

8. The political atmosphere in Athens is too complex to divulge here unfortunately, so only the relevant parts which affect the naval battle which follows have been lain out here.

9. Thucydides VIII.87. Tissaphernes allegedly went to collect a fleet of 147 ships from the Phoenicians, but never brought them back with him. Thucydides claims the reason was because of Tissaphernes' plan to prolong the war between Athens and Sparta, such a large number of ships would surely give the final advantage to one side over the other.

10. Neither Thucydides nor Diodorus actually name the overall commander of the fleet, but I am following Kagan's logic in identifying Thrasybulus in that role: namely his position within the fleet in the battle line. D Kagan, *The Fall of the Athenian Empire* (Ithaca, 1987) p 218, note 31.

11. Diodorus (XIII.39.4) places the two commanders on the opposite wings to Thucydides (VIII.104.3). I have chosen to follow Thucydides' description due to his temporal proximity to the events he narrates. Diodorus is a much later writer (first century BC) but made use of both Thucydides' account, and that of the fourth-century historian Ephorus (for whom we have only fragments of his work)

12. Diodorus XIII.40.1.

13. Diodorus XIII.39.5.

14. The rest of this paragraph is drawn from Diodorus (XIII.40.1–2). Diodorus' account offers an on-deck view of the battle, but misses many of the important tactical decisions made by the commanders. Thucydides, has the opposite problem, where his focus is on the battle-map view but offers no account of the actual combat. D. Kagan, *The Fall of the Athenian Empire*, p 222.

15. Cf D Kagan, *The Fall of the Athenian Empire*, pp 223–4. Kagan uses Diodorus' account of the fighting to explain the Athenian victory in this area of the battle, but I chose to place Diodorus' account in the general combat of the earlier stages. Diodorus' account relies on the Peloponnesians being the instigators of combat, but Thucydides' account implies that Thrasybulus' counter was driven by an Athenian offensive action, not a reactionary one.

16. Cf J S Morrison, J F Coates and N B Rankov, *The Athenian Trireme: The History and Reconstruction of an Ancient Greek Warship*, 2nd ed (Cambridge, 2000), pp 82–3. Morrison et al envisage the Athenians routing the enemy on both wings

with a double *periplous*, encircling the opposition and defeating them before driving home the victory in the centre. Unfortunately this interpretation is not stated in Thucydides nor Diodorus. The Syracusans, especially are never described as encircled, nor are they described as defeated until they saw their allies routed first.

17. Plutarch, *Alcibiades*, 28.4-5 states that he had forty ships, and broke through the enemy lines with twenty of his best. This seems unlikely because, even though he would still have been outnumbered, it would have been too large a fleet for the Peloponnesians to attack so foolhardily. I have kept with Diodorus' (XIII.50.2) figure.

18. The Battle of Cyzicus has three accounts, the longest being that of Diodorus (XIII.50). Xenophon's account (I.1.11-18) is short and contradictory, and Plutarch's account (*Alcibiades*, 28.4-6) is short and focussed on Alcibiades alone.

Chapter 10: The Battle of Arginusae (406 BC)

1. Xenophon, *Hellenica*, I.1.23. Translation is my own adapted version of Strassler's edition.

2. Xenophon knew Clearchus personally, and wrote about him in his *Anabasis*. Xenophon considered him a harsh man, but a good soldier and a great leader.

3. Clearchus' role was that of a *harmost*, a military governor. This gave him the power and the ability to rule like a minor king, however it did not give him the right nor the legitimacy to do so.

4. There is much debate as to whether Tissaphernes actually lost his position as a *satrap*, or if he kept control over the much smaller *satrapy* of Caria. Either way, his knowledge and experience did not go to waste and he became an advisor to the young Cyrus, although it was not a demotion he particularly enjoyed. For more on the tumultuous relationship between Tissaphernes and Cyrus see S Ruzicka, 'Cyrus and Tissaphernes, 407-401 B.C.', *The Classical Journal*, 80(3) (1985), pp 204-11.

5. This is, interestingly, the pay rate which Thucydides (III.17.3) claimed that the Athenians received at the outbreak of the Archidamian War. It is unlikely that the Athenian crews would desert their ships for the same pay that they received in Athens. This means that either the Athenians were not paying this amount any more, or that the Peloponnesians intended for Cyrus to pay them

that amount in full, as opposed to the Athenian policy of paying half before and half after an expedition (Thuc.VIII. 45.2). This, of course, assumes that the Athenian crews were actually Athenian people, because there is evidence that non-Athenian crew members were paid in full (Dem. 50.18).

6. It is worth noting that this is not Tissaphernes' own argument, but is the same argument which Alcibiades had convinced Tissaphernes of in the first place. Something described by Thucydides (VIII.46.1-5), and is reiterated in Xenophon (*Helenica*. I.5.9.).

7. Xenophon's account, followed here, is different to that given by Diodorus (XIII.71.1) who says Alcibiades left in a rush to deal with a possible uprising in Clazomenae. The most dramatic explanation for Alcibiades' absence comes from Plutarch (*Alcibiades*. 35.3) which describes him as a pirate trying to illicitly acquire more funds.

8. Antiochus personality is described as such by Diodorus (XIII.71.1), but Xenophon offers no explanation at all for the helmsmen's actions

9. The resulting battle of Notium is described by three main sources – Xenophon, *Hellenica*. 1.5.106, *Hell. Oxy.*. IV.1-3, Diodorus XIII.71 – which vary in their description in varying degrees. This narrative is an attempt to incorporate all three versions into a coherent structure. It follows from the analysis of A. Andrewes, 'Notion and Kyzikos: The Sources Compared', *The Journal of Hellenic Studies*, 102 (1982), pp 15-25, and relevant notes by P R McKechnie and S J Kern, *Hellenica Oxyrhynchia: edited with translation and commentary* (Warminster, 1993), pp 125-29.

10. Xenophon says the Athenians only lost fifteen triremes, which seems low but is not necessarily wrong on that basis. I have kept with twenty-two because both Diodorus and *Hell. Oxy.* give this number, and because it emphasizes how bad a defeat this was for the Athenians.

11. Pausanias, writing in the Roman Imperial period, describes this victory as a prime example of Lysander's wisdom (IX.32.6), suggesting how influential it was on his reputation.

12. Alcibiades went to his property around the Hellespont, imposing upon himself an exile from Athens.

13. The Greek is clear in the verb it uses, but often translators soften it to 'illicit affair with the sea' or 'playing the wanton with', which I feel loses the aggression in the Spartan's choice of words, and his sense of ownership over the sea.

14. The two sources here give very different accounts of the battle, with Diodorus splitting the fleets in half and staging two battles simultaneously. I have chosen to work with Xenophon's framework because he, rather unusually, spends a lot of time describing the layout of the Athenian line, which implies that he is sure in what he is saying.

15. Xenophon does not mention the omens, unusually. These come from the tradition used by Diodorus (XIII.97.5-98.1), and echoes the sentiment that Xenophon placed in the mouth of a helmsmen instead

16. Following J S Morrison, J F Coates and N B Rankov, *The Athenian Trireme: The History and Reconstruction of an Ancient Greek Warship*, 2nd ed (Cambridge, 2000), pp 90-91. Hamel offers a different model, which has the Athenian squadrons in a single line, supported from behind by another single line, giving the image of two rows of fifteen ships each. She further argues for the inclusion of an island within their lines, so as to artificially extend their lines. It is an interesting hypothesis, using Diodorus' account for the island, but I find the reasoning unconvincing. For the model see D Hamel, *The Battle of Arginusae: Victory at Sea and its Tragic Aftermath in the Final Years of the Peloponnesian War* (Baltimore, 2015), pp 47-50.

17. Xenophon only describes them as being in single file, which is ludicrous because that would be a file of ships almost 3 miles long and could easily be outflanked and attacked at the vulnerable sides. J. S.Morrison, J F Coates and N B Rankov, *The Athenian Trireme* (Cambridge, 2000), p 90.

18. Diodorus actually names this as Lysias, but Xenophon places him on the opposite wing. I have used Diodorus' description, but kept Xenophon's battle plan.

19. Hamel is understandably sceptical of this heroic death described in full by Diodorus, but I have left it in for the simple reason that it forms the majority of the battle narrative given to us by any of our sources. D Hamel, *The Battle of Arginusae* (Baltimore, 2015), pp 50-51.

20. Xenophon, *Hellenica* I.7.4; Diod. XIII.101.

21. For a brilliant overview and timeline of the trial for the generals see D Hamel, *The Battle of Arginusae* (Baltimore, 2015), pp 75-90.

22. Aristophanes, *Frogs*, 693-4. It was a loophole that allowed the Athenians to reward the slaves by making them free, and giving them citizen rights, but not make them Athenians.

Chapter 11: The Battle of Aegospotami (405 BC)

1. See Chapter 10: The Battle of Arginusae.
2. There is no evidence that the Spartans were yet aware of the trial of the generals in Athens, and the poor state of leadership that this now left the Athenians in.
3. The most obvious instance of this happening was when the great Spartan commander Brasidas was used in a similar capacity, see Chapter 5: The Battle of the Corinthian Gulf and Chapter 6: The Battle of Corcyra.
4. The placing of the arms inside the long sleeves (*korē*) was done to render the person harmless, in that they could not hold a weapon.
5. Xenophon (*Hellenica*, II.1.10-3) describes two separate meetings between the two, one before Cyrus received his father's summons, and one after. Xenophon's version describes Lysander being given money in the first meeting, and then in the second meeting gives Lysander access to his own personal income, the tribute from the cities which were considered his own personal property. I have followed Plutarch's narrative (*Lysander*, 9.1-2), which has only one meeting and does not have Cyrus offer a lump sum of money. Neither version is any less believable, but I have chosen the simplest narrative we have available.
6. See Chapter 10: The Battle of Arginusae for King Agis and his original realization of this Athenian strength.
7. Lysander's move north may have been his own intention, or else he received an order from the Spartan king Agis. He could have met Agis in a series of raids in Attica, which is described in Plutarch (*Lysander*, 9.2-3) and Diodorus (XIII.104.8) but not in Xenophon. I have not included these raids in the narrative because it is hard to corroborate with Xenophon's description of Lysander being based in Rhodes at this time. Also, Lysander did not have the luxury of security around the Ionian coast, as shown by the Athenian raids in the area, so the idea he would leave to attack Attica seems strange. Furthermore, Diodorus describes the raids as uneventful and actually refuses to give them a proper account, which brings their veracity into question somewhat.
8. These three orders do not all appear in any one source, but bring together what Xenophon, Plutarch and Diodorus all say about the end of the assault.
9. For problems identifying the exact location of this site see the overview by B Strauss, 'A Note on the Topography and Tactics of the Battle of Aegospotami', *The American Journal of Philology*, 108:4 (1987), pp 741-5. For another

interpretation try J Hale, *Lords of the Sea: How Trireme Battles Changed the World* (New York, 2009) pp 236–41, 356–9.

10. This is explicitly stated in Diodorus (XIII.106.1) and is implied by Xenophon (*Hellenica*, II.1.31-2).

11. This is not my estimate but that of D Kagan, *The Fall of the Athenian Empire* (Ithaca, 1987), p 382.

12. Reconstructing this battle is made extremely difficult by the seemingly incompatible accounts given by Xenophon and Diodorus, the two main sources of the engagement. Conventionally, scholars have often chosen to use only one of the sources, and have disregarded the other as full of lies. The preference of accounts often changes, so it is hard to discern which is most likely to be correct. I have chosen to follow the reasoning of Robinson, who presents a fair attempt (to my mind) of reconciling the two versions. Therefore, as a fair word of warning, you will not find this narrative in any one source. E. Robinson, 'What Happened at Aegospotami? Xenophon and Diodorus on the Last Battle of the Peloponnesian War', *Historia*, 63:1 (2014), pp 1-16.

13. For Alcibiades' disgrace and self-imposed exile see Chapter 10: The Battle of Arginusae.

14. Xenophon (*Hellenica*, II.1.25-6) does not give this information, he claims that Alcibiades advised the Athenians to move their camp to Sestos so that they would be able to resupply. He also states that from there they would be able to fight a sea battle at any time of their own choosing. It is difficult to work out what Xenophon is trying to achieve here. The advice to move the camp is obvious, but not stupid. Yet Alcibiades' claim of being able to dictate when the battle would occur goes in complete contrast to the past five days, in which it is quite plain that Lysander could keep refusing battle if he wished. Either Alcibiades is a fool, a nuisance, or he is trying to help and is rebuked for it.

15. Diodorus XIII.105.4

16. Why Lysander chose this day is not clear. He may have originally intended for it to last six days, wearing down the resources of his enemy and create this sense of security. Or, as Diodorus claims, he received some Athenian deserters who informed him of Philocles' own plan to attack the spy ships and this forced his hand. I am more inclined to believe the former solution, because it is simpler and does not require a bizarre literary antagonist (the deserter) to explain it.

Ultimately, if Lysander did not intend to attack what was his long term plan? The Athenians would have, at some point, sailed further down the Hellespont to a better camping point and stopped Lysander from ever entering the Aegean again. He had to act, and he knew it.

Chapter 12: The Battle of Catane (396 BC)

1. Polybius III.1.22.
2. Thucydides VI.2.6.
3. Herodotus VII.165; Diodorus XI.1.20. Diodorus claims that Carthage acted on the instructions of the Persian king Xerxes, and that the attack timed in with the Greek victory at Thermopylae. Herodotus does not link the two invasions, but does recount the Sicilian tradition, linking it with the Battle of Salamis instead. For analysis of the various sources and traditions see P Stylianou, *A Historical Commentary on Diodorus Siculus, Book 15* (Oxford: 1998), pp 53-4.
4. This was not a simple decision for the Carthaginians by any means. For analysis of the pros and cons of the decision see B Caven, *Dionysius I: War-Lord of Sicily* (New Haven: 1990), pp 28-30.
5. Our sources give astronomical numbers. This figure is Caven's and is based on later military commitments by Carthage in Sicily. B Caven, *Dionysius I: War-Lord of Sicily* (New Haven: 1990), p 32.
6. B Caven, *Dionysius I: War-Lord of Sicily* (New Haven: 1990), p 33.
7. The exact landing point of the army is not stated in our sources, but Diodorus (XIII.88.4) describes forty ships being moored at these two cities, implying that these might have been their original landing sites.
8. Dionysius had taken advantage of the political unrest following the defeat at Acragas and placed himself as the most powerful man in the city. The best account of Dionysius' rise to power, and his career, is still that of B Caven, *Dionysius I: War-Lord of Sicily* (New Haven: 1990), pp 50-8.
9. This has been questioned in the past by historians, because there is no mention of these ships being used again until the time of Alexander the Great: see W Tarn, *Hellenistic Military and Naval Developments* (Cambridge: 1930), pp 130-1. I have kept it here because Diodorus is so certain of this as a fact, he mentions it twice in quick succession (XIV.41.3, 42.2), and the argument against it is quite weak. For an argued link between the experiences at Selinus and the forms of weaponry being produced in Syracuse see W Murray,

The Age of Titans: The Rise and Fall of the Great Hellenistic Navies (Oxford, 2012), p 81.

10. This is not stated in Diodorus, but is the hypothesis of Caven, which seems a reasonable one. B Caven, *Dionysius I: War-Lord of Sicily* (New Haven: 1990), p 108.

11. Diodorus XIV.54.5.

12. Polyaenus V.2.9; Frontinus I.8.11.

13. P. Stylianou, *A Historical Commentary on Diodorus Siculus, Book 15* (Oxford: 1998), pp 73-5.

14. This battle is given only the smallest of space by our sources and is almost impossible to reconstruct. For a good analysis of the battle and its importance see A Papalas, 'The Battle of Alalia', *Syllecta Classica*, 24 (2013), pp 1-28.

15. L Rawlings, 'The Carthaginian Navy: Questions and Assumptions', in G Fagan and M Trundle, *New Perspectives on Ancient Warfare* (Leiden: 2010), pp 282-3.

Chapter 13: The Battle of Cnidus (394 BC)

1. The best source for this uprising is undoubtedly that of Xenophon, who was one of the Greek mercenaries in Cyrus' rebel army. Xenophon wrote his *Anabasis*, which tells the story of the uprising and the subsequent retreat of the surviving Greeks, from the centre of the Persian empire back to Byzantium.

2. S. Ruzicka, *Trouble in the West: Egypt and the Persian Empire 525-332 B.C.E.* (Oxford, 2012), pp 44-5.

3. For comparisons between the two situations see Ruzicka, *Trouble in the West: Egypt and the Persian Empire 525-332 B.C.E.* (Oxford, 2012), pp 29-35, 41-5.

4. *Karanos* was a position like commander-in-chief. The last person to be given this position was Cyrus the Younger, see Chapter 10.

5. Ctesias, fr 7; Xenophon, *Hellenica*, 3.4.11.

6. Thucydides 8.40-4.

7. This lake is described by the *Hellenica Oxyrhynchia* 9.3, but it is debatable as to whether the historian refers to this particular episode, or a slightly later one. I follow Ruzicka in describing this as a strategic strength of Caunus and therefore regarding it as a factor in Conon's decision making. S. Ruzicka, *Trouble in the West, Egypt and the Persian Empire 525-332 B.C.E.* (Oxford, 2012), pp 46-7; P.R. McKechnie and S.J. Kern, *Hellenica Oxyrhynchia* (Warminster, 1993), p 40.

8. Isocrates is surely exaggerating when he describes it lasting three years. C D Hamilton, *Sparta's Bitter Victories* (Ithaca, 1979), p 188; H D Westlake, 'Conon and Rhodes: The Troubled Aftermath of Synoecism', *Greek, Roman and Byzantine Studies*, 24 (1983), p 334.

9. The role of the Rhodians in the removal of the Spartans is contested. The hardest part to explain is how a popular uprising in Rhodes could force such a vast Spartan presence out of the city. A fleet of 120 ships is an enormous force, manned by tens of thousands of men, so it is more likely that the Spartans left of their own accord. See Ruzicka, *Trouble in the West, Egypt and the Persian Empire 525-332 B.C.E.* (Oxford, 2012), pp 47-8 and note 28 for the issues of reconstructing this sequence of events.

10. *Hellenica Oxyrhynchia*, 19.1-3.

11. Xenophon (IV.3.12) describes the Spartan fleet as being obviously outnumbered, which does not conform to the numbers given here by Diodorus. Xenophon was a dear admirer of Agesilaus, so this might be an example of him trying to protect the reputation of one of the king's family members.

12. The Persians did something similar during the Ionian War; ironically it was then to give the Spartans better sailors.

13. The idea of this defensive line comes from S Ruzicka, *Trouble in the West, Egypt and the Persian Empire 525-332 B.C.E.* (Oxford, 2012), pp 48, 56, who discusses its importance in relation to Persian interests

14. Peisander has received quite a bad review from modern historians, but it is important to keep in mind what he was facing, and the inability of anyone to predict what Conon's plans actually were.

15. Polybius (I.2) refers to the period of hegemony dating from their victory at Aegospotami to their defeat at Cnidus, lasting a twelve-year period.

Select Bibliography

Some works are repeated in different sections below. This is intentional.

Ancient Sources

Aeschylus, *Persians*.

Aristophanes, *Acharnians*.

    Frogs.

    Thesmophoriazusae.

Ctesias, *Persica*.

Demosthenes, *Speeches*.

Diodorus Siculus (Diodorus), *Library of World History*.

Frontinus, *Strategemata*.

Herodotus, *Histories*.

Pausanias, *Description of Greece*.

Plutarch, *Life of Alcibiades*.

    Life of Artaxerxes.

    Life of Cimon.

    Life of Lysander.

    Life of Nicias.

    Life of Themistocles.

    On the Malice of Herodotus.

Polyaenus, *Stratagems*.

Polybius, *Histories*.

Xenophon, *Anabasis*.

    Cyropaedia.

    Hellenica.

Unknown, *Hellenica Oxyrhynchia*.

McKechnie, P R, and S J Kern, *Hellenica Oxyrhynchia: edited with translation and commentary*, (Warminster, 1993).

Strassler, R, *The Landmark Thucydides: A Comprehensive Guide to the Peloponnesian War* (New York, 1996).

The Landmark Herodotus: The Histories (London, 2008).

The Landmark Xenophon's Hellenica (London, 2011).

For free translations on the internet there are no better resources than the Perseus Project, Lacus Curtius, and Livius. There are also numerous research projects online that are making valuable translations available to the wider public. See 'Websites' below for relevant URLs.

All Achaemenid Inscriptions referenced are available at the free depository of Livius.org (see 'Websites' below).

General Works

Acton, P, *Poiesis: Manufacturing in Classical Athens* (Oxford, 2014).

Bertosa, B, 'The Social Status and Ethnic Origin of the Rowers of Spartan Triremes', *War and Society*, 23 (2005), pp 1–20.

Casson, L, *Ships and Seamanship in the Ancient World* (Princeton, 1986).

Ducat, J, 'La société spartiate et la guerre', in F Prost (ed), *Armées et Sociétés de la Grèce classique: Aspects sociaux et politiques de la guerre aux Ve et IVe s. av. J.-C.* (Paris, 1999), pp 35–50.

Fagan, G, and M Trundle, *New Perspectives on Ancient Warfare* (Leiden, 2010).

Gabrielsen, V, *Financing the Athenian Fleet* (Baltimore, 1994).

Hale, J, *Lords of the Sea: How Trireme Battles Changed the World* (New York, 2009).

Jordan, B, 'The Meaning of the Technical Term "Hyperesia" in Naval Contexts of the Fifth and Fourth Centuries B.C.', *California Studies in Classical Antiquity*, 2 (1969), pp 183-207.

'The Crews of Athenian Triremes', *L'Antiquité Classique*, 69 (2000), pp 81–101.

Holladay, A, 'Further thoughts on trireme tactics', *Greece & Rome*, 35 (1988), pp 149-51.

Hornblower, S, *A Commentary on Thucydides: Volume I Books I–III* (Oxford, 1991).

Lazenby, J, 'The Diekplous', *Greece & Rome*, 34:2 (1987), pp 169-77.

'Essays and Reflections: Naval Warfare in the Ancient World: Myths and Realities', *International Historical Review*, 9:3 (1987), pp 438-55.

Meijer, F, 'Thucydides 1.13.2-4 and the Changes in Greek Shipbuilding', *Historia: Zeitschrift für Alte Geschichte*, 37:4 (1988), pp 461-3.

A History of Seafaring in the Classical World (New York, 2014).

Morrison, J S, 'Hyperesia in Naval Contexts in the Fifth and Fourth Centuries BC', *The Journal of Hellenic Studies*, 104 (1984), pp 48-59.

Morrison, J S, J F Coates and N B Rankov, *The Athenian Trireme: The History and Reconstruction of an Ancient Greek Warship*, 2nd ed (Cambridge, 2000).

Rees, O, *Great Battles of the Classical Greek World* (Barnsley, 2016).

Shaw, J T, 'Steering to Ram: The Diekplous and Periplous', in J T Shaw (ed.), *The Trireme Project: Operational Experience 1987-90: Lessons Learnt* (Oxford, 1993), pp 99-104.

Tritle, L, *A New History of the Peloponnesian War* (Oxford, 2010).

van Wees, H, *Ships and Silver, Taxes and Tribute: A Fiscal History of Archaic Athens* (London, 2013).

Wallinga, H T, *Ships and Sea-Power Before the Great Persian War: The Ancestry of the Ancient Trireme* (Leiden, 1993).

Whitehead, I, 'The Periplous', *Greece & Rome*, 34:2 (1987), pp 178-85.

Persian Conflict

Bowden, H, *Classical Athens and the Delphic Oracle: Divination and Democracy* (Cambridge, 2005).

Bridges, E, *Imagining Xerxes: Ancient Perspectives on a Persian King* (London, 2014).

Bury, J B, 'Aristides at Salamis', *Classical Review*, 10 (1896), pp 414-18.

Dandamaev, M, *A Political History of the Achaemenid Empire* (Leiden, 1989).

Evans, J, 'Notes on Thermopylae and Artemisium', *Historia: Zeitschrift für Alte Geschichte*, 1:4 (1969), pp 39-406.

Fink, D, *The Battle of Marathon in Scholarship: Research, Theories and Controversies since 1850* (Jefferson, 2014).

Fornara, C, 'The Hoplite Achievement at Psyttaleia', *The Journal of Hellenic Studies*, 6 (1966), pp 51-4.

Frost, F, 'A Note on Xerxes at Salamis', *Historia: Zeitschrift für Alte Geschichte*, 22:1 (1973), pp. 118-19.

George, P, 'Persian Ionia under Darius: The Revolt Reconsidered', *Historia*, 49:1, (2000), pp.1–39.

Grundy, G, 'Artemisium', *The Journal of Hellenic Studies*, 17 (1897), pp 212–29.

Hammond, N G L, 'The Battle of Salamis', *The Journal of Hellenic Studies*, 76 (1956), pp 32–54.

Hammond, N G L, and L J Roseman, 'The Construction of Xerxes' bridge over the Hellespont', *The Journal of Hellenic Studies*, 116 (1996), pp 88–107.

Hignett, C, *Xerxes' Invasion of Greece* (Oxford, 1963).

Keaveney, A, 'The Attack on Naxos: a "Forgotten Cause" of the Ionian Revolt', *The Classical Quarterly*, 38:1 (1988), pp 76–81.

Knight, W F J, 'The Defence of the Acropolis and the Panic before Salamis', *The Journal of Hellenic Studies*, 51:2 (1931), pp 174–178.

Kurht, A, *The Persian Empire: A Corpus of Sources from the Achaemenid Period* (New York, 2010).

Labarbe, J, 'Chiffres et modes de répartition de la flotte grecque à l'Artémision et à Salamine', *Bulletin de correspondance hellénique*, 76:1 (1952), pp 384–441.

Lazenby, J, 'Aischylos and Salamis', *Hermes*, 116:2 (1988), pp 168–85.

'The Diekplous', *Greece & Rome*, 34:2 (1987), pp 169–77.

Morrison, J S, 'The Greek Ships at Salamis and the Diekplous', *The Journal of Hellenic Studies*, 111 (1991), pp 196–200.

Myres, J, 'The Battle of Lade, 494 B.C. (Herodotus vi. 6–17. with map)', *Greece & Rome*, 1:2 (1954), pp 50–55.

Pritchett, W K, 'Toward a Restudy of the Battle of Salamis', *American Journal of Archaeology*, 63:3 (1959), pp 251–62.

Robertson, N, 'The True Meaning of the "Wooden Wall"', *Classical Philology*, 82:1 (1987), pp 1–20.

Rubincam, C, 'Herodotus and his Descendants: Numbers in Ancient and Modern Narratives of Xerxes' Campaign', *Harvard Studies in Classical Philology*, 104 (2008), pp 93–138.

Sacks, K, 'Herodotus and the Dating of the Battle of Thermopylae', *The Classical Quarterly*, 26:2 (1976), pp 232–48.

Scott, M, *Delphi: A History of the Centre of the Ancient World* (Princeton, 2014).

Sealey, R, 'Again the Siege of the Acropolis, 480 B.C.', *California Studies in Classical Antiquity*, 5 (1972), pp 183 91 .

Sidebotham, S, 'Herodotus on Artemisium', *The Classical World*, 75:3 (Jan-Feb, 1982), pp 177-86.

Strauss, B, 'Flames over Athens', *Arion: A Journal of Humanities and the Classics*, 12:1 (2004), pp 101-16.
Salamis: The Greatest Naval Battle of the Ancient World, 480 B.C. (London, 2005).

Tuplin, C, 'Marathon: In Search of a Persian Dimension', in Kostas Buraselis and Katerina Meidani (eds), *Μαραθών: η μάχη και ο αρχαίος Δήμος / Marathon: the Battle and the Ancient Deme* (Athens, 2010), pp 251-74.

van Wees, H, 'Those Who Sail are to Receive a Wage: Naval Warfare and Finance in Archaic Erteria', in Garrett Fagan and Matthew Trundle (eds), *New Perspectives on Ancient Warfare* (Leiden, 2010), pp 205-26.

Vasilev, M I, *The Policy of Darius and Xerxes towards Thrace and Macedonia* (Leiden, 2015).

Wallinga, H T, *Xerxes' Greek Adventure: A Naval Perspective* (Leiden, 2005).
'The Ionian Revolt', *Mnemosyne*, 37:3/4 (1984), pp 401-37.

Walters, K, 'Four Hundred Athenian Ships at Salamis?', *Rheinisches Museum für Philologie*, 124: 3/4 (1981), pp 199-203.

Waters, M, *Ancient Persia: a Concise History of the Achaemenid Empire, 550-330 BCE* (Cambridge, 2014).

West, S, 'Herodotus Portrait of Hecataeus', *The Journal of Hellenic Studies*, 111 (1991), pp 144-160.

Archidamian War

Bloedow, E F, 'Athens' Treaty with Corcyra: a Study in Athenian Foreign Policy', *Athenaeum*, 79 (1991), pp 185-210.

Gomme, A W, *A Historical Commentary on Thucydides: Volume I: Book I* (Oxford, 1945).

Hammond, N G L, 'Naval Operations in the South Channel of Corcyra 435-433 B.C.', *The Journal of Hellenic Studies*, 65 (1945), pp 26-37.

Hunter, V, *Thucydides: The Artful Reporter*, (Toronto: 1973).

Kagan, D, *Archidamian War*, (New York: 1974).

Kelly, T, 'Thucydides and Spartan Strategy in the Archidamian W?
American Historical Review, 87:1 (1982), pp 25-54.

Lech, M L, 'The Knights' Eleven OARS: In Praise of Phormio? Aristophanes' 546-7 *Knights*', *The Classical Journal*, 105:1 (2009), pp 19-26.

McKenzie, N (unpublished MA thesis), *Thucydides' Corinthians: an examination of Corinth in Thucydides' account of the outbreak of the Peloponnesian War* (University of Otago, New Zealand: 2010).

McKenzie, N, and P Hannah, 'Thucydides' Take on the Corinthian Navy. οἵ τε γὰρ Κορίνθιοι ἡγήσαντο κρατεῖν εἰ μὴ καὶ πολὺ ἐκρατοῦντο, "The Corinthians believed they were victors if they were only just defeated"', *Mnemosyne*, 66 (2013), pp 206-27.

Neumann, J, and J A Metaxas, 'The Battle between the Athenian and Peloponnesian Fleets, 429 B.C., and Thucydides' "Wind from the Gulf (of Corinth)"', *Meteorologische Rundschau*, 32, (1979), pp 182-8.

Roberts, M, *Two Deaths in Amphipolis: Cleon vs Brasidas in the Peloponnesian War* (Barnsley, 2015).

Salmon, J B, *Wealthy Corinth: a History of the City to 338 B.C.*, (Oxford, 1984).

Stahl, H-P, 'Narrative Unity and Consistency of Thought: Composition of Event Sequences in Thucydides', in A Rengakos and A Tsakmakis (eds), *Brill's Companion to Thucydides* (Leiden, 2006), pp 301-34.

Westlake, H D, 'Seaborne Raids in Periclean Strategy', *The Classical Quarterly*, 39: 3/4, (1945), pp 75-84.

Wick, T E, & T T Wick, 'Megara Athens, and the West in the Archidamian War: A Study in Thucydides', *Historia: Zeitschrift für Alte Geschichte*, 28:1 (1979), pp 1-14.

Sicilian Expedition

Bosworth, B, 'Athens' First Intervention in Sicily: Thucydides and the Sicilian Tradition', *The Classical Quarterly*, 42:1 (1992), pp 4-55.

Brunt, P A, 'Spartan Policy and Strategy in the Archidamian War', *Phoenix*, 19: 4 (1965), pp 255-280.

Gerding, H, 'Syracuse', in David Blackman et al (eds), *Shipsheds of the Ancient Mediterranean* (Cambridge, 2013).

Gomme, A W, A Andrewes, K J Dover, *A Historical Commentary on Thucydides, 4: Books V.25-VII*, (Oxford, 1970).

Jordan, B, 'The Sicilian Expedition was a Potemkin Fleet', *The Classical Quarterly*, New Series, 50:1 (2000), pp 63-79.

Kagan, D, *The Peace of Nicias and the Sicilian Expedition* (London, 1981).

Lazenby, J F, *The Spartan Army* (Barnsley, 2012).

Liebeschuetz, W, 'Thucydides and the Sicilian Expedition', *Historia: Zeitschrift für Alte Geschichte*, 17:3 (July, 1968), pp 289–306.

McKenzie, N, and P Hannah, 'Thucydides' Take on the Corinthian Navy. οἵ τε γὰρ Κορίνθιοι ἡγήσαντο κρατεῖν εἰ μὴ καὶ πολὺ ἐκρατοῦντο, "The Corinthians believed they were victors if they were only just defeated"', *Mnemosyne*, 66 (2013), pp 206–27.

Morrison, J S, J F Coates and N B Rankov, *The Athenian Trireme: The History and Reconstruction of an Ancient Greek Warship* (Cambridge, 2000).

Salmon, J B, *Wealthy Corinth: A History of the City to 338 B.C.* (Oxford, 1984).

Ionian War

Andrewes, A, 'Notion and Kyzikos: The Sources Compared', *The Journal of Hellenic Studies*, 102 (1982), pp 15–25.

Ehrhardt, C, 'Xenophon and Diodorus on Aegospotami', *Phoenix*, 24:3 (1970), pp 225–28.

Gray, V, 'The Value of Diodorus Siculus for the Years 411–386 BC', *Hermes*, 115:1 (1987), pp 72–89.

Hale, J, *Lords of the Sea: How Trireme Battles Changed the World* (New York, 2009).

Hamel, D, *The Battle of Arginusae: Victory at Sea and its Tragic Aftermath in the Final Years of the Peloponnesian War* (Baltimore, 2015).

Hunt, P, 'The slaves and the Generals of Arginusae', *The American Journal of Philology*, 122:3 (2001), pp 359–80.

Kagan, D, *The Fall of the Athenian Empire* (Ithaca, 1987).

Kapellos, A, 'Philocles and the Sea-Battle at Aegospotami (Xenophon *Hell.* 2.1.22–32)', *Classical World*, 106:1 (2012), pp 97–101.

McKechnie, P R, and S J Kern, *Hellenica Oxyrhynchia: edited with translation and commentary* (Warminster, 1993)

Morrison, J S, J F Coates and N B Rankov, *The Athenian Trireme: The History and Reconstruction of an Ancient Greek Warship*, 2nd ed (Cambridge, 2000).

Naiden, F, 'Spartan Naval Performance in the Decelean War, 413–404 BCE', *Journal of Military History*, 73:3 (2009), pp 729–44.

Robinson, E, 'What Happened at Aegospotami? Xenophon and Diodorus on the Last Battle of the Peloponnesian War', *Historia*, 63: 1 (2014), pp 1-16.

Ruzicka, S, 'Cyrus and Tissaphernes, 407-401 B.C.', *The Classical Journal*, 80(3) (1985), pp 204-11.

Salmon, J B, *Wealthy Corinth: A History of the City to 338 B.C.* (Oxford, 1984).

Strauss, B, 'A Note on the Topography and Tactics of the Battle of Aegospotami', *The American Journal of Philology*, 108:4 (1987), pp 741-5.

'Aegospotami Reexamined', *The American Journal of Philology*, 104:1 (1983), pp 24-35.

Westlake, H, 'Ionians in the Ionian War', *The Classical Quarterly*, 29:1 (1979), pp 9-44.

Wylie, G, 'What Really Happened at Aegospotami?', *L'Antiquité Classique*, 55 (1986), pp 125-41.

Turning of the Tide

Bouchet, C, 'Conon, Navarque Perse à Cnide en 394?', *Rivista di cultura classica e medioevale*, 49:2 (2007), pp 231-47.

Caven, B, *Dionysius I: War-Lord of Sicily* (New Haven: 1990).

Cook, J, 'Cnidian Peraea and Spartan Coins', *The Journal of Hellenic Studies*, 81 (1961), pp 56-72.

Di Stefano, C A, 'Motye: A bridge between Carthage and the Tyrrhenian Sea', in N Stampolidis (ed), *Sea routes from Sidon to Huelva: interconnections in the Mediterranean 16th–6th c. BC* (Athens, 2003), pp 194-5.

Hamilton, C D, *Sparta's Bitter Victories* (Ithaca, 1979).

Hutchinson, G, *Sparta: Unfit for Empire* (Barnsley, 2014).

Isserlin, B, and J. Du Plat Taylor, *Motya: a Phoenician and Carthaginian city in Sicily, I* (Leiden, 1974).

March, D, 'Konon and the Great King's Fleet, 396-394', *Historia: Zeitschrift für Alte Geschichte*, 46:3 (1997), pp 257-69.

McKechnie, P R, and S J Kern, *Hellenica Oxyrhynchia: edited with translation and commentary* (Warminster, 1993).

Murray, W, *The Age of Titans: The Rise and Fall of the Great Hellenistic Navies* (Oxford, 2012).

Papalas, A, 'The Battle of Alalia', *Syllecta Classica*, 24 (2013), pp 1–28.

Rawlings, L, 'The Carthaginian Navy: Questions and Assumptions', in G Fagan and M Trundle, *New Perspectives on Ancient Warfare* (Leiden, 2010), pp 253-87.

Ruzicka, S, *Trouble in the West: Egypt and the Persian Empire 525-332 B.C.E.* (Oxford, 2012).

Seager, R, 'Thrasybulus, Conon and Athenian Imperialism, 396-386 B.C.', *The Journal of Hellenic Studies*, 87 (1967), pp 95-115.

Strauss, B, 'Thrasybulus and Conon: A Rivalry in Athens in the 390s B.C.', *The American Journal of Philology*, 105:1 (1984), pp 37-48.

Stylianou, P, *A Historical Commentary on Diodorus Siculus, Book 15* (Oxford: 1998).

Tarn, W W, *Hellenistic Military and Naval Developments* (Cambridge, 1930).

Westlake, H D, 'Conon and Rhodes: The Troubled Aftermath of Synoecism', *Greek, Roman and Byzantine Studies*, 24 (1983), pp 333-44.

Websites

http://www.achemenet.com/

http://www.livius.org/aa-ac/achaemenians/inscriptions.html

http://penelope.uchicago.edu/Thayer/E/Roman/home.html

http://www.perseus.tufts.edu/hopper/collection?collection=Perseus:collection:Greco-Roman

Index